Between
Vengeance and
Forgiveness

Between Vengeance and

Facing History

Vengeance and

after Genocide and

Forgiveness

Mass Violence

Martha Minow

Foreword by
Judge Richard J. Goldstone

Beacon Press Boston

Beacon Press

25 Beacon Street

Boston, Massachusetts 02108-2892

www.beacon.org

Beacon Press books

are published under the auspices of

the Unitarian Universalist Association of Congregations.

Printed in the United States of America

03   8 7 6

This book is printed on acid-free paper that meets the uncoated paper
ANSI/NISO specifications for permanence as revised in 1992.

Text design by Sara Eisenman
Composition by Wilsted & Taylor Publishing Services

Library of Congress Cataloging-in-Publication Data
Minow, Martha, 1954–
    Between vengeance and forgiveness : facing history after genocide and mass
violence / Martha Minow ; foreword by Richard J. Goldstone.
        p.   cm.
    Includes bibliographical references and index.
    ISBN 0-8070-4506-3 (hardcover : acid-free paper)
    ISBN 0-8070-4507-1 (paperback)
    1. Genocide.   2. Political atrocities.   3. War crimes.   4. Crimes against
humanity.   5. Retribution.   6. Revenge.   7. Punishment.   8. Forgiveness.
I. Title.
HV6322.7.M56   1998
303.6—DC21   98-26846

For Margot Stern Strom

Foreword

Since 1991 I have been at the cutting edge of investigations into massive violence—in South Africa, the former Yugoslavia, and Rwanda. What has struck me again and again are the similarities in the manner in which perpetrators, victims, and bystanders react to massive human rights abuses. The callous manner in which innocent people are murdered, raped, and tortured. The shallow excuses produced by the perpetrators for such brutality; the calls for justice by the victims; the pleas of ignorance by bystanders. The above situations are universal and through this one must recognize that any people anywhere have the potential for evil on a massive scale, and that all victims, whoever they may be, need the opportunity to heal. No continent, no region, and no people are immune from it.

In this book Professor Minow examines in impressive detail the choices facing societies which emerge from a period of mass violence. She draws widely from the experience of nations in Latin America, Europe, and Africa. Her inspiration came from a conference which explored this subject. It was organized by Facing History and Ourselves, the Boston-based organization which produces educational programs aimed at teaching young people how to respond to violence and how to understand the Holocaust and other genocides.

It should be recognized that in a perfect society victims are entitled to full justice, namely trial of the perpetrator and, if found guilty, adequate punishment. That ideal is not possible in the aftermath of massive violence. There are simply too many victims and too many perpetrators. Even the most sophisticated criminal justice system would be completely overwhelmed. It is for this reason that such societies have to find other solutions. Some countries simply forget the past and attempt to induce a national amnesia in its people. Of course that is bound to fail—the victims do not, indeed cannot, forget. And their unanswered calls for retribution develop into hate and invariably that hate is directed collectively at the group from which the perpetrators came. In the former Yugoslavia and Rwanda the hate induced in that way provided the tool which evil leaders used to induce those under their power to commit genocide, crimes against humanity, and other gross violations of human rights.

In other countries wiser leaders recognized that in order to lay a foundation for an enduring peace, measures had to be taken to manage the past. It was acknowledged that history has to be recorded, calls for justice have to be heeded, and perpetrators have to be called to account. As Professor Minow shows us, it is dangerous to generalize or to offer armchair advice. There is no recipe for all such situations. In most cases the choices will be limited by political, military, and economic conditions. And, whatever solution is chosen, the results will be mixed. As she puts it: "There are no tidy endings following mass atrocity." That should not on any account be used as a reason to do nothing. I would suggest that the forms of response considered in this work are not necessarily exclusive or contradictory. In South Africa, the Truth and Reconciliation Commission legislation has not prevented some of the apartheid perpetrators from being prosecuted. In Bosnia and Herzegovina, if the people of that country desire it, there is much to be said for a nonamnesty type of truth commission to be established to complement the work of the United Nations War Crimes Tribunal. In Rwanda, too, serious consideration is being given to the setting up of a truth commission and there may be no other sensible way to manage the number of people awaiting trial in unacceptable prison conditions. Certainly in that brutally torn and damaged country imaginative solutions will have to be found if it is to recover from its most recent and bloodiest experience of murder, rape, and expulsion. I have no doubt that the present policy of publicly executing con-

victed perpetrators will be interpreted by many Rwandans as
acts of simple revenge and will not bring enduring peace and reconciliation to that country. That those executed were not given
fair trials only serves to exacerbate the situation. The government of Rwanda has a massive problem in consequence of a genocide in which over ten percent of its people were murdered in the
short span of three months. That it is frustrated at the slow pace
of trials in the International Tribunal is understandable. In no
way, however, is it justified in subjecting its people, regardless of
perceived public support, to this kind of barbarity. And, in no
way should it preclude the international community from condemning that policy.

There are many obvious problems attached to criminal prosecutions in the face of such massive atrocities. Professor Minow,
with insight, refers to the difficulties arising from selective prosecutions and how this can undermine perceptions of fairness. As I
write this foreword, the chief prosecutor of the Yugoslavia Tribunal has announced the withdrawal of indictments against fourteen of those indicted by the Tribunal. As Martha Minow states:
"This decision was taken in an attempt to balance the available
resources within the Tribunal and in recognition of the need to
prosecute cases fairly and expeditiously." One can only sympa-
thize with Justice Arbour who is faced with a growing number of
defendants who are all entitled to a trial within a reasonable
time. At the same time, the effect of withdrawing the indictments
is tantamount to the grant of an amnesty notwithstanding her
warning that they may one day be reindicted. I cannot but have
regard to the effect this decision must have on the many victims
of the atrocities with which those indicted stood accused. I wonder whether arrangements could not have been made for their
trial by national courts in Bosnia or in another European
country.

Victims are too frequently neglected. They are seldom if ever
on the agenda of the politicians or the military. If they were, it
would not have taken eighteen months for a chief prosecutor to
have been appointed to the Yugoslavia Tribunal by the UN Security Council and the well-armed NATO troops to have been

ordered to arrest Karadzic and Mladic as a priority to follow
swiftly the arrest of the others indicted by the Tribunal.

A word on the South African Truth and Reconciliation Commission. I must confess to have been a supporter of that institution from the beginning and to have been involved in discussions
which led to its establishment. Its success has exceeded by far my
expectations. It had the potential for failing abysmally. It could
have been ignored. The opposite is the reality. Over 7,000 applications for amnesty. Submissions and evidence from over 20,000
victims. The evidence has stopped denials of the many serious
human rights violations committed by the apartheid security
forces.

One only has to imagine where South Africa would be today
but for the Truth and Reconciliation Commission in order to
appreciate what it has achieved. Few South Africans have been
untouched by it. All sectors of its society have been forced to
look at their own participation in apartheid—the business community, the legal, medical, and university communities. A substantial number of white South Africans, all of whom willingly
or unwillingly benefited from this evil system, have experienced
regret or shame or embarrassment.

I have not heard a black South African complain that the
Truth and Reconciliation Commission has gone on too long or
suggest that it should come to a premature end. On the other
hand, I have heard many white South Africans complain that it is
enough of "opening wounds." To whose wounds, I have wondered, are they referring? Surely not their own. And, what makes
them think that the wounds of the victims have healed? And yet,
when I said this to the playwright Ariel Dorfman, he corrected
me in his always gentle and wise manner. He pointed out that
those white South Africans are also victims of apartheid. Their
discomfort with the truth is a symptom of their shame and that,
too, makes them victims. And that is the importance of Professor
Minow's pointing out that this discussion must include not only
the perpetrators and the victims, but also the "bystanders."

And, finally, I would refer to the problems of South Africans
talking past each other. A good example is the anguish caused to

Archbishop Tutu by former President de Klerk, during his appearance before the Truth and Reconciliation Commission. To apologize meaningfully for apartheid, President de Klerk would have had to admit that there was no justification at all for the policy he had helped implement during the whole of his political career, and which his father (also a Cabinet member) had implemented before him. He would have had to admit that it was a morally offensive policy. He did neither of those things. I do not believe I would be doing him an injustice by suggesting that his apology sprang from his perception that apartheid was a mistake, not because it was morally offensive but because it failed and that it was well meant in the interests of all South Africans.

The foregoing are just some of the many issues which are raised in this outstanding work. Each page I read evoked some memory, some recognition, of my own learning experience during the past eight years of my life. It is an essential resource for anyone interested in finding a means of curbing war crimes and human rights abuses in the next millennium. In her introductory chapter the author expresses the hope of developing a vocabulary for assessing the goals and limitations of each kind of response to atrocities. She has fulfilled that hope.

Judge Richard J. Goldstone
Judge, Constitutional Court, South Africa;
former Chief Prosecutor, International Criminal
Tribunals on the former Yugoslavia and Rwanda

1. Introduction

> *"You build your life around something that cannot be healed, . . .*
> *something for which there are no words." — Dori Laub*

> *"Wound and cure, in this sensitive area,*
> *are hard to tell apart." — Geoffrey Hartman*

Will the twentieth century be most remembered for its mass atrocities? The Holocaust of World War II. The killing fields of Cambodia. Argentina's "Dirty War" against subversion and regime of torture and killing. South Africa's apartheid and the violence deployed to sustain it. The Turkish massacre of the Armenians. The Romanian terror both before and after communism. The East German system of pervasive spying and lethal enforcement around the Berlin Wall. The slaughter by Stalin. The Americans at My Lai. Uganda, Chile, Ethiopian government repression, mass tortures, and murders. Military regimes using terror and repression in Eastern Europe, Greece, Uruguay, Brazil, and elsewhere. Each of these horrific events is unique, and incomparable. And yet, a century marked by human slaughter and torture, sadly, is not a unique century in human history. Perhaps more unusual than the facts of genocides and regimes of torture marking this era is the invention of new and distinctive legal forms of response. The capacity and limitations of these legal responses illuminate the hopes and commitments of individuals and societies seeking, above all, some rejoinder to the unspeakable destruction and degradation of human beings.

A most appalling goal of the genocides,[1] the massacres, systematic rapes, and tortures has been the destruction of the remembrance of individuals as well as of their lives and dignity: this is what joins the Holocaust and Final Solution, the Rape of Nanking, the mass killings of Cambodians, the genocide of Armenians during the Turkish Revolution, the massacre of Ibos in Nigeria, the killings of the Hutus, the Gulag, the tortures of "leftists" in Chile, the students in Argentina, the victims of apartheid.

Yet some of the incidents of mass violence are linked as well by wondrous, though painful and complex, transformations of the surrounding societies after the events. Less oppressive, and even democratic regimes, emerged, for example, in Argentina, Brazil, Poland, reunified Germany, and South Africa.[2] In the course of such transitions, societies have to struggle over how much to acknowledge, whether to punish, and how to recover. How to treat the continuing presence of perpetrators, and victims, and bystanders, after the violence has ended is a central problem, or better put, series of problems. A common formulation posits the two dangers of wallowing in the past and forgetting it. Too much memory or not enough; too much enshrinement of victimhood or insufficient memorializing of victims and survivors; too much past or too little acknowledgment of the past's staging of the present; these joined dangers accompany not just societies emerging from mass violence, but also individuals recovering from trauma.

This book explores how some nations have searched for a formal response to atrocity, some national or international reframing of the events. Groups of people and leaders of nations, at times, have refused to let forgetting or denial succeed. Groping for legal responses marks an effort to embrace or renew the commitment to replace violence with words and terror with fairness. The legal responses may seem puny and always insufficient after massacres, state-sponsored tortures, systematic raping of groups of women, bombing of children. Yet societies emerging from collective violence—such as Argentina and Rwanda—have on occasion sought to prosecute those who gave orders to kill and torture, those who enacted those orders, or those who benefited from those orders. Must all such societies pursue prosecutions in order to comply with international human rights standards? Alternative legal responses, recently invented, include East Germany's extension of public access to previously secret police files and Czechoslovakia's screening and removal of officials and civil servants involved in the old regime from public office, and Canada's grants of land as restitution to First Nations groups. These are less aggressive responses than prosecution, but they may satisfy people's needs both to know what happened and to establish a clear break with the past.

Some nations, like Brazil, name the names of those who were implicated in human rights violations. Others, like Chile and South Africa, create commissions of inquiry charged with gathering the stories of victims, the truth about what happened, and at whose hands. Many, including Germany after World War II and Switzerland more recently, secure reparations for individual victims and their families or for the groups most seriously damaged. Germany also authorized financial assistance for therapeutic services for such individuals. Meanwhile, mental health professionals in Scandinavia and in Latin America try to revamp therapy to respond to collective horror without removing its effects from politics.

Nations and cities have created memorials in the forms of public monuments and sculptures, museums, and days of memory. Individuals offer works of music, poetry, and drama. Requiring and devising programs of public education, including curriculum developed for schoolchildren, is another important response. Public education can convey versions of what happened to lift secrecy, celebrate the transition, and warn against future recurrences of the atrocities. Some nations permit or promote television talk shows and more informal settings to present confrontations between victims and those who tortured them or killed their relatives. These and other measures involve people outside the government and institutions outside the law.

Quite a different strategy, adopted, for example, in Chile, Greece, Uruguay, grants amnesty or immunity from prosecution to those involved in the horrors. Yet this approach can be—and in South Africa it has been—combined with official efforts to obtain information from oppressors about what really happened. The South African Truth and Reconciliation Commission illustrates an innovative and promising effort to combine an investigation into what happened, a forum for victim testimony, a process for developing reparations, and a mechanism for granting amnesty for perpetrators who honestly tell of their role in politically motivated violence.

4   These alternatives all share one feature. They depart from doing nothing. Yes, at best they can only seek a path between too much memory and too much forgetting. Yet they also try for a way between vengeance and forgiveness. Hannah Arendt contentiously asserted that in the face of genocides, we "are unable to forgive what [we] cannot punish and [we] are unable to punish what has turned out to be unforgivable."[3] Even if she is right, it would be wrong then to do nothing. Dwelling in the frozen space of inability and incapacity is unacceptable, unresponsive to victims, unavailing to the waiting future. This is what underlies attempts to act for victims in the affirmation of atrocity.

By exploring here what can and what cannot be accomplished through differing responses to collective violence, I hope to develop and to deepen a vocabulary for assessing the goals and limitations of each kind of response to societal-level atrocities. Survivors of violence often ache for retribution against identifiable perpetrators, and for public acknowledgment of what happened. Some want financial redress; psychological or spiritual healing seems crucial to others. Some survivors, and their fellow citizens, place higher priorities on moving ahead with life, building or rebuilding trust across previously divided groups, and establishing or strengthening democratic institutions. Many believe that the entire society needs to stand behind efforts to punish the wrongdoers, and to deter any such conduct in the future. People understandably may have great trouble sorting out priorities among these possibilities.

Even so, I hope to clarify the purposes animating responses to collective violence, and the relative capacities of different societal responses to meet those purposes. I do not seek precision here; nor do I mean to imply that we can wrap up these issues with analysis or achieve a sense of completion. Two reasons animate my resistance to tidiness. First, the variety of circumstances and contexts for each nation, and indeed each person, must inflect and inform purposes in dealing with the past and methods that work or can even be tried. It matters whether the new regime took over through combat or negotiation with the old leaders, and whether the wrongdoing involves a small portion or a large portion of the population; it matters whether the individual has a profound religious confidence in a divine realm of consequences for behavior on earth, or a strong desire to invest energy in surviving family members. Saying that context matters is not the end of the analysis. Rather, it is the beginning.

The second, and perhaps more crucial reason to resist any implication of exactness or closure in such matters is that *no* response can ever be adequate when your son has been killed by police ordered to shoot at a crowd of children; when you have been dragged out of your home, interrogated, and raped in a wave of "ethnic cleansing"; or when your brother who struggled against a repressive government has disappeared and left only a secret police file, bearing no clue to his final resting place. Closure is not possible. Even if it were, any closure would insult those whose lives are forever ruptured. Even to speak, to grope for words to describe horrific events, is to pretend to negate their unspeakable qualities and effects. Yet silence is also an unacceptable offense, a shocking implication that the perpetrators in fact succeeded, a stunning indictment that the present audience is simply the current incarnation of the silent bystanders complicit with oppressive regimes. Legal responses are inevitably frail and insufficient. As Larry Langer writes: "the logic of law will never make sense of the illogic of genocide."[4] But inaction by legal institutions means that the perpetrators prevailed in paralyzing the instruments of justice. Even new waves of massive violence turned upon the oppressors would offer more hope than inaction for the resurgence of ideals, of justice, of humanity. Yet new cycles of revenge and violence in the name of justice kill even that hope.

So this book inevitably becomes a fractured meditation on the incompleteness and inescapable inadequacy of each possible response to collective atrocities. It is also a small effort to join in the resistance to forgetting. It is an effort to speak even of the failures of speech and justice, truth-telling and reparation, remembering and educating, in the service of urging, nonetheless,

6   response. It is a missive to the next generation, in the next century, in the fearful acknowledgment that we are not done with mass violence, nor expert in recovering from it.

An estimated 20,000 Muslim women and girls were raped by Serb men between 1991 and 1995 in Bosnia as part of the collective violence in that region. Two women, Jadranka Cigelj and Nusreta Sivac, themselves survivors of this violence, labored to present their own stories and to gather those of more than 400 others who were detained, tortured, starved, and raped.[5] Their captors released Cigelj and Sivac with others from the Omarska internment camp after the international media started to uncover the violence. Devastated physically and mentally, both women found strength in telling their stories to the media. They helped make an award-winning documentary, *Calling the Ghosts*. They submitted testimony to the International Criminal Tribunal for the former Yugoslavia. In June of 1996, the tribunal issued indictments for the arrest of eight men and thereby launched the first prosecutions recognizing rape as a weapon of war and a crime against humanity.[6]

There is not, and could not be, a happy ending to this story. Five years after the event, nearly all the rapists remain free "as do the commanders who exploited rape as a weapon."[7] A few prosecutions recently began against those indicted for the rapes. Yet, the presiding judge called for shutting down the International Criminal Tribunal unless the United States or the NATO powers made the instigators of the Bosnian war available for trial. Julia Hall, a member of the team investigating women's issues in Bosnia for the nongovernmental organization Human Rights Watch reported in 1998 that "women are now saying they don't want to testify. They want to get on with their lives. Women want justice, and they have a need for justice. But they do not think they are going to get it."[8] The vision of international enforcement of human rights laws is both enlarged and vitiated by this incomplete, if not failed effort.

In a collaboration with people in an organization called Facing History and Ourselves, I have spent the past two years exploring the range of possible institutional responses to collective violence, genocide, apartheid, and torture. Facing History and Ourselves develops curricular materials and teacher-training sessions for high schools and middle schools around the United States, and increasingly the program consults with people in other countries who want schools to address the Holocaust, apartheid, and criminal regimes. What lessons can be learned—and what should be taught—to young people growing up in a world that has known, and still produces incomprehensible patterns of violence and torture? Would it be better to shield young people from the fact of those patterns until they grow up? The wager made by programs like Facing History and Ourselves is that young people would do better to learn about the horrors that have occurred at the hands of adults than to be subject to silence about the events that still shape their world. Young people, understandably, want to know what has been done, and what can be done, to respond, redress, and prevent future occurrences. They ask whether it is possible to find a stance between vengeance and forgiveness, a stance for survivors, bystanders, and the next generations.

Students should come to know that remarkable individuals, themselves victims and survivors, sometimes achieve a stance between vengeance and forgiveness. Jadranka Cigelj, one of the women from Bosnia who pursued international justice, found herself changing as she collected testimony from other survivors. Through a translator, she said,

> When you come out of a place like Omarska, you're filled with negative emotions and it's natural to seek revenge. To seek revenge you must hate. But I remember the story of an 86-year-old woman whose 14 family members were murdered and she had to bury all of them with her bare hands. And she said to me, "How can you hate those who are so repulsive?" I realized that the people I was directing my hatred toward were not worth that; they were only machines for murdering people.[9]

Cigelj continued,

> When you think of a 15-year-old girl whose entire world was destroyed, who was supposed to have the experience of moving

from childhood to womanhood under a moon somewhere in somebody's arms, when you think of how her youth was stolen and how she was turned into a wounded animal, you realize that what is important is to work toward a way to hold these people responsible and punish them. Then one day you wake up and the hatred has left you, and you feel relieved because hatred is exhausting, and you say to yourself, "I am not like them."[10]

For this extraordinary woman, herself a lawyer, the focus on prosecution, punishment, and documentation of victims' stories affords a way past revenge. This focus would not work for everyone, in all times and places. Remarkable personal strength is required, and a capacity to transform the impulse for revenge into a search for something larger. So is a particular cultural and perhaps even professional conception that establishing rape as a crime against humanity is such a larger something. Without a personal transformation, the focus on prosecution can entrench an adversarial thirst for revenge. That kind of thirst is seldom satisfied even by successful prosecutions, and failure in the prosecutorial structure can seem another betrayal.

But the possibility of prosecutions for war crimes can at least offer an armature for the rage and courage of individuals and nations devastated by mass atrocities. What other cultural and legal forms can afford structures for individuals to move from anger to the steady knowledge and commitment about being "not like them"? Are there harms that have too often gone unrecognized, unnamed, unredressed? Can and should there be alternatives to traditional institutional responses? Should working through the emotions of victims and survivors figure prominently in the goals for the nation or the world, or instead find a place as by-products of fact-finding, guilt-finding, and punishment? Is it possible for individuals to heal in the wake of mass atrocities? Is it meaningful even to imagine the healing of a nation riven by oppression, mass killings, torture?

The questions will outstrip any answers. As Ruby Plenty Chiefs once said, "Great evil has been done on earth by people who think they have all the answers."[11]

2. Vengeance and Forgiveness

"Forgiveness . . . seems to rule out retribution, moral reproach, nonreconciliation, a demand for restitution, and in short, any act of holding the wrongdoer to account." —Chesire Calhoun

"Boundless vindictive rage is not the only alternative to unmerited forgiveness." —Susan Jacoby

Perhaps there simply are two purposes animating societal responses to collective violence: justice and truth.[1] Justice may call for truth but also demands accountability. And the institutions for securing accountability—notably, trial courts—may impede or ignore truth. Democratic guarantees protecting the rights of defendants place those rights at least in part ahead of truth-seeking; undemocratic trials may proceed to judgment and punishment with disregard for particular truths or their complex implications beyond particular defendants. Then the question becomes: Should justice or truth take precedence? Of what value are facts without justice? If accountability is the aim, does it require legal proceedings and punishment? Do legal proceedings generate knowledge?[2] One answer calls for "[a]ll the truth and as much justice as possible";[3] another would stress punishment for wrongdoing, especially horrific wrongdoing. Only if we make prosecution a duty under international law will we ensure that new regimes do not lose courage, overstate the obstacles they face, and duck their duties to punish perpetrators of mass violence, argue experts such as Diane Orentlicher.[4] Yet only if we acknowledge that prosecutions are slow, partial, and narrow, can we recognize the value of independent commissions, investigating the larger patterns of atrocity and complex lines of responsibility and complicity.

Even this debate is too partial. Truth and justice are not the only objectives. At least, they do not transparently indicate the range of concerns they may come to comprise. There is another basic, perhaps implicit pair of goals or responses to collective violence—vengeance and forgiveness.

Vengeance: Although this word may sound pejorative, it embodies important ingredients of moral response to wrongdoing. We should pursue punishment because wrongdoers should get what is coming to them; this is one defense—or perhaps restatement—of vengeance. Vengeance is the impulse to retaliate when wrongs are done. Through vengeance, we express our basic self-respect. Philosopher Jeffrie Murphy explains, "a person who does not resent moral injuries done to him . . . is almost necessarily a person lacking in self-respect."[5] Vengeance is also the wellspring of a notion of equivalence that animates justice. Recompense, getting satisfaction, matching like with like, giving what's coming to the wrongdoer, equalizing crime and punishment, an eye for an eye; each of these synonyms for revenge implies the proportionality of the scales of justice.[6] Yet vengeance could unleash more response than the punishment guided by the rule of law, more even than the punishment consistent with the goal of forgiving those who have paid their price, or served their time.

The danger is that precisely the same vengeful motive often leads people to exact more than necessary, to be maliciously spiteful or dangerously aggressive,[7] or to become hateful themselves by committing the reciprocal act of violence. The core motive may be admirable but it carries with it potential insatiability. Vengeance thus can set in motion a downward spiral of violence,[8] or an unquenchable desire that traps people in cycles of revenge, recrimination, and escalation. In a book examining themes of punishment and forgiveness in literary works, John Reed notes that the danger of retaliation is "splendidly, if comically, illustrated by those Laurel and Hardy episodes when such a pattern of destructive retaliation, beginning with something as trivial as the inadvertent damaging of a shrub, may escalate rapidly to the trashing of vehicles and the virtual demolition of houses."[9]

Consider a more serious example: A Holocaust survivor portrayed in a recent novel explains to a man who has brutally lost a relative that to survive the death of people close to you, you need rituals. "In the camps there was no possibility of ritual—no corpses, no funerals, no sending or receiving condolences. So I created a ritual appropriate to the situation in which I found myself. . . . I spent three years tracking down the doctor who sent them to the gas" and upon finding him, "I created one last ritual . . . With these hands I strangled him." Only then, he explained, was he able to begin a new family and a new life. "It didn't bring them back from the dead," replied his interlocutor. The survivor answered, "It brought *me* back from the dead."[10]

Adam Michnick, the Polish Solidarity activist, opposed a proposal to purge communist collaborators from working in formerly state-run enterprises because of its implications of vengeance. He claimed that the logic of revenge "is implacable. First, there is a purge of yesterday's adversaries, the partisans of the old regime. Then comes the purge of yesterday's fellow-oppositionists, who now oppose the idea of revenge. Finally, there is the purge of those who defend them. A psychology of vengeance and hatred develops. The mechanisms of retaliation become unappeasable."[11]

Vengeance can lead to horrible excesses and still fail to restore what was destroyed initially. At a personal level, the result can be painful and futile vendettas. At a societal level, as the recent conflicts in Bosnia and Rwanda only too vividly demonstrate, memories, or propaganda-inspired illusions about memories, can motivate people who otherwise live peaceably to engage in torture and slaughter of neighbors identified as members of groups who committed past atrocities. The result can be devastating, escalating intergroup violence. Mass killings are the fruit of revenge for perceived past harms.

For Michnick, and for others, the way to avoid such escalating violence is to transfer the responsibilities for apportioning blame and punishment from victims to public bodies acting according to the rule of law. This is an attempt to remove personal animus, though not necessarily to excise vengeance.[12] Tame it, balance it, recast it as the retributive dimension of public punishment.[13]

Retribution can be understood as vengeance curbed by the intervention of someone other than the victim and by principles of proportionality and individual rights. Retribution motivates punishment out of fairness to those who have been wronged and reflects a belief that wrongdoers deserve blame and punishment in direct proportion to the harm inflicted.[14] Otherwise, wrongdoers not only inflict pain but also degrade and diminish victims without a corrective response. The retributive dimension insists on punishment not necessarily in search of deterrence or any other future effects, but instead as a way of denouncing previous wrongs and giving persons their deserts.[15] Yet assigning retribution to public prosecutors rather than reserving it for individual victims does not guarantee appropriate or respectable results, as Stalin's show trials and other abuses of public prosecution indicate.

In a powerful argument, philosopher Jean Hampton explains that retribution at its core expresses an ideal that can afford proper limitation, and thereby differ in theory from vengeance.[16] The ideal is equal dignity of all persons. Through retribution, the community corrects the wrongdoer's false message that the victim was less worthy or valuable than the wrongdoer; through retribution, the community reasserts the truth of the victim's value by inflicting a publicly visible defeat on the wrongdoer.[17] From Hampton's perspective, commitment to this ideal carries an internal limitation on retribution. The very reason for engaging in retributive punishment constrains the punishment from degrading or denying the dignity even of the defeated wrongdoer.[18] Thus, "[i]t is no more right when the victim tries to degrade or falsely diminish the wrongdoer than when the wrongdoer originally degraded or falsely diminished the victim."[19]

But whether retribution, properly understood and enacted, carries its own limitations, or whether limitations on retribution must be supplied from outside through competing ideals such as mercy and moral decency,[20] retribution needs constraints. Otherwise, it risks expanding into forms of harm that violate respect for persons, and that threaten the bounds of proportionality and decency. Moreover, giving in to emotions that often circle revenge and retribution can be self-defeating and illusory.

Traumatized people imagine that revenge will bring relief, even though the fantasy of revenge simply reverses the roles of perpetrator and victim, continuing to imprison the victim in horror, degradation, and the bounds of the perpetrator's violence. By seeking to lower the perpetrator in response to his or her infliction of injury, does the victim ever master the violence or instead become its tool? Satisfaction may never come. We should avoid hatred and revenge, Jean Hampton urges, not in order to be unreasonably saintly, but instead to be sensible.[21] Avenging the self can be too costly emotionally, by stoking consuming fires of hatred. Psychologist Judith Herman reports that "[p]eople who actually commit acts of revenge, such as combat veterans who commit atrocities, do not succeed in getting rid of their post-traumatic symptoms; rather, they seem to suffer the most severe and intractable disturbances."[22]

Moving from needs of victims to societal concerns, Jeffrie Murphy, a defender of retribution, urges recognition of the legitimate bounds of hatred and outrage over wrongdoing. Limitations are demanded for decency, for the sanity of the victims, and for the needs of an orderly society.[23] It is often impossible to get even because the wrongdoer is unreachable or because no proportional response could be conscionable.[24]

These concerns are nowhere better placed than in the context of collective violence, genocide, and mass atrocities. For at no other time does the need to condemn the misconduct seem more compelling; and at no other time does revenge bypass the usual societal constraints over the conduct of individuals, groups, or states. Michael Ignatieff explains,

> What seems apparent in the former Yugoslavia is that the past continues to torment because it is not the past. These places are not living in a serial order of time but in a simultaneous one, in which the past and present are a continuous, agglutinated mass of fantasies,

distortions, myths, and lies. Reporters in the Balkan wars often observed that when they were told atrocity stories they were occasionally uncertain whether these stories had occurred yesterday or in 1941, or 1841, or 1441.[25]

He concludes that this "is the dreamtime of vengeance. Crimes can never safely be fixed in the historical past; they remain locked in the eternal present, crying out for vengeance."[26] As Geoffrey Hartman puts it, "[t]he entanglement of memory and revenge does not cease."[27]

Finding some alternative to vengeance—such as government-managed prosecutions—is a matter, then, not only of moral and emotional significance. It is urgent for human survival.

Forgiveness: Reaching for a response far from vengeance, many people, from diverse religious traditions, call for forgiveness. The victim should not seek revenge and become a new victimizer but instead should forgive the offender and end the cycle of offense. When we have been injured by another's offense, we should seek to reconnect and recognize the common humanity of the other, and grant forgiveness to underscore and strengthen our commonality.[28] Through forgiveness, we can renounce resentment, and avoid the self-destructive effects of holding on to pain, grudges, and victimhood. The act of forgiving can reconnect the offender and the victim and establish or renew a relationship; it can heal grief; forge new, constructive alliances; and break cycles of violence.[29]

These aspirations may seem especially compelling following a period of mass atrocity. Finding a way to move on, as individuals and as a society, takes central stage. If the nation is turning or returning to democracy, forging new relationships of trust and foundations for collective self-government become urgent goals. Those very goals may be jeopardized by backward-looking, finger-pointing prosecutions and punishments.

José Zalaquett, a Chilean human rights activist, maintains that underneath truth, justice, and forgiveness lie the "twin goals of prevention and reparation in the process of moral reconstruction."[30] This formulation acknowledges that vengeance can be excessive or unquenchable, and that preoccupation with harms in the past can be debilitating for victims and bystanders. Instead, through forgiveness, victims can reassert their own power and reestablish their own dignity while also teaching wrongdoers the effects of their harmful actions. They can seek the reintegration of oppressors into society for their own sake, and for the sake of the larger projects of reconciliation and the rebuilding of a more fair and more humane world.

In theory, forgiveness does not and should not take the place of justice or punishment.[31] Forgiveness marks a change in how the offended feels about the person who committed the injury, not a change in the actions to be taken by a justice system.[32] Philosopher Jeffrie Murphy explains, "[b]ecause I have ceased to hate the person who has wronged me it does not follow that I act inconsistently if I still advocate his being forced to pay compensation for the harm he has done or his being forced to undergo punishment for his wrongdoing—that he, in short, get his just deserts."[33] Advocating punishment for a wrongdoer one has forgiven in fact is well supported by reference to the impersonal processes of a justice system, the inherent operations of a theory of deserts, or a commitment to treat offenders as full members of a community that demands responsibility by autonomous actors for their actions.[34] Forgiveness in this sense need not be a substitute for punishment. Even the traditional Christian call to forgive rather than avenge accompanies faith that vengeance will come—through the Divine.[35]

Yet, in practice, forgiveness often produces exemption from punishment. Especially when a governmental body adopts a forgiving attitude toward offenders, the instrument often takes the form of amnesty or pardon, preempting prosecution and punishment. This institutionalizes forgetfulness, and sacrifices justice in a foreshortened effort to move on. Moreover, such an effort to move on often fails because the injury is not so much forgiven but publicly ignored, leaving it to fester. After tireless work gathering the testimony of Bosnian Muslim women who had been rounded up, detained, and raped by Bosnian Serb soldiers, and helping to convince the International Criminal Tribunal for the Former Yugoslavia to bring indictments declaring rape a war crime, Jadranka Cigelj reflected on the failure of prosecutions five years later: "We are so disillusioned. We wonder if we shouldn't put all this behind us."[36]

Even when offered for moral reasons rather than realpolitik, forgiveness may appear to elevate the wrongdoer at least as someone worthy of forgiveness. Philosopher Chesire Calhoun warns that forgiveness "seems to rule out retribution, moral reproach, nonreconciliation, a demand for restitution, and, in short, any act of holding the wrongdoer to account."[37] Even if others maintain it is possible to forgive and still punish, forgiveness may mean ultimately forgetting or putting aside the harm. How can survivors of atrocity ever do that, emotionally? Even those who seek to forgive or move on need to face and address the fact and scope of the wrong that would occasion the forgiveness or forbearance.[38] Some may seek a way to reconcile with perpetrators, even perpetrators of atrocity, as a way to choose to be different from those perpetrators, to embrace a different set of values.[39]

Yet discerning and explaining the meaning of no punishment for war criminals, with or without official grants of immunity or amnesty, can be very difficult. If there is no punishment for those who ordered and committed the murders of hundreds and thousands of people, does the society imply forgiveness, or instead fear? Impediments to justice, especially in the context of war crimes prosecutions, "give rise to the suspicion that 'forgiveness' is nothing but a nice word for 'forgetfulness' and 'pardon' a synonym of 'amnesia.'"[40] Forgetfulness and amnesia, in turn, seem anathemas in response to mass violence because they let the perpetrators prevail in blotting out memories and avoiding punishment. Victims and witnesses who seek to forget ironically may assist the perpetrators by keeping silent about their crimes. Silence about violence locks perpetrators and victims in the cruel pact of denial, literally and psychologically.

Donald Shriver, who has written eloquently about the need for forgiveness in politics, also vividly explains the problems with forgetting atrocities: "Pain can sear the human memory in two

crippling ways: with forgetfulness of the past or imprisonment in
it. The mind that insulates the traumatic past from conscious
memory plants a live bomb in the depths of the psyche—it takes
no great grasp of psychiatry to know that. But the mind that
fixes on pain risks getting trapped in it. Too horrible to remember, too horrible to forget: down either path lies little health for
the human sufferers of great evil.''[41]

Human rights activist Aryeh Neier warns that public forgiveness in particular runs the risk of signaling to everyone the need
to forget. When governments or their representatives "usurp the
victim's exclusive right to forgive his oppressor," they thereby
fail to respect fully those who have suffered.[42] Governmental forgiveness that means exemption from punishment also forecloses
the communal response, the acknowledgment of harm, that vengeance, and indeed justice, demand. Even if the rigor of prosecution and punishment are not pursued, some other form of public
acknowledgment, overcoming communal denial, is the very least
that can be done to restore dignity to victims.

Observers of South Africa's Truth and Reconciliation Commission note that although many who were victimized are prepared
to forgive or reconcile with police officers and government officials from the apartheid regime, the survivors recoil when perpetrators greet victims with open arms and handshakes.[43] In these
cases, forgiveness is assumed, rather than granted. A survivor
may think, "should you not wait for me to stretch out my hand
to you, when I'm ready, when I've established what is right?"[44]
Forgiveness is a power held by the victimized, not a right to
be claimed. The ability to dispense, but also to withhold, forgiveness is an ennobling capacity and part of the dignity to be
reclaimed by those who survive the wrongdoing. Even an individual survivor who chooses to forgive cannot, properly, forgive
in the name of other victims.[45] To expect survivors to forgive is
to heap yet another burden on them.

Perhaps forgiveness should be reserved, as a concept and a
practice, to instances where there are good reasons to forgive. To
forgive without a good reason is to accept the violation and deval-
uation of the self. Some acts of forgiveness raise questions about

whether the victim has enough self-respect or strength to view the injury as a violation.[46] If forgiveness involves letting go of warranted resentment, then the forgiver needs a good reason to let go. If the offense injured and devalued the victim, then the victim must have some very good reason to overcome the anger and hatred toward a person who committed such unjustified and inexcusable harm.[47] Expressing outrage, making clear what is unacceptable, and refusing relationships with those who commit evil are responses especially justifiable after mass violence.[48] There may be no good reason to forego blame and condemnation. "[H]ow could one even *consider* reconciling oneself with people such as Hitler or Stalin or Charles Manson, who really may not have any decency left in them—nor even any possibility of decency?"[49]

In ordinary, everyday instances of wrongdoing, a reason to forgive arises, for some, when a wrongdoer changes, becomes "a new person" who repents his or her wrongs. But repentance for participation in a mass atrocity may simply be insufficient. Because no subsequent change of heart or regret could begin to be commensurate with the violations done, forgiveness seems out of place.[50]

Yet, especially for some people working from a Christian tradition, forgiveness may not even require repentance by the wrongdoer. Instead, they hope that the act of forgiving may transform the wrongdoer, softening her or his heart and reinviting her or him into the moral community of humanity.[51] Left with the unrepentant and apparently indecent offender, the victim who considers forgiving must abandon hope for the offender's own contrition, or else vest in the act of forgiveness inspiration, or pressure, to change that wrongdoer.[52] Some religious traditions support such stances; some do not.

Hoping that the process of forgiveness can itself transform the wrongdoer depends upon a script that must be shared by the forgiven and the forgiver. John Reed explains: "The forgiven must act likewise and be forgiving. Moreover, to be forgiven, one must first acknowledge fault."[53] If both participants play their part, the process can heal the offender and also restore a sense of dignity and self-respect to the offended person.[54] Thus, a reason to forgive might be to set in motion this process, and thereby seek to break cycles of violence by transforming perpetrators and victims. Yet many people do not share this script. Pardon does not transform all perpetrators. Making contrition a precondition for pardon simply increases the likelihood that contrition will be feigned. Granting forgiveness to transgressors who show no contrition or regret cannot be justified in hopes of changing the unrepentant offender. If the initial angry thirst for retribution was righteous, then it rightly calls for a restoration of the balance of rights and wrongs. Simply forgiving the recalcitrant wrongdoer does not accomplish that task, although it may aid the victim's own process of healing.

Victims have much to gain from being able to let go of hatred, even when the perpetrator is unrepentant. Rabbi Harold Kushner argues that victims should forgive not because the other deserves it but because the victim does not want to turn into a bitter resentful person.[55] Victims should release the anger for their own sake.[56] Indeed, especially after mass atrocities, life could seem so precious that not a moment should be wasted in grudges or hatred toward the perpetrators. Dumisa Ntsebeza, a commissioner of the South Africa Truth and Reconciliation Commission who himself spent years incarcerated under the apartheid regime, explained that there could be generosity toward perpetrators because "there is so much to do in the time that remains of one's freedom."[57]

Some psychological or religious views suggest that forgiveness can help to transform perpetrators and victims, or simply victims. Even bystanders, advocates claim, can be helped by forgiveness in ways they cannot by judicial action.[58] The South African Truth and Reconciliation Commission created a register for submissions and comments by people who are neither direct victims of apartheid atrocities nor direct perpetrators. In the flood of comments initially received, a recurring refrain was "I should have done more to fight the atrocities."[59] In participating in a process that combines truth-telling and a spirit of forgiveness with personal contrition, even bystanders can join the effort for reconciliation.

A general endorsement of the therapeutic benefits of forgiveness, though, confuses "specific acts of deserved forgiveness with a policy of unconditional forgiveness."[60] A victim consumed with hatred and revenge fantasies could find some relief directly through professional psychological help rather than forgiveness of the murderer. Learning to manage or extinguish pain and resentment, becoming able to sleep and get on with life, to coexist with former enemies, are valuable goals; but they do not require, entail, nor necessarily accompany grants of forgiveness.[61]

Fundamentally, forgiveness cannot be commanded. No friend, cleric, or official can force another to grant forgiveness to an offender. A victim who considers forgiving must summon compassion, benevolence, love, or a profound sense of the flaws shared by all human beings, victims and offenders alike.[62] Some victims instead summon righteous indignation, an urgent need to condemn and punish, or a generous desire, coupled with passion to bear witness and to prosecute, in order to prevent any repeated horror for anyone else.

Individual human beings are just that, individual human beings, both before and after anyone is victimized and then labeled as a victim. Individuals respond uniquely and differently to horror. At least the responses are their own. To demand different ones may be yet another form of degradation and denial of their very being. If forgiveness is announced by someone who was not wronged, perhaps by a public official claiming to speak on behalf of victims, it is a call to forgetting or putting aside the memories, not the act of forgiveness itself. Forgiveness can slip into forgetting or else elude those from whom it must come. Geoffrey Hartman, scholar of literature and the Holocaust, writes: "Amnesty is lawful amnesia; and what takes place at this highly formalized level may also take place in the domain of the social or collective memory."[63] Perhaps amnesty conditioned upon acknowledgment of the particular acts of violence takes a different shape.[64] If vengeance risks ceaseless rage that should be tamed, forgiveness requires a kind of transcendence that cannot be achieved on command or by remote control.[65]

Vengeance and forgiveness are marks along the spectrum of human responses to atrocity. Yet they stand in opposition: to forgive is to let go of vengeance; to avenge is to resist forgiving. Perhaps justice itself "partakes of both revenge and forgiveness."[66]

So I return to the central question: Might paths lie between vengeance and forgiveness? Susan Jacoby suggests:

> A wife need not forgive an unashamedly brutal husband in order to avoid dousing him with gasoline and setting him on fire; a concentration-camp survivor need not pray for God's blessing on the Nazis in order to refrain from personally settling scores in the manner of spy-novel avengers; a society need not set murderers free if it refuses to put them to death; the leaders of adversary nations need not throw their arms around one another in order to restrain themselves from destroying the world in a nuclear holocaust.[67]

Jacoby urges a search for the right forms of retribution and the right forms of forgiveness.

I suggest a similar spirit but—an expanded—scope of possibilities. What responses do or could lie between vengeance and forgiveness, *if legal and cultural institutions offered other avenues for individuals and nations?* For nations recovering from periods of massive atrocity, the stakes are high, the dangers enormous. Members of those societies need to ask not only what should count as a good reason to forgive, and not only what are the appropriate limits to vengeance. They need to ask, what would it take, and what do our current or imagined institutions need to do, to come to terms with the past, to help heal the victims, the bystanders, and even the perpetrators? What would promote reconstruction of a society devastated by atrocities? What could build a nation capable of preventing future massacres and incidents or regimes of torture?

One path between vengeance and forgiveness pursues therapeutic goals. Promoting healing for individual victims, bystand-

22   ers, and even offenders points to potential aims in response to
mass atrocity. Recognizing healing as a value prompts new questions. What relative importance should the therapeutic goals
have for victims, bystanders, and offenders, and what weight
should therapeutic purposes bear in relation to the search for
truth, the demand for justice, the urge for retribution, and the
call of forgiveness? What place should a psychological frame of
analysis have in assessing alternative responses to collective
atrocities by individuals and societies? What if any sense is there
in drawing analogies between the psychological needs and therapeutic responses appropriate to individuals, and issues involving
entire groups of people, and even societies?

The striking prevalence of therapeutic language in contemporary discussions of mass atrocities stands in contrast to comparable debates fifty years ago. What is gained, and what is lost,
through the attention to psychological healing, in contrast with
gathering facts or securing punishments? Does the effort to overcome denial and to search for a complete factual picture deserve
the highest priority after genocide? When is the language of healing itself an insult to those whose devastation is inconsolable,
untellable, unassimilable? Therapeutic purposes contrast starkly
with political ones, although in practice the two influence one
another. The topic of forgiveness, for instance, is sometimes
addressed in political terms. Who should have the power to forgive, or to withhold forgiveness, who should be forced to beg for
it?[68] The most important political response to mass violence,
some argue, is to change the political structure. Restore democracy, dismantle the military that presided over torture cells,
remove the officials who ran the bureaucracy of oppression.
These changes could have great psychological consequences for
those removed from power and for survivors of their abuses. Yet
the point of such intervention is political; the method of response
is institutional.

Political concerns are often aimed at another set of goals, also
lying somewhere between vengeance and forgiveness. The first is
creating a climate conducive to human rights, a democratic process that seems to many a crucial rejoinder to mass violence. To

mark the defeat of terror; to set in place safeguards against future collective atrocity; to communicate the aspiration that "never again" will such abominations happen—these are all significant human rights accomplishments that may be set in motion by political means. When terror was state sponsored, vital responses would establish the legitimacy and stability of a new regime.

Promoting reconciliation across divisions created by, or themselves causing, the collective violence is still another goal. Such reconciliation would assist stability, and democracy, but it also would require other measures: restoring dignity to victims would be part of this process, but so would dealing respectfully with those who assisted or were complicit with the violence. Otherwise, new rifts and resentments are likely to emerge and grow.

Each of these purposes propels and repels alternative responses that a nation can pursue when emerging from mass atrocity. Potential responses to collective violence include not only prosecutions and amnesties, but also commissions of inquiry into the facts; opening access to secret police files; removing prior political and military officials and civil servants from their posts and from the rolls for public benefits; publicizing names of offenders and names of victims; securing reparations and apologies for victims; devising and making available appropriate therapeutic services for any affected by the horrors; devising art and memorials to mark what happened, to honor victims, and to communicate the aspiration of "never again"; and advancing public educational programs to convey what happened and to strengthen participatory democracy and human rights. What can be hoped for, and what cannot, from these responses to collective violence?

Observers of contemporary Western art suggest it resists the paradigm that contrasts punishment and forgiveness, a paradigm that dominated earlier Western art. For example, the novels of Joseph Conrad never depict forgiveness nor even render it conceivable, but instead manifest the cruelty of human existence.[69] In even more recent chronicles of revenge, no public punishment nor prospect of forgiveness appears. Instead, people who have been victimized have no expectation that anyone, human or divine, will assume their psychic burden. Thus, they must discharge it themselves or be crushed, with no legitimate outlet for rage.[70]

There is in these stories a lack of closure, and the impossibility of balance and satisfaction, in the face of incomprehensible human violence. Saul Friedlander, a historian who attempts to address the Holocaust, argues that it is imperative for people to render as truthful an account as documents and testimonials will allow, *without giving in to the temptations of closure*, because that would avoid what remains inevitably indeterminate, elusive, and inexplicable about collective horrors.[71] Crucial here, Friedlander reminds us, is an effort to introduce individual memories and individual voices in a field dominated by political decisions and administrative decrees.[72] For all who would know the history, the voices of individual victims can puncture seeming normality and prevent flight from the concreteness of despair, pain, and death.

3. Trials

"That four great nations, flushed with victory and stung with injury, stay the hand of vengeance and voluntarily submit their captive enemies to the judgment of the law is one of the most significant tributes that Power has ever paid to Reason."
—Justice Robert Jackson, U.S. prosecutor at Nuremberg

"Many experts on Nuremberg, including Telford Taylor, who was the chief prosecutor for the U.S. military tribunal, argue that Nuremberg's cry for human rights would have carried further if the tribunal had not stepped on so many legal principles itself."
—Tina Rosenberg

To respond to mass atrocity with legal prosecutions is to embrace the rule of law. This common phrase combines several elements. First, there is a commitment to redress harms with the application of general, preexisting norms. Second, the rule of law calls for administration by a formal system itself committed to fairness and opportunities for individuals to be heard both in accusation and in defense. Further, a government proceeding under the rule of law aims to treat each individual person in light of particular, demonstrated evidence.[1] In the Western liberal legal tradition, the rule of law also entails the presumption of innocence, litigation under the adversary system, and the ideal of a government by laws, rather than by persons. No one is above or outside the law, and no one should be legally condemned or sanctioned outside legal procedures. The rule of law creates a community in which each member is both fenced in and protected by the law and its institutions. To bring these ideas to state-sponsored or state-countenanced mass murders, tortures, and deprivations of human rights requires a belief that even these massive horrors can and should be treated as punishable criminal offenses perpetrated by identifiable individuals.[2] As Judge Richard Goldstone, the first lead prosecutor for the International Tribunals for the former Yugoslavia and Rwanda comments, "the success of the international tribunals will be tested by whether the trials were fair," not by the number of prosecutions or convictions.[3] Applying the rule of law in these cases expresses the hope that legal institutions can handle such issues without betraying the ideals of law for the exigencies and pressures of politics, personal biases, or yet a new phase in the cycles of revenge and power struggles.

A trial in the aftermath of mass atrocity, then, should mark an effort between vengeance and forgiveness. It transfers the individuals' desires for revenge to the state or official bodies. The transfer cools vengeance into retribution, slows judgment with procedure, and interrupts, with documents, cross-examination, and the presumption of innocence, the vicious cycle of blame and feud. The trial itself steers clear of forgiveness, however. It announces a demand not only for accountability and acknowledgment of harms done, but also for unflinching punishment. At the end of the trial process, after facts are found and convictions are secured, there might be forgiveness of a legal sort: a suspended sentence, or executive pardon, or clemency in light of humanitarian concerns. Even then, the process has exacted time and agony from, and rendered a kind of punishment for defendants, while also accomplishing change in their relationships to prosecutors, witnesses, and viewing public. Reconciliation is not the goal of criminal trials except in the most abstract sense. We reconcile with the murderer by imagining he or she is responsible to the same rules and commands that govern all of us; we agree to sit in the same room and accord the defendant a chance to speak, and a chance to fight for his or her life. But reconstruction of a relationship, seeking to heal the accused, or indeed, healing the rest of the community, are not the goals in any direct sense. Getting out the facts through an adversarial test, applying clear norms to conduct, reaching a judgment based on facts and norms, all seek the separation of the adjudicated wrongdoer from others through sentencing to prison or death. The trial works in the key of formal justice, sounding closure through a full and final hearing, a verdict, a sentence.

When any nation or international body seeks to prosecute indi-

viduals for war crimes or domestically perpetrated mass violence, it embraces and builds upon the complex legacies of the
Nuremberg and Tokyo trials conducted after World War II. By
the end of the twentieth century, politicians, leaders, and human
rights activists cited these trials as landmark contributions to the
struggles for a just world order. The World War II war crimes
trials represent the possibility of legal responses, rather than
responses grounded in sheer power politics or military aggression. The images of defendants, preserved on film, display not
the horrors of their acts but the methodical, careful processes of
litigation.

In their own time, however, the Nuremberg and Tokyo trials
were condemned by many as travesties of justice, the spoils of the
victors of war, and the selective prosecution of individuals for
acts more properly attributable to governments themselves.[4] Yet,
perhaps due to the haze of half-century distance, and the celebratory tone of anniversary-marking events, these critiques today
hardly surface in popular consciousness. Instead, the World
War II trials receive credit for helping to launch an international
movement for human rights and for the legal institutions needed
to implement such rights. Domestic trials, inspired in part by the
Nuremberg trials, include Israel's prosecution of Adolph Eichmann for his conduct during World War II; Argentina's prosecution of 500 members of the military junta involved in state
terrorism and the murder of 10,000 to 30,000 people; Germany's prosecution of border guards and their supervisors
involved in shooting escapees from East Germany; and Poland's
trial of General Jaruzelski for his imposition of martial law.

It is hard not to notice, however, the enormous gap in time
between the Nuremberg trials and any comparable effort to prosecute war crimes in international settings. Indeed, not until the
recently convened International Criminal Tribunals for the
former Yugoslavia and for Rwanda in the early 1990s did
international institutions undertake any similar efforts. The
intervening forty years included many atrocities, and this fact
undermines claims that the Nuremberg trials deterred mass violence. The failure of international bodies to craft a legal response

to the mass murders in Cambodia, South Africa, and Kurdistan, just to name a few, cast further doubt on the long-term effects of the Nuremberg trials.[5] One pale effort, an informal mock tribunal established by philosophers Bertrand Russell and Jean-Paul Sartre, "tried" the United States in 1967 for its conduct in Vietnam.[6] Ironically, U.S. leaders at the time invoked Nuremberg to justify U.S. policy in response to Hanoi's aggression and to resist any judicial evaluation of the U.S. action.[7] It seems impossible to separate the disinterest of the United States in building tribunals for war crimes during this period from the fact that it was the United States' own conduct that was triggering calls for such adjudication. Forever after, efforts to create tribunals for war crimes would raise questions for many inside the United States about its own accountability to such tribunals.

If the power and influence of the Nuremberg trials stopped short of establishing sequels for five decades, so did they fail to encourage many domestic states to prosecute participants in massive human rights violations. Decisions not to prosecute, and often to grant amnesty, frequently reflect efforts to protect newly formed, or rebuild, fragile democratic regimes. A successor regime may seek to move on after collective violence, or hope to avoid the confrontational atmosphere generated by trials in order to rebuild a democratic nation. Or the new government may simply lack the political and economic power, or freedom from the prior military and judicial powers, to prosecute leaders and followers for atrocities committed in the recent past. Such decisions thus represent different considerations, some principled, some practical, that depart from the "duty to prosecute" that some authors glean from the international covenants emerging after Nuremberg.[8]

Most intriguing about the response of trials to mass atrocities is the close proximity of idealism and cynicism surrounding the entire project. The idealism animates stirring but often shrill and impractical claims, such as the "duty to prosecute." Such arguments often are made by scholars remote from the actual worlds of domestic nations struggling with transitional justice.

The cynicism infuses the resistance of ordinary citizens as well as their leaders to contribute money or other resources to the efforts to build international law enforcement or peace-keeping institutions.

As I explore here, I think that idealists need at minimum to acknowledge the profound critiques and limitations of the trial response to atrocities. Yet cynics need to ask: What can be imagined and built, even in the face of critiques and limitations? Indeed, how much is cynicism itself the problem? How might what has been imagined and built instruct societies, and individuals, about the proper place of prosecutions for unspeakable violence?

Three Critiques

After the defeat of the Axis powers, the Allies in World War II simply could have summarily executed their enemies. This option actually for a time was advocated by Joseph Stalin, by the British Foreign Office, and later by Winston Churchill.[9] By deciding instead to hold trials, the Allies sought to establish an international body of rules to guarantee peace and human rights with institutions sufficiently strong to enforce those rules. Roosevelt, Churchill, and Stalin issued a statement at the Moscow Conference on November 1, 1943, conveying this commitment. Representatives of their nations then constructed a Charter of the International Military Tribunal. Resisting revenge and the continuation of war, the tribunal turned to principle, fact-finding, and public debate.

That International Military Tribunal was intended as an innovation. It would adopt the principles of law for the international sphere. Known rules, not force, should judge actions. Governments themselves would be constrained against arbitrary conduct. These ideas sit at the foundation of the rule of law. Limiting governmental arbitrariness is fundamental fairness, including opportunities for individuals to be heard and a full chance for any who face criminal charges to defend their individual actions and to refute allegations of culpability before an impartial tribunal. Symbolism on many levels can express these ideals: Nuremberg was selected not only because its facilities were intact. It had been the location of the early 1935 anti-Semitic laws.[10] Holding trials there began to transform the associations with that place, and thus symbolized how law can transmute horror into hope.

Yet at the time of the Nuremberg trials, critics leveled many charges, some public, some private. The International Tribunal operated without precedent and thus lawlessly; it was merely a front for the Allies military power; it violated liberal notions requiring separation of the functions of lawmakers, prosecutors, judge, and jury; it applied new norms to conduct occurring before the norms were announced; it wrongly prosecuted individuals for acts of state; and it neglected to prosecute the Allies for bombing Dresden, Hiroshima, and Nagasaki, or anyone from the Soviet Union for conduct that was arguably as reprehensible as conduct committed by Germans.[11] Victors' justice, and sloppy at that, some critics publicly charged. Privately, then–Chief Justice Stone of the United States Supreme Court labeled the trial a "high class lynching party."[12] If true, these criticisms would be telling precisely because they betrayed the tribunal's promise to bring the rule of law to bear on the horror of mass atrocity. The criticisms thus put into question whether the tribunal replaced or perpetuated revenge and war with fair formalities designed to secure justice. The Allied firebombing of Tokyo, destruction of Dresden, and atomic bombing—especially of Nagasaki, after Hiroshima had already been bombed—remained outside the tribunal's scope of inquiry.[13]

Three interrelated aspects of the critiques deserve assessment not only in the context of the World War II tribunals, but also for the current trials in Bosnia and Rwanda. The first is retroactivity. Individual defendants in these trials faced charges under norms that had not been previously announced or broadcast, in a forum using procedures that also had not existed previously, in violation of the rule of law's commitment to apply clear, preexisting norms. The second is politicization. Rather than standing as independent institutions removed from political pressures and calculations, the tribunals' very construction and deployment allegedly enacted politics, undermining the ideals of impartiality and universal norms. The final aspect can be named selectivity. Only a small portion of those who could be charged with violations became the target of prosecutions for actions. Proper prosecutorial discretion generally reflects efforts to identify those most responsible or the most serious offenders; some selectivity, however, reflects the chance involved in finding and arresting violators. Some elude arrest and prosecution by escaping, or dying, or concealing their identities, their conduct, or the evidence implicating them. Some avoid arrest because their nation or political party or ethnic group remains enough of a victor or ruling power. As a result, the actual set of individuals who face prosecution is likely to reflect factors far removed from considered judgments about who deserves prosecution and punishment.

In sum, critics at the time of the Nuremberg and Tokyo trials cited retroactivity, politicization, and selectivity as objections. The same dangers are apparent in the International Criminal Tribunals for the former Yugoslavia and for Rwanda, and in domestic prosecutions for human rights violations. The dangers do indeed tarnish the rule of law ideal. The question is when, and whether enough mettle remains in that ideal to make the effort at prosecutions worthwhile.

In his opening statement as lead prosecutor before the Nuremberg tribunal, Justice Robert H. Jackson of the United States Supreme Court powerfully stated both the commitment to the rule of law and an acknowledgment that the procedures at hand departed from the practices well-established in the prosecuting nations.[14] In words that helped launch the tribunal's reputation for adherence to the rule of law he also explained:

> If these men are the first war leaders of a defeated nation to be prosecuted in the name of the law, they are also the first to be given a chance to plead for their lives in the name of the law. Realistically, the Charter of this Tribunal, which gives them a hearing, is also the source of their only hope . . . [and] a fair opportunity to defend them-

selves—a favor which these men, when in power, rarely extended to their fellow countrymen. Despite the fact that public opinion already condemns their acts, we agree that here they must be given a presumption of innocence, and we accept the burden of proving criminal acts and the responsibility of these defendants for their commission.[15]

On the exact issue of adherence to the rule of law, the Nuremberg trials presented central problems, as Jackson himself acknowledged. Retroactivity could not be entirely refuted as an objection to the prosecution. The norms guiding the prosecution were not explicitly or specifically in place at the time of the offenses, despite the general commitment to apply only preexisting laws to particular cases. Elements of domestic law could be invoked as bans against torture and murder. Crimes against the law of nations had emerged in customary law, but only restricted examples, such as piracy on the high seas, had widespread consensus.[16] Norms about conduct during war certainly had foundation in customary laws and in treaties, but lacked clear connection to individual penal culpability. Nor did fully articulated crimes against peace or crimes against humanity, as such, clearly exist, although the Kellogg-Briand Pact gave some context to these norms. Not until the 1945 creation of the International Military Tribunal did there exist a formal, specific statement of norms, the very norms to be used in the newly created tribunal against defendants to be charged with violations previously committed during World War II.[17] Nor did there exist norms of defense against the kinds of charges mounted at the Nuremberg and Tokyo trials. What should count as a justification or an excuse? When should a statute of limitations bar prosecution?

By any measure of human decency, the Nazis' ruthless effort to exterminate the Jewish people of Europe, ethnic minorities, homosexuals, persons with disabilities, gypsies, and political opponents obviously violated any notion of duty, reasonableness, or fairness. That is why the charge of retroactivity does not seem much to matter. Perhaps, then and now, it would seem offensive to hew to the idea that no binding national or international norm in existence at the time forbade these actions. The sheer unprecedented scale of the deportation, murder, and ill-treatment of civilians, the slave labor policy, and the specific per-secution of the Jews stand today as the most uncontroversial examples of human rights violations. Yet, as the defense attor-neys in Nuremberg immediately argued and as observers have debated ever since, no prior law made it clear that individuals could be charged with the crime of waging aggressive war; the same held true for crimes against humanity, including murder, extermination, enslavement, and persecution on the basis of views or identities. Nor, claimed the defense, did then-existing law prohibit deportation, forced labor, or following the orders of a superior officer.[18]

The tribunal rejected the defense argument that the charges depended upon criminal laws adopted after the events alleged. By relying on treaties condemning wars of aggression before the onset of World War II, and by restricting "crimes against human-ity" to those committed in conjunction with waging a war of aggression, the tribunal acknowledged the constraints imposed by the rule of law. At the same time, however, the tribunal demon-strated how to stretch the constraints set by the rule of law, and thereby to dislodge the reassurance they intended to provide.[19] Even scholars devoted to the articulation of law as neutral princi-ples acknowledged that the Nuremberg proceeding thus could be viewed as political rather than legal, but defended the proceeding as nonetheless "more civilized than a program of organized vio-lence against prisoners."[20]

Once established, the Nuremberg tribunal and even the "some-what nebulous" notion of crimes against humanity[21] no longer could be viewed as unprecedented.[22] Yet, as already noted, the precise precedent established includes application of laws to con-duct committed before the clear statement of the laws, in sharp contrast with the basic notions of the rule of law. Indeed, one former Nuremberg prosecutor argues that the most important contribution of Nuremberg is the development of a kind of international law that grows, and is always in the process of becoming.[23]

34   Thus, the Nuremberg trials are commonly cited for establishing that there is no injustice in punishing defendants who knew they were committing a wrong condemned by the international community, even in the absence of "a highly specified international law."[24] Nuremberg itself establishes such international law that takes precedence over both claims of state authority and claims of obligation under state law.[25] Efforts to justify such principles in terms of natural law, common sense, or justice cannot fully override the sheer power of victors to apply what they want to losers. However, at least at the time of the Nuremberg trials, most Germans reported that they viewed the proceedings as fair and just.[26]

By the 1950s, the United Nations undertook efforts to codify the Nuremberg principles, including the drafting of the Genocide Convention and proposals for a permanent international criminal court. Establishment of the criminal court halted, even as allegations of war crimes mounted against the United States' involvement in Vietnam, and against other nations in the subsequent decades. Multilateral conventions continued to articulate aspects of international crime, including terrorism, yet no permanent tribunal was established to deal with international war crimes. Although the trials at Nuremberg and to a lesser extent those held in Tokyo undergird an idea of international law enforcement as a tradition that would endure, such trials were not even actually conducted by international tribunals. Instead, joint occupation courts established by the occupying powers over defeated nations held the trials.[27] These trials could look as much conditioned upon military victory as on a vision of world peace.

Nuremberg precedents, the Hague and Geneva Conventions, and two Protocols of 1977 articulate humanitarian norms accepted in international law. The risks of retroactive application of norms are far less severe for the International Tribunal established in 1992 to respond to violations of international humanitarian law committed in the territory of the former Yugoslavia.[28] The International Criminal Tribunal for Rwanda argu-

ably poses weightier issues of retroactivity; its mandate includes
armed conflict of a noninternational character which arguably
extends human rights norms beyond universally accepted international law. Yet even the tribunal for the former Yugoslavia
rests on a generous interpretation of the United Nations' authority to respond to threats to international peace and security.[29]
For the tribunal must resolve questions that have never before
been answered in international settings, and some that have
never been dealt with in any legal setting. The tribunal was asked
to address whether to characterize rape in the context of ethnic
conflicts as a violation of international law. The tribunal must
consider and resolve heretofore unanswered normative questions about the nature of intent required for genocide; whether
ethnic cleansing is genocide; the scope of the concept of grave
breaches; and the scope of criminal responsibility for failures of
command responsibility.[30] New resolutions of procedural issues
may seem less significant for purposes of retroactivity. Nonetheless, crucial differences in practice—and in the meanings of the
substantive norms—would result from resolution of procedural
issues, such as whether a person can be tried *in absentia* and
whether duress should constitute a defense to crimes against
humanity. Unless rulings on these unprecedented matters are
made prospective only without application to events in the past,
the tribunal's decisions inevitably have the character of applying
norms to people who did not know at the time of the conduct in
question the content of the norms by which they could be judged.

A striking example of the complexities of applying norms retro-
actively occurred in the very first appeal taken before the tribunal. Dražen Erdemović was a Croat, married to a Serb, who
joined the Bosnian Army out of financial need after a failed effort
to emigrate to Switzerland with his wife. He then participated in
mass slaughter of Muslim civilians after the Srebrenica enclave
fell, in July 1995.[31] After receiving a sentence of ten years, he pursued review before the appeals chamber on the grounds that he
was acting under duress and extreme necessity, with resulting
diminished mental capacity. Indeed, at the time he submitted his

guilty plea, Erdemović expressed remorse and sobbed while offering this additional explanation on the record:

> Your Honour, I had to do this. If I had refused, I would have been killed together with the victims. When I refused, they told me: "If you are sorry for them, stand up, line up with them and we will kill you too." I am not sorry for myself but for my family, my wife and son who then had nine months, and I could not refuse because then they would have killed me.[32]

The trial court itself had invented for the first time a process for a guilty plea, and did not have a mechanism in hand for treating a guilty plea joined with an explanation. The governing language of the relevant procedural code itself suggested that a trial follow a guilty plea, so the initial question on appeal dealt with sources of law and norms to be reviewed establishing the process for a defendant who offered a guilty plea. The appeals panel of six judges produced four thoughtful, learned opinions that canvassed possible sources of law on the viability of duress as a defense to crimes against humanity. Unanimous in the view that the plea itself was voluntary, the appellate judges divided over the question at hand. Three judges, in two opinions, reasoned that duress does not afford a complete defense to crimes against humanity. A majority of the judges did conclude that the plea was not informed; Erdemović was not fully apprised that, by pleading guilty, he would lose his right to trial and to assert his lack of criminal responsibility.[33] Therefore, a majority concluded that the case had to be remitted to a new trial chamber to give Erdemović an opportunity to replead "in full knowledge of the nature of the charges and the consequences of his plea."[34]

Whether duress should provide any kind of defense to crimes against humanity is a fascinating, troubling issue that should interest any moral philosopher, lawyer, or student of mass atrocities.[35] It is moving to witness the seriousness of the tribunal appeals judges and their prodigious efforts to scour and integrate all available sources of domestic law, international legal principles, and moral theory on the subject. Yet, regardless of the particular conclusions reached in the case, the application of those conclusions to Erdemović himself involves application of norms that were not known to him or to anyone else when he participated in the massacre. The retroactive quality is mitigated by the judgment allowing him to plead anew. But the mix of brand-new procedures, theories of defenses, and ultimate normative standards involved in this case appears in many of the cases before the International Tribunal. There is a certain quality of "making it up," from the decision to proceed, to a presentencing hearing without a trial after the guilty plea, to the assessment of the defense of duress. It is not out of bounds, but instead crucial, that outside observers care enough to question the fairness, neutrality, and predictability of the enterprise. Otherwise, the mechanism for accountability is itself unaccountable.

Beyond issues of fairness, neutrality, and predictability posed by retroactive application of norms, the rule of law is potentially subverted when the trial tribunal is patently or profoundly dependent on political actors and developments for its operations, resources, and decisions. This may be the case with the tribunal for the former Yugoslavia. In a situation that was almost the opposite of the circumstances surrounding the Nuremberg and Tokyo tribunals, the response to Bosnia occurred while those charged with the crimes remained in power. These actions have been widely understood as symbolic international efforts undertaken after no nation indicated a willingness to risk the loss of its own soldiers to stop the massacres.[36] Especially given the paltry resources appropriated and the failed efforts to generate support for more direct international response to the war, ethnic cleansing, and tortures in the former Yugoslavia, the creation of the tribunal seemed a political response rather than an embrace of the rule of law.

Madeleine Albright, as United States Ambassador to the United Nations, explicitly celebrated the commitment to law represented by the creation of the tribunal. She also reasoned that "unlike the world of the 1940s, international humanitarian law today is impressively codified, well understood, agreed upon and enforceable. The debates over the state of international law that so encumbered the Nuremberg trials will not burden this trial."[37] As an aspirational and inspirational statement, it is commendable. Nonetheless, the claim of international consensus does not by itself create it or eliminate remaining ex post facto concerns. No clear source shows that international law includes the full range of criminal and penal authority enjoyed by nation states. Therefore, the UN Security Council authorized resorting to the domestic law of the former Yugoslavia to fill any gaps,[38] further rendering ambiguous the precedent under creation at the international level. Additionally, the new tribunals originated with the Western-dominated Security Council, unavoidably anchoring the law in power politics.

Similar concerns about retroactivity permeate domestic prosecutions in Eastern Europe after the fall of communism. In Hungary, for example, scholars charged that retroactive changes in criminal law, including the statute of limitations, should not permit indictments and punishments that would not have been authorized at the times of the acts.[39] The parliament proceeded to enact a law declaring that the statute of limitations for treason, murder with premeditation, and injuries causing death committed between December 21, 1944, and May 2, 1990, did not begin until May 2, 1990. Otherwise, the statute of limitations law would prevent justice, and leave untouched the perpetrators' own efforts to consolidate government power as a total shield against accountability. The president of Hungary refused to sign the bill, however, and the Constitutional Court declared it unconstitutional.[40] Not only should the law be viewed as continuous, between the communist period and the present, the court ruled, but also the effort to overcome political rationales for failures to prosecute could produce new and dangerous contaminations between law and politics.[41]

The connections between law and politics are stark in the creation and operation of the International Tribunal for Rwanda. The political and ethnic slaughter in 1994 in Rwanda directed at the ethnic Tutsi minority population and Hutu opposition— with massacres of some 800,000 African people, a tenth of the nation's population—created an excruciatingly clear need for international legal response, given the albeit modest and incomplete precedent of the Yugoslavia Tribunal, created after 150,000 whites were killed. International commentators and especially African nations successfully pressed the Security Council to create a parallel tribunal for Rwanda, if only to avoid charges of rank racism and ethnocentrism. The United Nations stretched the thin basis of Charter authority invoked for the Bosnia Tribunal even further to apply it to a conflict *within* one nation. This conflict had to be deemed a threat to international peace and security.[42]

Most discussions of both tribunals center on the practical difficulties faced in arresting indicted offenders from Bosnia and in gathering sufficiently detailed and reliable evidence from both Bosnia and Rwanda to prosecute in locales removed in time and place from the offenses. With chronic understaffing and severely limited resources, lack of cooperation from states involved in the conflict, and dependence upon states for apprehending the indictees, these practical problems could prove insurmountable. Yet a deeper challenge is to rescue the ideal of applying law to atrocity from what are so palpably political uses of legal forms. For their very resources and continued operations, the tribunals remain fundamentally dependent upon the political views and wills of the members of the UN General Assembly.

Even to enforce orders related to gathering evidence and arresting offenders, the tribunals must rely on explicitly political calculations made by other bodies. Until NATO-supported arrests gave the Hague effort new life, European military officers and diplomats speculated that no trial would make sense without a previous or simultaneous international commitment to pursue a military victory in the former Yugoslavia.[43] On this view, the trial process cannot replace military efforts and instead stands contingent upon them. Alternatively, to proceed with the arrest and trials of leaders would undermine efforts not only to negotiate but to stabilize arrangements for peace.[44] Then, after the Dayton Peace Accords, it was feared that arrests would jeopardize the peace. Judges and prosecutors involved in the tribunals themselves publicly wondered whether starting the process of arrests and trials and then failing to proceed could be worse than never having started at all.[45]

Political alignments of powerful nations remain crucial to any international tribunal's existence, funding, and management. Dependence on political processes risks undermining the scrupulous lawfulness of the tribunals. Thoughtful observers of the American legal system emphasize that law can never be entirely separated from politics.[46] Yet collapsing the two, and making law dependent on the vagaries of politics, risks jeopardizing the very aspiration of law to be impartial, fair, and steady, and thereby distinct from strategic power and individual personalities.

The final danger—patent selectivity in prosecution—is at one level the simple difficulty of justifying why some people are prosecuted and others are not. Can selection be judged as a matter of fairness rather than arbitrariness? Do power and personality rule? Yet the selectivity concern has more complex dimensions. It arises from the crucial idea of individual criminal responsibility embedded in the Western ideal of the rule of law. To prevent lingering assignments of collective guilt, blame and punishment must be restricted to specific individuals and based on specific proof, itself tested through the adversary process. The emphasis on individual responsibility offers an avenue away from the cycles of blame that lead to revenge, recrimination, and ethnic and national conflicts. Yet, as developed in Nuremberg and since, the notion of individual criminal responsibility for mass atrocities also stems from a recognition of individual duties to international norms that transcend national obligations.

In the former Yugoslavia, the difficulties in arresting major figures and establishing an evidentiary trail to them leaves the tribunals dealing with low-level operatives who can be charged with individual responsibility for their actions and whose arrests pose less risk of destabilizing the peace. Yet in the absence of trials of their superiors who gave them orders, inducements, and threats, such trials risk seeming either trivial or overblown. In Rwanda, the international tribunal has in custody many important figures, and the domestic tribunal has incarcerated 120,000 others in deplorable conditions for their alleged involvement in the massacres. The domestic law in Rwanda permits, and the domestic prosecutors plan to pursue, the death penalty in many cases, while the International Tribunal's most severe sanction is life imprisonment, not death. A genuine possibility, then, is that leaders tried by the International Tribunal will receive term sentences while those influenced by or ordered by them will receive death sentences.[47] The selectivity and arbitrariness in such a pattern threatens any sense of fairness or rationality.

Some of these difficulties were foreshadowed at the time of the Nuremberg and Tokyo trials. The Nuremberg Tribunal, staffed by representatives of the Allies, proceeded initially with a criminal prosecution of twenty-four individual Germans. Admittedly selective, if not token, these officials stood in for the thousands involved in knowingly causing the deaths of more than twenty million people and the unspeakable suffering of many more millions. Subsequent trials at the tribunal prosecuted additional individuals, but still only a tiny fraction of those actually involved.[48]

The prosecution of leaders for all acts performed by participants as part of a common plan struck some as a violation of the notion of individual responsibility.[49] The Tokyo Tribunal's issuance of the death sentence for Kirota Koki, the prime minister, for sharing responsibility with the military for the Rape of Nanking, expressed condemnation for the horrors. Yet it also suggested that the military leaders lacked any personal responsibility and that the military itself had no culpability or obligation to change.[50]

An even more basic conflict with the rule of law might occur in the very prosecution of individuals for what law professor Mark Osiel has called, "administrative massacre," or "large-scale violation of basic human rights to life and liberty by the central state in a systematic and organized fashion, often against its own citizens, generally in a climate of war—civil or international, real or imagined."[51] As Osiel explains, "[e]pisodes of administrative massacre . . . characteristically involve many people acting in coordinated ways over considerable space and time, impeding adherence" to the stricture of proving willful acts of particular defendants.[52] Prosecutions of foot soldiers involved in massacres can render vivid portrayals of the process by which ordinary people become swept up in complex and well-orchestrated campaigns of fear and violence. Yet the inability of the trial process to proceed against all or even many such foot soldiers risks making those trials that do proceed seem arbitrary and grossly incomplete.

The prosecution of a few border guards for shooting people who tried to escape during the last days of the Berlin Wall illustrates these difficulties. Tina Rosenberg gives a vivid account of the complex biographies and world events underlying the 1991 prosecution of four border guards for manslaughter and attempted manslaughter of Chris Gueffroy, the last victim of the Berlin Wall security policy.[53] Gueffroy was shot during his attempt to escape East Berlin over the Wall just nine months before the Wall fell during the "Velvet Revolution" of 1989. Rosenberg suggests that the German government indicted the four security guards on duty at the time because the evidence had been well assembled by Gueffroy's mother at her own expense, because the case afforded the new government a high profile occasion to put "on trial both the Berlin Wall and the system that had built it," and because the case was a lead-in to an indictment of the actual officials who had set the 1974 policy that firearms should be used "without consideration" to stop border crossings.[54]

One could say that the four guards, Ingo Heinrich, Andreas Kühnpast, Peter-Michael Schmett, and Michael Schmidt simply had the bad luck to be on duty so close to the fall of the Wall. Or one could say instead that they were no less guilty than any of the other guards who had killed at least 474 individuals among the thousands who tried to escape during the twenty-eight years that the Wall separated East and West Berlin.[55] In any case, the prosecution and the defense agreed that the four guards simply had been following orders. The two sides disagreed only over whether following orders—that phrase made suspect when

invoked by German defendants at Nuremberg—should constitute an excuse.

The prosecution tried to establish that other guards avoided
the orders to shoot "without consideration" and had not suffered great penalty. The defense responded that defiance would
have produced military prison sentences for the guards. Based on
the practices of the secret police files, Rosenberg notes that
refusal to follow orders could have led to penalties not only for
the soldier but also for his children.[56] At trial, the defense maintained that the state was prosecuting ordinary men for not being
heroes, and "that for forty years the East German political system had made its first order of business the assurance that heroes
not be produced."[57] Many observers also criticized the prosecution for retroactivity, for seeking to punish soldiers for what had
been understood as a legal act when committed.[58] Victors' justice, politics disguised as law, an effort by West Germans to
humiliate East Germans; these critiques surrounded the trial
itself.[59] Even the prosecutor maintained at trial that none of the
defendants belonged in jail.[60]

Indeed, the East German security force deliberately drafted
individuals as border guards who evidenced stability, no potential for conflict, and strong family ties—to reduce the risk of
their own escapes.[61] Border guard training aimed to create collective thinking and a siege mentality.[62] The trial established that
the four individuals on trial were trained to follow orders and
that the guards were under constant pressure to shoot, both to
secure rewards for the regiment and to avoid condemnation and
punishment as individuals.[63] There was no suggestion that the
guards had any knowledge that their conduct would violate the
Helsinki Accords and emerging international law norms forbid-
ding shooting out of wartime. Testifying at the trial were some of
the guards' superior officers, themselves at liberty, unindicted,
and even paid for missing work during the court process.[64]

The West German judge presiding over the case concluded
that, "The Nazis showed us that not everything that is legal is
right. The court was waiting for any defendant to question
why—why was it, for example, that the order to shoot was tem-

porarily suspended or that border guards who shot were transferred away from their divisions? Why was no one allowed to talk about it? Why were their names eliminated in documents? One's conscience cannot be turned off in the last quarter of the twentieth century when the killing of another human being is allowed."[65] The judge acquitted two of the defendants, issued an attempted manslaughter conviction with a suspended sentence for one who sprayed the ground but did not hit Gueffroy, and convicted the one who had fired the fatal shot of manslaughter with a three-and-one-half-year prison sentence, despite the prosecution's own request for two years of probation.[66] The sentence was overturned on appeal, producing two years of probation.[67] In subsequent trials, no other guard who had followed orders to shoot received a jail sentence.[68]

The prosecutors and court in the border guard trial tried to establish the responsibility of each individual, as well as the duty of each to think independently. Yet the trial itself, and others like it, seemed unfair to the watching public in the former East Germany.[69] Prosecution of the guards but not of their superiors in particular seemed unjust. So did the court's failure to acknowledge or comprehend the context of indoctrination and military control governing the guards' conduct, and the assumption that West German moral and ethical judgments could fairly be applied to the East German border guards.

Selectivity in prosecutions has undermined perceptions of fairness elsewhere. After his surprise election in 1983, Argentina's President Raúl Alfonsín launched bold domestic prosecutions of leaders in the "Dirty War" and in the military process of "disappearances."[70] Former military presidents and leaders were tried and sentenced. Initial trials gave public acknowledgment to the years of violence and human rights abuses. But parliamentary and military opposition, as well as fears of a judiciary out of control, pushed even President Alfonsín to back off from further prosecutions. The results were a "full stop" law and a "due obedience" enactment exempting officials, soldiers, and police from punishment for human rights violations if they had acted within the scope of due obedience to authorities.[71] This made the pattern of existing and halted prosecutions so evidently selective and partial as to challenge seriously the fairness of the entire process.

In addition to the fairness problem, selectivity in prosecution risks creating martyrs out of the few who are subject to trial and punishment.[72] The distinction between law and politics seems all but erased and the truth-seeking process seems subordinated to public spectacle and symbolic governmental statements—and thus the perpetrators begin to look like victims of the prosecutorial regime.

Where the trial process follows war or other polarizing conflicts, the failure to pursue prosecutions on both sides renders those that are pursued suspect. Thus, the failure to indict Allied offenders, including Russian leaders, in the Nuremberg process undermined its fairness in the eyes of some critics.[73] When one violation but not another generates prosecution, this selectivity creates further risks of perceived unfairness. In this vein, some observers of the World War II Tokyo trials objected to the silence about crimes committed in Asian regions under Japanese control.[74] Radmila Nakarada, a researcher at the Institute of European Studies, argued that the creation of the International War Crimes Tribunal for the former Yugoslavia itself amounted to so selective and partial a response to genocides as to "represent a clear amnesty for all those responsible for committing similar war crimes in Vietnam, Algeria, Panama, South Africa or Iraq."[75]

A different cause of selective prosecution is short resources. There may simply not be enough courtrooms, lawyers, witnesses, experts, or time for prosecuting all who deserve it in places like Rwanda, East Germany, or Brazil.[76] Even the trials that proceed face evidentiary difficulties, especially given the remoteness and reluctance of witnesses, and the costs and limitations of forensic experts who exhume and study bodies. Prosecutions for atrocities spotlight the close connections between law and politics, and the danger that politics will overtake law. When imposed by victors who have vanquished enemies, prosecutions may seem, or even be, simply show trials, putting on theatre to express domination rather than justice. Soviet courts specialized in show trials and thereby stoked cynicism about the law that persists after the fall of that regime.

The dependence of the tribunals addressing atrocity on explicit political processes and considerations lead some, like Mark Osiel, to defend deliberate myth-making at least by tribunals addressing mass violence in liberal societies that intend to subscribe to the rule of law. Osiel argues that trials following mass violence can help a nation consolidate memories and engage in "secular rituals of commemoration," even to the point of rendering the distinction between truth and falsity problematic.[77] Such lengths are justified, Osiel says, in order to create a meaningful framework for publicly exploring traumatic memories of political violence.[78] Osiel suggests that collective memory probably can only be enshrined through trials if the intention to achieve this end is concealed from the public audience;[79] revealing an orchestrated plan to shape the content and message would corrode public confidence in the fairness and open-endedness of the trial. Yet even Osiel presses that in a *liberal* society, such show trials must adhere to the legal rules of procedural fairness and personal culpability. "The most gripping of legal yarns must hence be classified as a failure if its capacity for public enthrallment is purchased at the price of violating such strictures."[80]

These strictures include preventing retroactive application of norms; otherwise the trial invites cynicism about the entire trial enterprise as an enactment of the rule of law. Yet, as Osiel suggests, even adherence to formal procedural restrictions will not shield the audiences of mass trials from cynicism. The central premise of individual responsibility portrays defendants as separate people capable of autonomous choice—when the phenomena of mass atrocities render that assumption at best problematic.[81] Those who make the propaganda but wield no physical weapons influence those with the weapons who in turn claim to have been swept up, threatened, fearful, mobilized. Those who frame the trial do so to shape a public memory and communal solidarity—yet the focus on select individuals cannot tell the complex connections among people that make massacres and genocides possible.[82] If the goal to be served is establishing consensus and memorializing controversial, complex events, trials are not ideal.[83] Even if they were adequate to the task, the theatrical devices and orchestration required threaten the norms of law that are a crucial part of the lesson, at least in societies committed to the rule of law.

Trials following mass atrocities can never establish a complete historical record, despite all hopes. Sir Hartley Shawcross, the British chief prosecutor at Nuremberg, put the hopes well; he explained that "this Tribunal will provide a contemporary touchstone and an authoritative and impartial record to which future historians may turn for truth and future politicians for warning."[84] Yet subsequent historians expose the partiality and distortions in the record left by the trial due to the prosecutorial emphasis on crimes against peace rather than crimes against humanity, making war, rather than anti-Semitism and racism, the central explanation for the Holocaust.[85] Defendants in war crimes trials tell their version of the story at trials, and like other defendants, they often lie, further compromising the historical record.

Even more devastating is the apparent shortfall between the capacity of the trial form with its rule of law and the nature of mass atrocities. Hannah Arendt wrote her friend Karl Jaspers in 1946 that the Nazi crimes exposed the limits of law, for no punishment could ever be sufficient, and that explained why the defendants at Nuremberg seemed so smug.[86]

Resisting Cynicism

Nonetheless, or perhaps, precisely in the face of potential cynicism and despair, Nuremberg launched a remarkable international movement for human rights founded in the rule of law; inspired the development of the United Nations and of nongovernmental organizations around the world; encouraged national trials for human rights violations; and etched a set of ground rules about human entitlement that circulate in local, national, and international settings. Ideas and, notably, ideas about basic human rights spread through formal and informal institutions. Especially when framed in terms of universality, the language of rights and the vision of trials following their violation equip people to call for accountability even where it is not achievable. Hannah Arendt herself, who so exquisitely articulated the limits of law in the face of the Holocaust, and who remained skeptical of a bill of rights attached to an international body such as the United Nations, searched for a "law above nations" founded in cooperation across nations.[87] The Nuremberg trials inspired even their critics to develop conceptions of law that might begin to assure human dignity, even when nations failed to do so. The spirit of the Nuremberg trials is widely credited with inspiring the Bosnia and Rwanda Tribunals. In turn, the contemporary trials breathe new life into the Nuremberg principles while branding defendants as indicted international criminals.[88]

The fifty-year anniversary of the Nuremberg trial process offered dignitaries around the globe the chance to speak to its legacy. Almost uniformly, the speeches emphasized the accomplishments and inspirations. A good example is U.S. Supreme Court Justice Stephen Breyer's address, "Crimes against Humanity," held at the Capital Rotunda to mark Yom Hashoah, the Day of Remembrance on April 16, 1996.[89] He described the Nuremberg trial as "the most important trial that could be imagined."[90] Breyer offered three arguments to endorse this assertion. First, he pointed to the sheer work of collecting evidence as directed by the trial process. Over one hundred thousand captured German documents, and millions of feet of film and photographs led to the creation of seventeen thousand pages of trial transcript. In the face of that record, no one then, now, or in the future, can responsibly deny the crimes "and no tradition of martyrdom of the Nazi leaders can arise among informed people."[91] Breyer concluded that Jackson accomplished his goal to "establish incredible events by credible evidence."[92]

Second, Breyer celebrated the Nuremberg legacy that "nations feel that they cannot simply ignore the most barbarous acts of other nations." Those who commit such acts cannot neglect "the ever more real possibility that they will be held accountable and brought to justice under law."[93] Finally, the trial enables others to learn from the past and to warn those in the future. Thereby, it contributes to the aspiration for justice.[94]

Breyer's words, like the words of others who celebrate the legacy of the Nuremberg trials, are inspiring, if a bit lacking in concrete detail. Similarly, commentators remember the Tokyo trial as an advance in the human struggle for justice and deterrence of future harms. On one of its anniversaries, a symposium participant asserted: "The Tokyo trial was—or purported to be—a legal proceeding; but its purpose was as much historical as legal: to establish once and for all the record of Japanese misdeeds in the Pacific. Even as it looked to the past, it looked also—or tried to look—into the future: to establish norms of international conduct."[95] And some say similarly hopeful things about the tribunals for the former Yugoslavia and Rwanda, despite their limited accomplishments to date.

Is it possible to shield listeners from the deflating cynicisms, the easily demonstrated shortcomings, and the failures of the project of prosecutions after mass atrocities? No perfect shield can, or should, be created, but toning down the claims for the trial response might help preserve their legacy. Perhaps, paradoxically, it would be worth the gamble to embrace the somewhat mysterious power of belief and aspiration in motivating people to create organizations, hold meetings, demand changes, and generate an environment infused by norms of human rights. The challenge is to found the beliefs in claims that cannot be refuted easily and thus cannot cascade quickly into renewed doubt and cynicism.

Thus, I do not think it wise to claim that international and domestic prosecutions for war crimes and other horrors themselves create an international moral and legal order, prevent genocides, or forge the political transformation of previously oppressive regimes. Expansive claims may be tempting in order to convince international and national audiences to fund and support trial efforts, but exaggerated assertions are bound to yield critical and even hostile disappointment.

Justice Jackson's own defense of the prosecutorial effort at

50   Nuremberg was more modest than the assertion of deterrence offered by others since. He called for modest aspirations especially because wars are usually started only in the confidence that they can be won. Therefore, he acknowledged, "[p]ersonal punishment, to be suffered only in the event the war is lost, is probably not to be a sufficient deterrent to prevent a war where the war-makers feel the chances of defeat to be negligible."[96] Does the risk of punishment for human rights violations make the leaders of authoritarian regimes reluctant to surrender power in the first place?[97] Individuals who commit atrocities on the scale of genocide are unlikely to behave as "rational actors," deterred by the risk of punishment. Even if they were, it is not irrational to ignore the improbable prospect of punishment given the track record of international law thus far. A tribunal can be but one step in a process seeking to ensure peace, to make those in power responsible to law, and to condemn aggression.[98]

Trials can create credible documents and events that acknowledge and condemn horrors. Thus they help to articulate both norms and a commitment to work to realize them.[99] Even when sharply limited in their numbers, their reach, or their results, indictments, prosecutions, and convictions can build up the materials of international human rights and the notions of individual responsibility, conscience, and human dignity that imbue them. Accordingly, trials should not be pursued where there is no chance for fairness or perception of fairness; where the tribunal is entirely subject to a particular nation's self-interest; or where there are overwhelming disparities between the resources and will needed to undertake trials and the capacities of lawyers and judges, witnesses and offenders, actually in hand.

Even when marred by problems of retroactive application of norms, political influence, and selective prosecution, however, trials can air issues, create an aura of fairness, establish a public record, and produce some sense of accountability. Then claims for the power of the rule of law can grow, even in the face of demonstrable failures in its implementation. The current high regard at least voiced by world leaders and scholars especially for the Nuremberg trials suggest that it is possible to build an evolving consensus about international norms even in the face of legally grounded objections. The fact that leaders trace the new international tribunals and domestic trial efforts to Nuremberg means that the historical example, however flawed or mythological, affords new precedents whose flaws may, too, be overlooked generations hence.

Bertrand Russell, the British mathematician, philosopher, and peace activist who launched a mock international tribunal during the Vietnam War, wrote, "The dilemma is the same in every country. There are great injustices and laws fail."[100] Tina Rosenberg adds, "Trials that seek to do justice on a grand scale risk doing injustice on a small scale; their goal must not be Justice but justice bit by bit by bit. Trials, in the end, are ill suited to deal with the subtleties of facing the past."[101] Some trials may do better than that, at least by creating a permanent record to be consulted by future generations. Some may permit national debate and private acknowledgments. In any case, to find the trial process wanting against the aspiration of truly dealing with the complex past is not to find it worthless as a response to atrocity. The challenge is to combine honest modesty about the promise of trials with a willingness to be inspired—and to combine inspiration with the hard, grubby work of gathering evidence and weaving legal sources into judgments.

4. Truth Commissions

*"ignorance about those who have disappeared /
undermines the reality of the world."* —Zbigniew Herbert

*"But the truth will not necessarily be believed, and it is putting too
much faith in truth to believe that it can heal."* —Michael Ignatieff

*"[T]here is a need for understanding but not for vengeance,
a need for reparation but not retaliation, a need for* ubuntu
but not for victimisation." —Postamble, South African
Interim Constitution, 1993

Imprisoned for twenty-seven years for his political work, the freed Nelson Mandela then helped to negotiate the peaceful end of South Africa's apartheid. A crucial item in the negotiation was how the new government should deal with the events and consequences of the apartheid period. The outgoing leaders made some form of amnesty for those responsible for the regime a condition for the peaceful transfer to a fully democratic society. The interim constitution, a remarkable document of negotiated political transformation, called for a process for freeing participants in apartheid from prosecution. It gave explicit reference to the African concept, *ubuntu*, meaning humaneness, or an inclusive sense of community valuing everyone. Yet precisely the commitment to *ubuntu* made it urgent to establish human rights during the transition, and to help the entire nation confront its past.

The African National Congress (ANC), led by Mandela, wanted a truth commission, an official investigation into the facts of atrocities, tortures, and human rights abuses. The ANC had already launched two independent inquiries into human rights abuses committed by its own members, especially in ANC training camps in Angola. This process unearthed facts about tortures and deaths committed within ANC activities, embraced

and elevated human rights standards, and set a tone concerning
values that departed from those that prevailed under apartheid.
Some ANC leaders thought a similar but more extensive truth
commission to inquire into the massive atrocities committed by
apartheid officials would help to honor victims and also offer
some answers to burning questions about what really had happened under apartheid. The National Party, led by the old
regime, advocated a reconciliation commission. The chief concern here was amnesty for participants in the activities approved
and ordered by the apartheid government.[1]

After a negotiated settlement between the major parties in the
early 1990s, the world awoke on April 27, 1994, to globally
transmitted pictures of the dramatic day of South Africa's first
democratic elections. People of all colors and races waited
patiently in massive lines to vote, and then hung around to celebrate the experience. The multiparty negotiating forum and
the last apartheid Parliament adopted the Interim Constitution
in 1993. It included in its final paragraphs an unusual self-reflec-
tion: a description of the document itself as a bridge from the
past of a deeply divided society to a future committed to human
rights, democracy, and peaceful coexistence. Toward those ends,
the document directed the Parliament to adopt a law providing
for the mechanisms and criteria for granting amnesty for conduct "associated with political objectives and committed in the
course of the conflicts of the past."

On July 19, 1995, the Parliament fulfilled this charge in creating a Truth and Reconciliation Commission (TRC), with a Committee on Human Rights Violations, a Committee on Amnesty,
and a Committee on Reparation and Rehabilitation.[2] The Parliament's decision to create the TRC reflected a lengthy process of
consultation with many different groups. This process built upon
but also distinguished the South African effort from previous
truth commissions undertaken elsewhere. Like a few other commissions, the TRC was launched by a democratic legislative act.[3]
Yet only the TRC grew from extensive public debate and involvement in its design.[4]

Similar inquiries into human rights violations elsewhere grew

54 from quite different processes. The Commission on the Truth for
El Salvador was established pursuant to the Salvadoran Peace
Accords negotiated under United Nations auspices.[5] The
National Commission for the Disappearances of Persons in
Argentina resulted from a presidential decision.[6] Other truth
commissions and inquiries resulted from executive decisions;
some analogous efforts involved nongovernmental organizations.[7] A group of international nongovernmental organizations
joined with Rwandan human rights organizations to create a
short-lived commission for Rwanda.[8] Nelson Mandela previously appointed the commission to investigate torture and brutality at the ANC detention camps run outside of South Africa
when the ANC was still an outlawed political party, and then a
second commission to pursue further complaints about the
camps.[9]

A privately initiated investigation in Brazil, undertaken with
the financial and political support of the Catholic archbishop of
São Paulo and the World Council of Churches, involved four
years of a sophisticated, secret effort to photocopy and analyze
verbatim transcripts of military trials without letting any officials know. Technically, nothing illegal was involved; the million
pages of archival records were public documents, and lawyers
entitled to check them out did so, and returned them in the allot-
ted time.[10] Teams of photocopiers, statisticians, couriers, and
lawyers worked for four years on the project, although most of
them did not know the others, or even the content of the pages in
their hands. Twelve volumes of materials resulted. The coordina-
tors also enlisted two still-unnamed journalists to write a suc-
cinct, summary volume. That volume, *Brasil: Nunca Mais*
(*Brazil: Never Again*), documenting 144 political murders and
1,800 incidents of torture, became an unprecedented best-seller
in Brazil.[11] The book interspersed chapters on background and
context with excerpts from testimony in the files. The ground-
swell of public response to the book's revelations helps to explain
why Brazil then signed the United Nations Convention Against
Torture.[12]

After the transition of power in South Africa, national leaders

and scholars joined with people drawn from the international
community to study these and other previous truth commissions
and conducted discussions in public hearings and other settings.[13] Some people worried about this process. University of
Cape Town professor André Du Toit, a long-time human rights
activist in South Africa, has commented, "As religious leaders
and churches became increasingly involved in the commission's
work, the influence of religious style and symbolism supplanted
political and human rights concerns."[14] The language of forgiveness invoking religious community grew as the commission took
shape.

Yet, when South Africa's justice minister Dullah Omar
reflected on the goals embedded in the Act, he stressed the value
of the process of public deliberation in creating legitimacy for the
undertaking.[15] He also emphasized how the drafters remained
mindful of the larger context of negotiation and compromise
between former adversaries, as well as theoretical analysis of
principles of justice and international law.[16] The religious and ethical commitments and standing of leaders in South Africa, such
as Nelson Mandela and Archbishop Desmond Tutu, set the tone
of reconciliation and forgiveness. The practical sense of security
once the black majority obtained voting rights combined with
the continuing recognition that whites retained vital power over
economic resources to support a process for forging national
unity.

Based on the experiences in other countries, South Africans
concluded that "to achieve unity and morally acceptable reconciliation, it is necessary that the truth about gross violations of
human rights must be: established by an official investigation
unit using fair procedures; fully and unreservedly acknowledged
by the perpetrators; made known to the public, together with the
identity of the planners, perpetrators, and victims."[17] Crucially,
Omar and others decided that the commitment to afford
amnesty was the price for allowing a relatively peaceful transition to full democracy.[18] Amnesty would be available but only
conditionally: to individuals who personally applied for it and
who disclosed fully the facts of misdeeds that could be fairly char-

56   acterized as having a political objective. Trading truth for
amnesty, and amnesty for truth, the commission was intended to
promote the gathering of facts and the basis for the society to
move on toward a strong democratic future.

Members of Griffith Mxenge's family, Steve Biko's family, and
other survivors of murdered activists joined to file a lawsuit challenging the TRC's very existence. They claimed that the amnesty
provisions violated the rights of families to seek judicial redress
for the murders of their loved ones. The newly created Constitutional Court heard the case, and rejected the claim.[19] The court
reasoned that neither the South African Constitution nor the
Geneva Convention prevented granting amnesty in exchange for
truth.

Stinging in the minds of many is the widespread practice of
granting amnesty following collective atrocities. In Brazil, the
armed forces granted themselves amnesty before permitting the
civilian government to be restored; in Uruguay, the civilian government granted amnesty apparently after a private agreement
with military leaders to do so.[20] Against those images, amnesty
seems closer to impunity than to justice or accountability.

Yet the amnesty process employed by the TRC, however con-
tested and complex, is different. It is not a blanket grant. Prosecutions and civil suits remain potential options against any
perpetrators who do not apply for amnesty, and against those
whose applications are denied. There is an important difference
between the TRC's individual grants of clemency or pardon that
follow a finding of guilt, and other amnesties granted prior to
prosecution, and often accorded to a group to wipe out the
offenses entirely.[21] The conditional amnesty process does not
foreclose truth-seeking, but instead promotes it. The commission
could secure statements and explanations of specific acts of torture and murder otherwise unavailable, especially because outgoing authorities destroyed records and closed ranks. Thus, as its
name signals, the Truth and Reconciliation Commission combines a notion of restorative justice with the search for truth.[22]

The commission is charged not only with obtaining the facts,
but also with working to overcome ignorance or denial among

the general community and among government officials. It turns
the promise of amnesty, wrested from political necessity, into a
mechanism for advancing the truth-finding process. The commission also aims to restore and devise recommendations for reparation. Its goal is to express government acknowledgment of the
past, to enhance the legitimacy of the current regime, and to promote a climate conducive to human rights and democratic processes. Only if the recommendations for reparations are followed with concrete actions, though, will these aims promise to
bear fruit.

Do the aspirations of the South African Truth and Reconciliation Commission represent "second-best" goals in the face of
practical political constraints? Or do the TRC's objectives identify an admirable alternative to prosecutions needed to implement national and international norms in response to collective
violence and state-sponsored atrocities? Does the TRC chart an
exemplary path between vengeance and forgiveness? Or does
this truth commission illustrate an inevitable residue—of feeling,
moral outrage, and justice's demands—that exceeds the reach of
legal institutions?[23]

I suggest that even in light of some of the basic goals of prosecution, truth commissions can afford benefits to a society. If the
goal of healing individuals and society after the trauma of mass
atrocity is elevated, truth commissions could well be a better
option than prosecutions, although limitations in the therapeutic
value of commissions for individuals and limitations in our
knowledge of societal healing make this a line of future inquiry
rather than a current conclusion.

Second Best?

A truth commission looks like a less desirable choice if prosecutions for human rights violations serve as the model for institutional responses to state-sponsored violence. As Professor
Stephan Landsman has argued, prosecuting human rights violations can substantially enhance the chances for establishing the
rule of law and signaling that no individuals are outside the reach
of legal accountability.[24] Prosecution also provides a means for

punishing wrongdoers, while enhancing a society's ability to deter future human rights violations. Prosecution may be essential as well for the healing of social wounds caused by serious violations, on the theory that a society cannot forgive what it cannot punish.[25]

In contrast, a commission of inquiry charged with investigating and reporting on human rights violations may seem a pale and inadequate substitute.[26] Most commentators assert that criminal prosecution is the best response to atrocities, and truth commissions should be used only as an alternative when such prosecutions are not possible.[27] As explored in the previous chapter, practical reasons often interfere with or prevent prosecutions: insufficient material resources, inadequate numbers of trained staff qualified and available to pursue prosecutions, or lack of enough power or courage to proceed against offending leaders, police, and military officials. When political realities preclude prosecutions, the prosecutorial road not taken may haunt and diminish the remaining avenues.[28]

And yet a different set of reasons for forgoing prosecution relates to the inherent limitations of trials rather than to failures and limitations of the nation's capacity to conduct trials. Litigation is not an ideal form of social action. Voltaire once said, "I was never ruined but twice: once when I lost a law suit, and once when I won one."[29] The financial and emotional costs of litigation may be most apparent when private individuals sue one another, but there are parallel problems when a government or an international tribunal prosecutes. Victims and other witnesses undergo the ordeals of testifying and cross-examination, usually without a simple opportunity to convey directly the narrative of their experiences. The chance to tell one's story and be heard without interruption or skepticism is crucial to so many people, and nowhere more vital than for survivors of trauma. So, too, is the commitment to produce a coherent, if complex, narrative about the entire nation's trauma, and the multiple sources and expressions of its violence. If the goals are to gain public acknowledgment for the harms and accounts, as full as possible, of what happened, the trial process is at best an imperfect means.

For those two goals, a truth commission may actually be better suited, especially when the commission is authorized by or influential with the government and capable of producing a report with wide public distribution. Some of the full story would never be known, absent grants of immunity to those who can tell it. South Africa's unusual effort combines a truth commission with conditional grants of amnesty to offenders who participate in the process to provide honest and full accounts of their behavior. Prosecutions thus could proceed against any other alleged perpetrators. A quasi-judicial body evaluates the stories through independent investigations, and decides whether to accept the application for amnesty. Applications from people whose crimes are deemed "disproportionately" heinous or not motivated by politics can be turned down, leaving them to face criminal prosecution and civil suits.[30] Although borne of the political compromise necessary to ensure peaceful transition of power, the amnesty process also reflects the ANC's prior discoveries of the value of disclosures by apartheid insiders, traded for safety.[31]

The trade of amnesty for testimony affords the chance to use participation by some to gain participation by others. Five mid-level political officers sought amnesty and implicated General Johan van der Merwe as the one who gave the order to fire on demonstrators in 1992.[32] The general then himself applied for amnesty before the commission, and confessed that he had indeed given the order to fire; he in turn implicated two Cabinet-level officials who gave him orders. Evidence of this kind, tracing atrocities to decisionmakers, is likely to be held only by those who participated. It is extremely difficult to unearth through the adversarial process of trials. Taking testimony, pursuing independent investigations, and conditioning grants of amnesty on truthful testimony assist the TRC in its task of building a thorough record of the collective violence.

The task of making a full account of what happened, in light of the evidence obtained, requires a process of sifting and drafting that usually does not accompany a trial. Putting narratives of distinct events together with the actions of different actors demands materials and the charge to look across cases and to connect the

stories of victims and offenders. Truth commissions undertake to
write the history of what happened as a central task. For judges
at trials, such histories are the by-product of particular moments
of examining and cross-examining witnesses and reviewing evidence about the responsibility of particular individuals.

The sheer narrative project of a truth commission makes it
more likely than trials to yield accounts of entire regimes. Yet,
just as no historical account can fully grasp the entire truth of
events, a commission report will be limited. A commission
may serve as a representative of the "public," to afford public
acknowledgment of harms, or it may instead seem marginal,
unimportant, or unrepresentative. Also, truth commissions
usually work under tight time limitations—the TRC had a
maximum of two years—and often have severe constraints
on resources, further hampering how much can be known,
recorded, and transmitted.[33] Mass atrocities explode the frames
of reference usually available for historical investigations, with
the result that a report that claims to be comprehensive will be
defective precisely on those grounds.

The most distinctive element of a truth commission, in compar-
ison with prosecution, is the focus on victims, including forgotten victims in forgotten places.[34] Additionally distinctive in the
South African case is the emphasis on reconciliation and healing.
Regular broadcasts of the commission's hearings bring victims'
stories and pain to public view. Pumla Gobodo-Madikizela, a
psychologist serving on the human rights committee, reports
that many victims conceive of justice in terms of revalidating oneself, and of affirming the sense "you are right, you were damaged, and it was wrong."[35] The human rights committee seeks to
offer such validation as it takes testimony from survivors and
family members of those who were tortured and murdered.

The focus on victims resulted in part from the structure of the
TRC. Although its authorizing Act establishes three committees
to carry out its work—the Committee on Human Rights Violation, the Committee on Amnesty, and the Committee on Reparation and Rehabilitation—the Committee on Human Rights

Violation started first, and established a process for the testimony of victims. These well-publicized hearings quickly set the tone and public impression of the TRC. The Act specifies that individuals who wish to apply for amnesty have up to twelve months from the adoption of the Act to do so.[36] The Committee on Reparation and Rehabilitation on the other hand had to await applications from individuals, or referrals based on findings of the human rights and amnesty committees about individual victims and societal needs.

Timothy Garton Ash comments that as a result of this structure, "the amnestied killer immediately walks free" while his victim must wait for decisions about reparations.[37] Yet this implies that the process of testifying and of being heard by the official TRC human rights committee is of no independent value to the individual victims or the nation as a whole. It is precisely the contrary view that warrants attention: Could it be that speaking to official listeners of the past atrocities accomplishes something important for the individual victims, and for the listening nation?

Healing through Testimony and Inquiry

If the affirmative case for truth commissions rests on the goal of healing, then the working hypothesis is that testimony of victims and perpetrators, offered publicly to a truth commission, affords opportunities for individuals and the nation as a whole to heal. With the aim of producing a fair and thorough account of the atrocities, a truth commission proceeds on the assumption that it helps individuals to tell their stories and to have them acknowledged officially. Also assumed here is the premise that a final report can create a framework for the nation to deal with its past. Echoing the assumptions of psychotherapy, religious confession, and journalistic muckraking, truth commissions presume that telling and hearing truth is healing.

Tina Rosenberg, a journalist immersed in the subject of collective violence in Latin America, Eastern Europe, and South Africa, finds parallels between truth commissions and the therapeutic process that helps individual victims deal with post-traumatic stress disorder.[38] She notes that in both contexts individuals need to tell their stories to someone who listens seriously and who validates them with official acknowledgment; in both settings, individuals must be able to reintegrate the narrative of atrocity into their whole life stories.[39] She adds, "If the whole nation is suffering from post-traumatic stress disorder, this process would be appropriate for the whole nation."[40]

On the contrary, some say: Individuals, and nations, can have too much memory.[41] Perhaps this only happens when it is the wrong kind of memory: superficial, or overflowing without a catch basin.[42] Or perhaps it happens when the truth attends to a past without affording a bridge to the future. Lawrence Weschler invoked W. S. Merwin's prose poem "Unchopping a Tree" as a warning about the limitations of truth commissions.[43] Merwin examines step-by-step how one would reassemble a tree that is destroyed so completely that its leaves, branches, and twigs have all come apart. After the painstaking steps to reassemble the tree, part by part, it stands. But the breeze still can touch only dead leaves. Healing is an absurd or even obscene notion for those who have died. Survivors of mass atrocity may feel as though in fact they have died, or live among the dead. Perhaps endurance, not healing, is what survivors at best can seek.[44]

The problem is not too much truth but that "truth" can never be full enough, or sufficiently embracing enough, to connect profoundly difficult perceptions of what happened. Michael Ignatieff reminds us: "Either the siege at Sarajevo was a deliberate attempt to terrorize and subvert the elected government of an internationally recognized state or it was a legitimate preemptive defense of the Serbs' homeland from Muslim attack. It cannot be both."[45]

Difficulties remain even if truth-seeking is justified on the hope that testimony and fair investigation, undertaken in good faith, could afford opportunities for individuals and societies to recover after periods of terror and violations of human rights. Victims, perpetrators, and bystanders stand in different relationships to the underlying events and to the prospect of healing, and tracing the effects of participation in or knowledge of the truth commission's work for each group would be insuperable.

Further complicating matters, particular individuals may be viewed as victims, perpetrators, and bystanders. A student watches his parents being harassed by secret police; the student joins protest or freedom-fighting groups and then is arrested; the student emerges willing to use terrorist tactics against the secret police, and sets off bombs that kill civilians.[46] Another person emerges from a session of torture ready to work as an informant for the secret police.[47] How and when can such people confess to others what they have done while also telling of their own trauma? How can they forgive themselves and work through horror? When it comes to the goal of national healing, it is simply unclear whether theories and evidence of individual recovery from violence have much bearing.

The language of healing casts the consequences of collective violence in terms of trauma; the paradigm is health, rather than justice. Justice reappears in the idea that its pursuit is to heal victims of violence and to reconcile opposing groups. At the same time, the formal justice system recurs in discussion of healing as a potential barrier or provocation for renewed trauma.[48] Healing and justice seem most compatible for groups poised to reclaim or restart a nation under terms conducive to democracy. They are less compatible where the victimized group has been expelled or so decimated that it has no nation in which to reconcile and rebuild.

The very vocabularies of healing and restoration are foreign to the legal language underpinning prosecutions. Emotional and psychological healing did not figure largely in the initial national and international debates in response to the Holocaust. Yet healing recurs in contemporary discussions, perhaps reflecting the popularization of psychological ideas over the course of the twentieth century. Another source may be the experiences of survivors of atrocities, and their families. From the vantage point of passing decades, survivors and often their children emphasize the need to heal and to learn to live again.

Scholars and therapists have begun to explore the dimensions of healing that could emerge for individuals, and perhaps for societies, after collective violence. For example, Eric Santner writes of the trauma experienced by victims and by observers of the Holocaust, the dangers of prematurely invoking normalcy before the trauma has been worked through, and the continuing need in newly reunified Germany in particular to work through the trauma of the Nazi period.[49] Drawing explicitly on the works of Sigmund Freud and Saul Friedlander, Santner defines trauma as the overstimulation of a person's psychic structures so that the individual needs to reinvent or repair the basic ways of making meaning and bounding the self and others. For a trauma victim, for example, regulating the flow of information across the boundaries of the self may require profound reconstruction.[50] Santner writes, "To take seriously Nazism and the 'Final Solution' as massive trauma means to shift one's theoretical, ethical, and political attention to the psychic and social sites where individual and group identities are constituted, destroyed, and reconstructed."[51]

Similarly, Robert Jay Lifton emphasizes that victims of violence experience trauma that breaks the lifeline, and leaves to the survivor the task "of formulation, evolving new inner forms that include the traumatic event."[52] And Judith Herman develops a theory of trauma and recovery that connects the experiences of Holocaust victims, U.S. soldiers in Vietnam, battered women, child abuse victims, and incest survivors.[53] The initial injury for victims, according to Herman, follows two stages: relinquishing autonomy, connections with others, and moral principles in the face of terror and domination; and then, losing the will to live.[54] Other observers recount the effects of chronic fear and daily unspoken terror on survivors of totalitarian regimes, including hopelessness, emotional breakdowns, and repetition and recurrence of traumatic events in the guise of personal problems.[55] Those who survive often have difficulties controlling their anger, overcoming suicidal thoughts, remembering the traumatic events, being able to stop reliving the events, and sustaining relationships, beliefs, and a sense of meaning.[56] Herman argues that "[d]enial, repression and disassociation operate on a social as

well as individual level,"[57] and that the need for fantasies of
revenge are aspects of trauma that can be worked through.[58]

Herman stresses the importance of learning to recover memories and to speak of atrocities in order to heal. Survivors cannot
simply pick up prior relationships, because they come to view all
relationships through the "lens of extremity."[59] Nor can survivors simply resume their previous identities. They need to find
ways to incorporate the memories of the self "who can lose and
be lost to others," and the self who learned firsthand about the
capacity for evil, within others and within herself or himself.[60]
Through a process of truth-telling, mourning, taking action and
fighting back, and by reconnecting with others, Herman argues,
even individuals severely traumatized by totalitarian control
over a prolonged period can recover.[61] Empowerment—restoring a sense of power and control—and reconnection—reviving a
sense of identity and communality—become the building blocks
for healing. Reaching out to help others and to prevent future victimization can help survivors regain a sense of purpose and reason to live.[62]

It remains to be seen how these ideas relate to traumas that
are inextricable from political conflict and struggle. Herman
acknowledges the therapeutic value of collective political action
and legal initiatives for some trauma survivors,[63] but she focuses
on the direct relationship between a trauma survivor and a professional therapist—or therapy groups conducted by a professional therapist. When the truth-telling occurs in the more
formal setting of commission hearings, can any of the important
dimensions of a trusting relationship between survivor and
helper emerge? How do political movements against oppression
affect both the experience of psychological trauma and the value
of therapeutic responses?[64] How important is it for a therapist to
use the language of injustice and oppression to support the
victim?[65]

The potential restorative power of truth-telling, the significance of sympathetic witnesses, and the constructive roles of perpetrators and bystanders each suggest promising features of a
truth commission. Let us consider each in turn, and then return

to the contrast between the levels of individual and national wounds and healing, the differences between healing and justice, and issues of implementation and amnesty.

The Restorative Power of Truth-Telling: "The fundamental premise of the psychotherapeutic work is a belief in the restorative power of truth-telling," reports Herman.[66] The same premise undergirds a truth commission that affords opportunities for victims to tell their stories. In both settings, the goal is not exorcism but acknowledgment; in both settings, the story of trauma becomes testimony. Know the truth and it will set you free; expose the terrible secrets of a sick society and heal that society.[67] Is this an assertion that can be tested or instead an article of professional, cultural, or religious faith? Without answering this question fully, anecdotal evidence suggests the healing power of speaking about trauma.

Inger Agger and Soren Jensen have worked therapeutically for years with refugee survivors of persecution. They emphasize the significance of testimony, in both the private, confessional sense and the public, juridical sense.[68] Similarly, Richard Mollica explains that the trauma story is transformed through testimony from a telling about shame and humiliation to a portrayal of dignity and virtue, regaining lost selves and lost worlds.[69] Therapists working with survivors of political torture have found the process of developing and revising testimony an important element of healing.[70] Facing, rather than forgetting, the trauma is crucial if a victim hopes to avoid reproducing it in the form of emotional disturbances. A group of Chilean therapists conclude:

> we have found that the person or the family needs to recount the traumatic experience in detail, and express the emotions it produced. This permits integration into a coherent history of events that were necessarily disassociated, allowing the person to feel the pain of the losses experienced. It opens up the possibility for grief and mourning, and facilitates the development of a more coherent self-image.[71]

By confronting the past, the traumatized individuals can learn to distinguish past, present, and future.[72] When the work of knowing and telling the story has come to an end, the trauma then belongs to the past; the survivor can face the work of building a future.[73]

Coming to know that one's suffering is not solely a private experience, best forgotten, but instead an indictment of a social cataclysm, can permit individuals to move beyond trauma, hopelessness, numbness, and preoccupation with loss and injury.[74] The clandestine nature of torture and abuses by repressive governments doubles the pain of those experiences with the disbelief of the community and even jeopardy to the victim's own memory and sanity. Holding in the account of what happened exacerbates the trauma. In contrast, speaking in a setting where the experience is acknowledged can be restorative. One individual who was blinded by an apartheid-era police officer who became known as the Rambo of the Peninsula spoke before the Human Rights Committee of the TRC and then was asked how he felt about coming there to tell his story. He replied: "I feel what has been making me sick all the time is the fact that I couldn't tell my story. But now I—it feels like I got my sight back by coming here and telling you the story."[75] Testifying publicly before an official body can transform the seemingly private experience into a public one. Manouri Muttetuwegama chairs the Presidential Commission on Disappearance in the southern provinces of Sri Lanka, and has already heard thousands of testimonies from petitioners. She reports how eager people are to tell their stories, shed the constraint of silence, and provide vivid accounts of their tragic experiences.[76]

Pumla Gobodo-Madikizela, the psychologist serving on the South African Truth and Reconciliation Commission, reports that one mother testified before the commission about her pain in losing a child to torture and then death. She said later that she did not intend to cry before the commission, but nonetheless, she did cry. Knowing the testimony was broadcast, she concluded, "I wanted the world to see my tears." There can be pride and

strength in seeing oneself as an actor on the world stage, and as
one who can educate the world while also exposing personal suffering in a public way. Tears in public will not be the last tears,
but knowing that one's tears are *seen* may grant a sense of
acknowledgment that makes grief less lonely and terrifying.

Some people, however, may feel exploited by media coverage
of their grief. Accordingly, the TRC provides opportunities for
many to participate without the intrusion of media coverage. By
February, 1998, the TRC had obtained statements from 20,000
people in addition to those given in public hearings.

With or without public broadcast of the testimony, the sheer
act of speaking in a setting where you are believed can be affirming for those who have been victimized. Mzykisi Mdidimba
told Tina Rosenberg that testifying about being tortured
at the age of sixteen "has taken it off my heart." He continued: "When I have told stories of my life before, afterward I
am crying, crying, crying, and felt it was not finished. This time,
I know what they've done to me will be among these people
and all over the country. I still have some sort of crying, but also
joy inside."[77]

Thomas Buergenthal, one of three commissioners in the
United Nations Truth Commission for El Salvador, reported that

> many of the people who came to the Commission to tell what hap-
> pened to them or to their relatives and friends had not done so
> before. For some, ten years or more had gone by in silence and pent-
> up anger. Finally, someone listened to them, and there would be a
> record of what they had endured. They came by the thousands, still
> afraid and not a little skeptical, and they talked, many for the first
> time. One could not listen to them without recognizing that the
> mere act of telling what had happened was a healing emotional
> release, and that they were more interested in recounting their story
> and being heard than in retribution. It is as if they felt some shame
> that they had not dared to speak out before and, now that they had
> done so, they could go home and focus on the future less encum-
> bered by the past.[78]

This is, of course, the perception of an outside observer, not a survivor. Yet it does reflect a first-hand observer's reaction to survivors who had the opportunity to testify before a truth commission.

Some individuals may find it therapeutic to testify even when they personally dislike or refuse a psychological framework for their suffering. Agger and Jensen describe an individual they identify as "K" who survived, exhibited symptoms of post-traumatic stress, but insisted he had no psychological problems. "K . . . did not understand why he was to talk with a therapist. His problems were medical: the reason why he did not sleep at night was due to the pain in his legs and feet. He was asked by the therapist . . . about his political background, and K told her that he was a Marxist and that he had read about Freud and did not believe in any of that stuff: how could his pain go away by talking to a therapist?"[79]

K agreed to tell his story to the therapist, however, after the therapist explained two points relevant to K's own purposes. First, part of her task involved collecting information about prison practices in his country. Also she recounted that she had seen how people who had nightmares about their experiences of torture could be helped by telling others about what happened.[80] Perhaps others who decline to or are unable to meet with a therapist would find benefits in telling their stories in a truth commission setting.[81] Yet there are dangers that a truth commission focuses so much on victims that it deters participation by those who view themselves as survivors, not victims.[82]

A truth commission could help individual victims who testify, and even those who do not, to locate their experiences within the larger setting of political violence. Commission investigators take the testimony seriously by confirming, challenging, or clarifying it, and developing the broader context for the violations. Those too afraid or in too much pain to testify can gain some benefit from hearing the testimony of others who tell of experiences parallel or partially similar to their own. Integrating personal experiences of devastation with the larger context of political oppression can be crucial to a therapeutic result. One mother in Chile felt guilty about the death of her young son who was shot by a police squad after she let him cross the street to watch television with neighbors. In therapy with professionals committed to acknowledging the context of political terror in Chile, the woman learned that her son was shot as part of mass political repression, "and that her private and personal loss was caused by a sociopolitical situation. One of the things that helped her in her private mourning was attaining an emotional understanding of the fact that the police, and not she, had killed her son."[83] The therapists note that the legal action she subsequently initiated against the police also proved therapeutic.

Yet to be effectively therapeutic, the act of narrating experience with oppression should move beyond a plain statement of facts to include also the survivor's emotional and bodily responses and reactions of others important to her. Herman explains that "[a] narrative that does not include the traumatic imagery and bodily sensations is barren and incomplete . . . The recitation of facts without the accompanying emotions is a sterile exercise, without therapeutic effect."[84] Similarly, for healing to occur, the testimony should include attention to how the individual has tried to understand what happened, and how those understandings can be reintegrated with the individual's values and hopes.[85] Ensuring these elements is likely to exceed the time, attention, and expertise of a truth commission. Yet unless the commissioners and staff of a truth commission attend to these dimensions of an integrated personal narrative of meaning, emotion, and memory, the therapeutic effects for testifying victims will be limited. The arduous process of working through trauma that individual therapists can create is not created by a truth commission, but the commission process can offer therapeutic moments.

The Presence of Sympathetic Witnesses: The benefits of truth-telling depend in no small measure on the presence of sympathetic witnesses. Survivors recount the painful stories in the course of establishing trusting relationships and receive acknowl-

edgment and validation from others.[86] Many who come forward
to speak before the South African TRC explain how they want
the commission to witness their pain or the evidence of their lost
loved ones.[87] Therapists who work with survivors of traumatic
violence have discovered how crucial a moral, sympathetic, and
politically attentive stance is to the therapeutic relationship; the
therapist must take a moral stance and not remain neutral nor
focused solely on the subjective sphere.[88]

Thus, therapists working with survivors of political repression
have concluded that "[t]he primary challenge to the therapist, in
fact, is to maintain the link between psychotherapeutic work
and the sociopolitical phenomena in which the symptoms are
rooted."[89] The therapist and the patient need to build a bond of
commitment premised on an explicit political, social, and psychological alliance.[90] Therefore, "[i]t is taken for granted that the
patient's disturbance is the result of a traumatic experience
inflicted purposefully and criminally for political reasons."[91]
Acknowledgment by others of the victim's moral injuries is a central element of the healing process.[92] "The therapist is called
upon to bear witness to a crime. She must affirm a position of solidarity with the victim."[93] When survivors speak of their relatives
who "died," one psychologist instead emphasizes the fact that
they were murdered.[94] Reestablishing a moral framework, in
which wrongs are correctly named and condemned, is usually
crucial to restoring the mental health of survivors.

Recognizing the indignity of the abuses similarly is vital in com-
municating to the victimized, and to the rest of the nation, that
individuals do matter. Although it is not easy to demonstrate that
the simple gathering of testimony accomplishes this task, failure
to take such steps would most likely convey that individuals
and their pain do not matter. That indifference compounds
victimization.[95]

The very establishment and structure of a truth commission
that receives testimony from survivors affords witnesses for the
stories of those survivors who testify. The TRC human rights
committee hearings give victims the chance to tell their stories
before sympathetic listeners, and create a public setting devoted

to documenting the atrocities and locating individual trauma in the larger political context. These opportunities can afford chances for individuals to heal. By identifying someone's suffering as an indictment of the social context rather than treating it as a private experience that should be forgotten, a commission can help an individual survivor make space for new experiences.[96] Even if the commission cannot create the bond of commitment that therapists seek with a client, public acknowledgment of harms can help individual survivors reestablish a capacity to trust people, even the government.

The TRC presents its hearings with a tone of care-giving and a sense of safety.[97] It does not cross-examine survivors of torture and other alleged human rights violations. And yet it must appear fair and sufficiently neutral to encourage amnesty applications from perpetrators. This can conflict with the national need for a body that can condemn the wrongdoing. The appearance of evenhandedness is assisted by the division of work into a more formal, court-like amnesty committee and a more informal, compassionate human rights committee. Precisely because it is not a court, the human rights committee avoids chilling reminders to victimized people of the hostility and insensitivity of courts under apartheid. It also avoids the taint of a judiciary too often complicit with the human rights abuses of the apartheid regime. Treating those who testify about human rights abuses as persons to be believed, rather than troublemakers or even people with a burden to prove their story, the TRC offers a stark contrast with adversarial hearings and inquests. Because the testimony escapes the tests of cross-examination, however, its truth value lies in its capacity to elicit acknowledgment and to build the general picture of apartheid's violations.[98]

The TRC hearings are regularly broadcast on radio and television, with a weekly show recapping the sessions. In one televised session, Singqokwana Ernest Malgas, now confined to a wheelchair partly due to injuries from torture, tried to describe the techniques of torture he endured, and broke down in sobs which he tried to hide with his hands. Malgas is an ANC veteran who was imprisoned in Robben Island for fourteen years. During that time, his house was repeatedly firebombed and police burned one of his sons to death with acid.[99] As Malgas hid behind his hands before the TRC committee, family members and a staff person tried to comfort him and help him recover the ability to speak. Seated across the room was Archbishop Desmond Tutu, the head and founder of the commission. Hearing the man testify and cry, Archbishop Tutu buried his head in his hands and then bowed, prone, before the table between them. Perhaps he was carefully holding his own horror from view, or seeking to prevent his own sympathetic pain from displacing attention from the testifying victim. In either case, this moment, caught in a broadcast, exemplifies the complex and deeply emotional process of acknowledging, bearing witness to, and mourning the atrocities committed under apartheid, while also restoring dignity to those whose very being had been so deeply violated.

Justice Albie Sachs of the South African Constitutional Court notes that "Tutu cries. A judge does not cry."[100] At times, the commissioners join witnesses in singing, or bowing their heads in prayer. The public process of acknowledgment brings recognition even to stories that are already known by those who testify and those who listen.

Pumla Gobodo-Madikizela reports that many victims are grateful that their pain is honored by the South African commissioners' sympathetic attention to their stories. Yet no one should pretend that the process of testifying before a truth commission involves the establishment of trusting relationships on a level called for by the model of therapy. Dr. Gobodo-Madikizela notes that although the TRC provides assistance to victim-witnesses before and after their testimony, it falls short of full therapeutic services. Perhaps the commission will recommend such services as an aspect of future reparations, but the very experience of testifying often calls for more immediate psychological assistance. Other groups, such as The Centre for the Study of Violence and Reconciliation, which contributed to the establishment of the TRC, offer counseling and referral for survivors and family victims, but the need outstrips the available resources.

In addition, a truth commission typically pays no attention to the psychological needs of commission members and others who listen to victims of torture and violence. What should the listeners do with the disturbing images and emotions that the testimony is bound to engender? With whom can they talk and work through their reactions? Studies of therapists who work with trauma victims indicate that the listeners' needs also matter not only due to humanitarian concerns but also to increase the chances of successful results for the victims. Sympathetic listeners who work with survivors may be engulfed by anguish, overcome by despair, and awash with mourning.[101] All of these reactions are understandable responses to identifying with the survivors, feeling guilty for causing the patient to reexperience pain in the retelling, dwelling with the contagious hopelessness of victims, becoming overwhelmed by the enormity of reported suffering and confronting such human evil.[102]

Yet even more disturbing may be moments when the listeners identify with bystanders and even with perpetrators.[103] If these feelings are not understood and managed, the therapist—or commission member—may become self-doubting, patronizing, or burned-out.[104] At the same time, listeners can grow if they learn to balance immersion in the experiences and feelings of victims with a sense of humor and engagement in the fullness of life.[105] These insights underscore the importance of therapeutic assistance for those who testify and for those who listen in the truth commission process.

Tasks for Perpetrators and Bystanders: Therapists who work with victims of collective violence emphasize the need for social repair. A therapist explains: "[V]ictims need to know that their society as a whole acknowledges what has happened to them."[106] Such general, social acknowledgment is needed also for bystanders, who often experience guilt because they avoided harm or else participated, through ignorance and denial, in the regimes producing collective violence.[107]

Sources such as the *New York Times* assert the therapeutic value for whites in having the chance to watch the TRC testimony of victims on television. "The hearings are therapeutic not only for the victims. The televised statements of victims and criminals can open the eyes of whites who ignored or justified apartheid's crimes, a crucial ingredient of reconciliation and for creating a democratic culture."[108]

The fact of the broadcast may enable viewers to share in the process of acknowledgment, mourning, and sympathetic listening. It also may add dimensions of voyeurism, and it is not clear how the televised hearings affect viewers, or for that matter, participants. Yet, if the sheer fact of a public audience can help acknowledge suffering and wrongdoing, the broadcasting is valuable. If the broadcast extends across the nation, it can create a shared experience for a much-divided nation. It remains to be seen, however, whether people from different quarters see the same thing and empathize with the same witnesses or instead line up with those whose positions most resemble their own.

Other mechanisms besides watching can involve bystanders more directly in the process of creating a shared national narrative. The TRC created a Register of Reconciliation for people to write their reactions even if they are not victims or have no reason to seek amnesty. The flood of comments ("I didn't know . . ." or "I should have done more to help resist . . .") received in an initial wave suggests ways that the commission's process provides a beacon for bystanders as they reorient themselves with the new national agenda. The TRC steers the victims toward reconciliation; it officially describes the register as affording "members of the public a chance to express their regret at failing to prevent human rights violations and to declare their commitment to reconciliation."[109] When less than six months remained for the TRC's work, the entries in the registry dropped off substantially. Archbishop Tutu made a public plea for more participation by whites and urged their participation in the official process to enable reconciliation.[110] Yet the nonparticipation may reflect many complex motives, including disillusionment with the process after an initial heady rush of high expectations.

The TRC also invited members of the business community, journalists, and judges to offer submissions for amnesty for their complicity with apartheid, but received almost no responses. No individual members of the judiciary came to seek amnesty for their own personal acts performed in the apartheid courts. Only a few leading judges signed and submitted a document acknowledging that the judiciary as an institution enforced apartheid and failed to protect people from torture.[111] Inquiries into the role of businesses as beneficiaries of apartheid—and the conduct of medical professionals and journalists in supporting it—help fill out the patterns of complicity relevant to a full account. They also illustrate how the disclosures of the past can engage representatives of leading institutions in an embrace of the new vision for the nation. But they fall short of statements accepting or noting individual responsibility for acts, omissions, or complicity with the regime of violence and oppression.

The hearings and the final report of a truth commission can give context to the human rights violations, and remind a viewing public of the human costs that were suppressed or unknown. Tina Rosenberg asserts, "People need to see the human cost," such as "the woman who says, 'The police came in and broke my sewing machine.' It's the small stories that have gone missing."[112] Moving beyond statistics to real people of blood, flesh, and tears, a commission that gathers individual testimony can present human consequences of atrocities that are otherwise unfathomable and overwhelming.

A truth commission can also cut through myths, rumors, and false pictures about the past. The report on El Salvador confirmed what some suspected, and what others refused to believe, while separating truth from rampant lies and rumors.[113] According to one of its drafters, the report put an end to inflammatory charges and countercharges, overcame denial of terrible truths, and allowed the nation to focus on the future.[114] Although skeptics could disagree, the report did establish credibility through the commission's deliberative process and its apparent honesty.

Perhaps acknowledgment of wrongs is most helpful to the victimized and the entire society when it comes from perpetrators,[115] yet no sincere acknowledgment can be ordered or forced. The legislation in South Africa does not require anyone to seek

amnesty. Nor does it require those who do seek amnesty to show
contrition.[116] Still, the amnesty available to perpetrators on the
condition that they testify fully before the TRC about their politically motivated crimes and misconduct has elicited confessions,
with details, of acts of torture, shootings, and bombings. Gathering this information can provide some measure of comfort to
the victimized who want to know where a loved one is buried,
whether he or she was tortured before dying, who ordered the
raid, or whether the suicide note was forged. The collected information from amnesty applicants will help provide a fuller picture
of the past. It will partially overcome the risk of impunity and
immunity from exposure for those who committed violations of
human rights. Of course, some details, perhaps many, will never
publicly be known.

On occasion, those seeking amnesty acknowledge such acts
were wrong, not merely justified by political beliefs. Some have
even proffered apologies and requests for forgiveness. When General Johan van der Merwe confessed that he was the one who
gave the order to fire on demonstrators in 1992,[117] he did not
only crack the secrecy and anonymity of the apartheid regime.
When the police general confessed to his order to fire on the demonstrators, he also said he was sorry. Archbishop Tutu said later,
"It was an incredible moment. I said we should just keep quiet a
bit and put our heads down for a minute."[118]

Other moments before the TRC do not have this quality.
A police captain admitted his role in the shooting of thirteen
people, and asked the victims' families for forgiveness. Instead,
he was met by what a *New York Times* reporter describes as
"low grumbling," clarified later as a clear resistance to the notion
that amnesty and truth could heal wounds.[119] Other alleged perpetrators lie to the commission, distort their actions, respond
with arrogance and adversariness, or admit their crimes in mono-
tones, with no embarrassment.

Some victimized individuals want to forgive but lack the basic
information about whom to forgive; here, a truth commission
may help identify names. A teen-aged daughter of a murdered
South African activist indicated she wanted to forgive but didn't

know who committed the murder; then her father's murderers applied for amnesty.[120] Others do not want to and certainly do not have to forgive perpetrators. South African Justice Minister Dullah Omar emphasizes that in his view, "forgiveness is a personal matter. However, bitterness can only exacerbate tensions in society. By providing victims a platform to tell their stories and know the destiny of their loved ones, one can help to achieve a nation reconciled with its past and at peace with itself."[121]

The healing sought by the TRC does not require apologies or forgiveness. On behalf of bystanders and perpetrators, as well as victims, it seeks to reestablish a baseline of right and wrong, to humanize the perpetrators and to obtain and disclose previously hidden information about what happened, who gave orders, where missing persons ended up. Commissioner Ntsebeza explains that victims of apartheid are not only those on the receiving end of gross violations of human rights, but also family members who learn of the offenses committed by their loved ones, and even perpetrators, warped and sometimes broken by their conduct as spies, torturers, and murderers.[122] This generosity of vision that extends the hope for healing to perpetrators is a distinctive feature of the TRC.[123]

A truth commission is charged to produce a public report that recounts the facts gathered, and render moral assessment. It casts its findings and conclusions not in terms of individual blame but instead in terms of what was wrong and never justifiable. In so doing, it helps to frame the events in a new national narrative of acknowledgment, accountability, and civic values.[124] Trial records do not seek a full historical account beyond the actions of particular individuals. A commission, though, can try to expose the multiple causes and conditions contributing to genocide and regimes of torture and terror. Close historical analysis of testimonies and documents expose the influences of economic privation, intergroup hostility, demagogic politicians, totalitarian structures, passive bystanders who felt ineffective, disengaged, or panicked—or complacent about their benefits from the repressive regime. The commission can also crucially detail how leaders and cultural practices dehumanized particular groups of individuals, and how military and police practices emerged with no accountability to the public.[125] Complex analyses can do more than verdicts of guilt or innocence to produce a record for the nation and the world, and a recasting of the past to develop bases for preventing future atrocities.

Healing a Nation

Can a therapeutic process work for collectivities? Are truth commission mechanisms, which already fall short of the elements necessary for full therapeutic relationships and treatment for individuals, able to promote reconstruction of whole societies? National healing and reconciliation takes precedence over individual healing in the design of the TRC, but it would be wrong to suggest that a commission by itself could accomplish the reconstruction of a society devastated by violent and hostile divisions. Yet there are promising roles that a commission can play.

Father Bryan Hehir observes that truth commissions function at three levels: 1) personal catharsis through talking about terrible personal trauma; 2) moral reconstruction, by producing a social judgment and moral account of the historical record; and 3) political consequences, to take action such as prosecutions or instead to desist after assessing the risks of further violence and instability.[126] In this view, the social reconstruction occurs as the commission provides an accounting of the atrocities and articulates the moral stance needed to name the horrors, and also to move on.[127]

It remains an open question whether through taking testimony and publishing reports, a truth commission can also help to reconcile groups that have been warring or otherwise engaged in deep animosities. Even a minimal form of reconciliation would require capacities for constructive cooperation between those most victimized and those who committed, ordered, or countenanced their victimization. Crucial here would be demonstrable evenhandedness and honest acknowledgment of injuries and wrongs committed by the competing sides without losing hold of the distinction between those who abused government power and those who resisted the abuses.[128] The TRC is committed to exposing abuses by the liberation forces as well as by apartheid officials and supporters, and perhaps this commitment to the injuries on both sides can support reconciliation over time. Yet the very effort to articulate the moral baseline must treat the crimes of apartheid as worse than the crimes of the ANC or other antiapartheid activists in terms of scale and motive.[129] Some observers object that the entire TRC operates as a political witch hunt designed to discredit the former National Party government even more than it has been already.[130]

In addition, a truth commission focused on the experiences of victims may tilt the writing of history in terms of victimhood rather than rights in a democratic, political order. André Du Toit, an academic activist involved in the formation of the TRC, worries that the focus on victims, caregiving, and the Christian notion of forgiveness may lead some people to refuse to participate. "The survivors [who do not identify as victims] do not relate to this situation. They respond by saying, 'we have had these experiences, but we do not want to present ourselves as victims in need of healing. We do not necessarily agree with the message of forgiveness. What political purpose does the story serve when it is framed in this way?' "[131]

Treating truth commissions as focused on therapy seems to ignore politics, shortchange justice issues, and treat survivors and their recovery as a means toward a better society rather than as persons with dignity and entitlements to justice.[132] Yael Tamir, an Israeli philosopher, listened to an exchange of views about the relative importance of victim testimony and common civic rights in truth commissions, and commented: "I am uneasy about this psychological perspective because the catharsis of one person is the suffering of another. How does this work in cases where everybody has done something wrong to somebody else?"[133]

Even where everyone has done something wrong to someone else, the wager of the TRC is that reconciliation can be better reached if the emphasis is on securing in public form the fullest possible truth. Then there is a chance to acknowledge human rights violations committed by each side rather than to blame and punish only those who devised and implemented apartheid.

Yet, many long-time antiapartheid activists cannot accept the archbishop's call for reconciliation and forgiveness across South Africa. To Churchill Mxenge, the brother of Griffith Mxenge, an antiapartheid lawyer murdered under apartheid orders, the archbishop's stance seems a betrayal of his own promises made at Griffith's funeral to ensure that justice would be done.[134] The surviving brother recounted to Tina Rosenberg, "I try to put myself in Tutu's position . . . Tutu is a man of the cloth, a man who believes in miracles. But I cannot see him being able overnight to cause people who are hurt and bleeding simply to forget about their wounds and forget about justice . . . Unless justice is done it's difficult for any person to think of forgiving."[135]

Churchill Mxenge had the chance to convey his views to Archbishop Tutu directly on a television show with several family members of apartheid victims. Tutu offered the explanation of political necessity: amnesty was extended to avoid military upheaval. When Tina Rosenberg later asked the archbishop whether he was honoring his commitment to justice, he replied by identifying different kinds of justice: "Retributive justice is largely Western. The African understanding is far more restorative—not so much to punish as to redress or restore a balance that has been knocked askew. The justice we hope for is restorative of the dignity of the people."[136]

Archbishop Tutu does not speak for all black South Africans, and certainly not for all South Africans, in this aspiration. This very dissension, ideally, could be part of the story narrated by a truth commission. Honesty about the complexity of the past and transparency about the commission's own deliberations can help prevent the production of a victors' report. A fact-finding commission can expose the multiple causes and conditions contributing to genocide and to regimes of torture and terror, and it can distribute blame and responsibility across sectors of society.

Many in South Africa proudly embrace the TRC's search for nonviolent responses to violence.[137] From their vantage point, it is an act of restraint not to pursue criminal sanctions, and an act of hope not to strip perpetrators of their political and economic positions. Yet it is also an act of judgment that prosecutions would impose too great a cost to stability, reconciliation, or nation building. Acknowledging the dimension of political necessity should not obscure the dimension of courage. When a democratic process selects a truth commission, a people summon the strength and vision to say to one another: Focus on victims and try to restore their dignity; focus on truth and try to tell it whole. Pursue a vision of restorative justice, itself perhaps a major casualty in the colonial suppression of African traditions. Redefine the victims as the entire society, and redefine justice as accountability. Seek repair, not revenge; reconciliation, not recrimination. Honor and attend in public to the process of remembering. Cynthia Ngewu, mother of one of the individuals known as the Guguletu Seven, expressed the vision beautifully: "This thing called reconciliation . . . if I am understanding it correctly . . . if it means this perpetrator, this man who has killed Christopher Piet, if it means he becomes human again, this man, so that I, so that all of us, get our humanity back . . . then I agree, then I support it all."[138]

These bold ambitions may be doomed. To create such high expectations is to invite disappointment. Yet the wager is that setting these goals at least to some degree redirects people's understandable desires for vengeance and recrimination. The democratic origins of the TRC help to consecrate that redirection through a process of broad participation. A truth commission imposed by the nation's executive or an international body may have even more difficulty conveying the messages of reconciliation. It might instead seem merely an insincere or ineffective sop to those who demand some response to the atrocities. Articulating goals more modestly than the TRC's—such as gathering names and accounts of victims and documenting the scope of killings, torture, and other atrocities—could save truth commissions from generating cycles of high hopes and bitter disappointments.

The TRC's pursuit of restorative justice is also in jeopardy if it presages no changes in the material circumstances of those most victimized. Characterized as only one step in the process of reconciliation, the TRC is designed to propose specific economic reparations and also to assist the development of a society stable enough to pursue land reform, redesign of medical and educational systems, and other reforms to redress the massive economic imbalances in the country. The TRC committee on reparations will recommend to the president specific acts requested by the victimized, such as funds for gravestones, as well as collective reparations in the form of monuments, parks, and schools named for victims and survivors, and individual stipends to support medical and therapeutic treatment. Its authorizing Act also creates a special fund to meet the immediate needs of those who testify. The longer term vision of social transformation holds out the idea of redemption for suffering, and yet if progress toward this vision is not made, skepticism about the goals of healing and reconciliation will surely mount.[139]

Cautions

Truth commissions require cooperation by private and public parties, and work best if they have authority to obtain official records.[140] Yet the very atrocities under review may well have destroyed the confidence of private parties in such an undertaking, and may have left in place police departments, cabinet officers, and military leaders resistant to cooperating. When F. W. de Klerk, who with Mandela received the Nobel Peace Prize for steering the peaceful transition, withdrew participation from the TRC, many observers believed that he threw the entire process in jeopardy.[141] De Klerk threatened to sue the TRC for "not being impartial"; he argued that in his one-day appearance he had been badgered while ANC officials received probing or rigorous questioning. Winnie Mandela, the ex-wife of the first postapartheid president and inspirational leader, also strained the TRC and dominated international news coverage when she refused to acknowledge her own participation in alleged human rights violations, and by demanding a public hearing which she in turn tried to turn into a popularity contest.[142]

To secure cooperation from key leaders, truth commissioners may have to contemplate departing from ideal procedures. To establish its own legitimacy and consonance with democratic processes, a truth commission should operate publicly and openly. Yet without ensuring confidentiality, it may never obtain information from witnesses who genuinely and understandably feel still at risk.[143] A truth commission should also steer clear of partisan loyalties and conflicts, and yet public hearings involving divisive leaders can run directly into those tides.

There may be systematic bias in who is willing to testify, who thinks his or her suffering is worthy, who is willing to come forward as a victim, and who is willing to accept responsibility as a perpetrator. Observers of the TRC indicate that a disproportionate number of those coming to testify are women.[144] Also, notably, most of the women do not speak about themselves as victims, but about their husbands, or sons, or other men in their lives. The women tell of men who were brutalized, killed, made to disappear. Recently, a report on gender issues in the TRC cited the absence of women's testimony about their own direct suffering as cause for concern.[145] The commissioners responded by creating hearings specifically focused on women's own experiences. One woman volunteered testimony about a sexual violation committed by police that she found extremely humiliating; she had not mentioned the incident in her written statement.[146] Do the women feel that their own bodily suffering is unimportant? Is there shame that prevents discussions of rape or sexual offenses against women?[147] This sadly would exacerbate a huge underlying problem.

Yet it would also be a misfortune if a truth commission were devalued because it elicits women's testimony about their loved ones. Women's voices are so rarely heard in societal responses to collective violence. The women who testify, indeed everyone who testifies, render vivid and palpable the human faces of suffering, and survival. The strength and devastation displayed when survivors speak of those they have lost sheds light on the endurance and fragility of human bonds. As the poet Robert Lowell wrote, "We are poor passing facts," and so we must give "each figure in the photograph / his living name."[148]

Ironically, those who run oppressor regimes also understand the significance of intimate relationships to human meaning and

dignity. The same report on gender issues in the TRC painstak-
ingly, and painfully, notes the ways in which women often were
tortured by police and prison practices under apartheid through
exploitation of their care for loved ones. Threats to kill a child,
or false claims to have done so, often were used in interrogation
sessions. The gender report urges the commission members to
recognize these kinds of tactics as forms of torture. Somehow,
the commission's ultimate report must balance attention to the
breaches of individual autonomy and dignity with attention to
the violations of vital networks of care and affection wrought by
a regime of hatred and violence.

An additional dilemma involves whether to elicit testimony
from children who themselves experienced or witnessed atrocities. Not to do so would mean missing important stories and
denying children the potentially affirming experience of being
heard and believed; to do so could mean further inflicting
trauma, or dealing with the fragments and confusions of children's memories. The TRC decided not to take testimony from
anyone under eighteen years old, but to hear from adults who
could report on their experiences as children.

Perhaps the greatest practical problem lies here: if journalists,
historians, and philosophers endlessly debate what is truth and
whether facts can ever be separate from interpretation, it is
unlikely that drafters of truth commission reports can resolve
such issues, especially in the politically charged contexts of societies emerging from collective violence. Just report the facts, urges
José Zalaquett, from his experience with the Chilean truth commission;[149] do not worry about testing the truth of particular
pieces of testimony but instead work to acknowledge how the
society must understand the testimony, urges Dennis Thompson,
an American political theorist.[150] One need not descend into
enduring debates over the existence of truth or its accessibility to
humans to sense the difficulties in writing a truth commission
report. It may be possible to identify and distinguish forensic
truth—based on medical and testimonial evidence about what
happened, where, and to whom—from explanatory truth—
encompassing explanations, emerging from dialogue, and con-

necting with larger social and economic contexts of both past and future. Yet interpretations are impossible to separate from all but the most specific facts, and interpretations guide the selection of facts as relevant. Interpretations are contestable and potentially divisive. As professional historians attest, the possibility of new and contrasting interpretations keeps them in business. A South African satirist, Pieter-Dirk Uys, once remarked: "Remember, the future is certain. It is the past that's unpredictable."[151]

Some of the skepticism about truth and its interpretation must be held at bay. Natalie Zemon Davis, the historian who has written vividly about ambiguities in the historical records concerning people's identities, desires, crimes, and reasons,[152] has described how she was jolted in conversations with Eastern European historians after the 1989 "Velvet Revolutions." They wanted to know what can only be described as facts: how many bodies are in the mass grave? Did the bullet shots enter from the front or the back? These kinds of facts stand apart from any meaningful dispute about what is real, or open to human grasp.[153]

Even assuming some careful effort to report fully the brute facts, to negotiate the line between facts and interpretation, in a responsible manner, and to explain candidly the commissioners' disputes and degrees of confidence drafters of a report face dilemmas not only about what to report, but also to whom. Perhaps nothing presents the dilemmas more vividly than the issue of naming names.[154] On the one hand, if names of those who participated in and those who commanded acts of torture, rape, murder, and terror are uncovered through victim testimony and other investigation, they are precisely what should be reported to fill the need to know what happened, and to fulfill the promise to provide full truthful accounting. The United Nations Truth Commission for El Salvador concluded, "Not to name names would be to reinforce the very impunity to which the Parties instructed the Commission to put an end."[155]

On the other hand, a truth commission does not, and could not, follow the strict requirements of due process at work in the judiciary. It does not presume to try people or establish guilt and innocence. In that light, naming names could seem to violate due process and the basic fairness that an emerging democratic society most fundamentally needs. Perhaps a truth commission should report to a prosecuting authority the names uncovered through its investigation. Or perhaps the truth commission should employ standards for fact-checking akin to the procedures that establish grounds for accuracy among journalists and historians.

A Spectrum of Goals

Perhaps, as some say, there are simply two purposes animating societal responses to collective violence: justice and truth.[156] Then the question becomes, which of these two purposes should take precedence? "What is the point of knowledge without justice? Should justice or truth be the guiding aim of accountability? Is punishment through the criminal justice system a suitable means of arriving at knowledge?"[157] One answer calls for "[a]ll the truth and as much justice as possible;"[158] another would stress punishment for wrongdoing, especially horrific wrongdoing. Only if we make prosecution a duty under international law will we ensure that new regimes do not chicken out and overstate the obstacles they face, argues Diane Orentlicher.[159] Yet only if we acknowledge that prosecutions are slow, partial, and preoccupied with the either/or simplifications of the adversary process, can we recognize the independent value of commissions investigating the larger patterns of atrocity and the complex lines of responsibility and complicity.

As this chapter has explored, even these purposes capture only a narrow portion of the potential goals for societal responses to collective violence. Justice requires at least particular truths. Truth-seeking may occur without the trials that can produce just punishments. Truth and justice are not the only objectives, or at least they do not transparently indicate the range of concerns they may come to comprise.

Instead, I have identified twelve overlapping aspirations:

1. overcome communal and official denial of the atrocity and gain public acknowledgment;

2. obtain the facts in an account as full as possible in order to meet victims' need to know, to build a record for history, and to ensure minimal accountability and visibility of perpetrators;

3. end and prevent violence; transform human activity from violence—and violent responses to violence—into words and institutional practices of equal respect and dignity;

4. forge the basis for a domestic democratic order that respects and enforces human rights;

5. support the legitimacy and stability of the new regime proceeding after the atrocity;

6. promote reconciliation across social divisions; reconstruct the moral and social systems devastated by violence;

7. promote psychological healing for individuals, groups, victims, bystanders, and offenders;

8. restore dignity to victims;

9. punish, exclude, shame, and diminish offenders for their offenses;

10. express and seek to achieve the aspiration that "never again" shall such collective violence occur;

11. build an international order to try to prevent and also to respond to aggression, torture, and atrocities;

12. accomplish each of these goals in ways that are compatible with the other goals.

In light of this list, truth commissions are not a second-best alternative to prosecutions, but instead a form better suited to meet many of the goals. Indeed, to serve the goals of healing for individuals and reconciliation across social divisions even better, truth commissions would need to diverge even more than they usually do from prosecutions, and to offer more extensive therapeutic assistance and relief from threats of prosecution.

When the societal goals include restoring dignity to victims, offering a basis for individual healing, and also promoting reconciliation across a divided nation, a truth commission again may be as or more powerful than prosecutions. The commission can help set a tone and create public rituals to build a bridge from a terror-filled past to a collective, constructive future. Individuals do and must have their own responses to atrocity, but the institutional framework created by a society can either encourage desires for retribution or instead strengthen capacities for generosity and peace.

This suggests that the most difficult aspiration is the last one: It is far from clear that a truth commission can achieve therapeutic and reconciliatory goals at the same time that prosecutions proceed. Although South Africa currently permits prosecutions of those individuals who do not obtain amnesty from the TRC, all of the practical dimensions of prosecutions could work against the goals of healing, reconciliation, and full truth-telling. Nonetheless, a rich understanding of healing from atrocity gives an important place to the operations of a justice system, including prosecution and punishment of perpetrators, if the process is not to unleash new violence and thirst for revenge. Prosecutions and truth commissions share, fundamentally, the effort to cabin and channel through public, legal institutions the understandable and even justifiable desires for revenge by those who have been victimized.

The repertoire of societal responses to collective violence must include prosecutions, but it must not be limited to them. Investigatory commissions, most fully developed in the South African Truth and Reconciliation Commission, challenge the assumption that prosecutions are the best form of response. Consider the story of General Magnus Malan, army chief and later defense minister. Charged with authorizing an assassination squad that mistakenly killed thirteen women and children in 1987, General Malan was the subject of one of the few prosecutions before the completion of the work of the TRC in South Africa. The prosecution of Malan grew from nine months of investigation and trial took nine more, costing twelve million rand. In 1996, General Malan was found not guilty, despite numerous allegations that continued to be made after the trial ended. Then, in 1997, General Malan volunteered to speak before the TRC. He expressly did not seek amnesty but instead seemed to want the chance to tell his own story. He acknowledged cross-border raids; he described how he set up a covert unit to disrupt Soviet-backed liberation movements. He denied approval of assassinations or atrocities. He also made clear his opposition to the operation of the TRC itself, as a witch-hunt, but said that he came forward to take moral responsibility for the orders he had given.[160]

Fact-finding commissions open inquiry into the varieties of possible responses and the multiple purposes they may achieve. Truth commissions emphasize the experiences of those victimized; the development of a detailed historical record; and the priority of healing for victims and entire societies after the devastation to bodies, memories, families, friendships, and politics caused by collective violence. A truth commission could generate the evidence to support prosecutions. Or, when the fullest accounts and participation are sought in a nation marked by deep and historic divisions, a truth commission represents a potential alternative to prosecutions. Whether these implement or complement justice, they are worthy of human effort in the continuing struggles against mass atrocities.

5. Reparations

"[A]pology speaks to something larger than any particular offense and works its magic by a kind of speech that cannot be contained or understood merely in terms of expediency or the desire to achieve reconciliation." —Nicholas Tavuchis

"Compensation can never compensate." —Joseph W. Singer

The South African Truth and Reconciliation Commission launches not only an inquiry into what happened, but also a process intended to promote reconciliation. Other truth commissions seek information to support prosecutions. The information unearthed by the TRC may lead to some legal charges and trials, but its central direction, enhanced by its power to grant amnesty to perpetrators on the condition that they cooperate fully, moves away from prosecutions toward an ideal of restorative justice. Unlike punishment, which imposes a penalty or injury for a violation, restorative justice seeks to repair the injustice, to make up for it, and to effect corrective changes in the record, in relationships, and in future behavior. Offenders have responsibility in the resolution. The harmful act, rather than the offender, is to be renounced. Repentance and forgiveness are encouraged.[1]

By design, the TRC includes a committee devoted to proposing economic and symbolic acts of reparation for survivors and for devastated communities. Monetary payments to the victimized, health and social services, memorials and other acts of symbolic commemoration would become governmental policies in an effort to restore victims and social relationships breached by violence and atrocity. The range of money, services, and public art suggests the kinds of steps that can be pursued in the search for restorative justice.

Restorative justice has academic and political advocates in many countries. They draw on diverse religious and philosophical traditions.[2] Christian sources stress the universality of human suffering and the redemptive power of forgiveness. Jewish sources look to Talmudic treatments of restitution and repair.[3] New Zealand and Australia have drawn upon Maori traditions to develop state experiments in restorative justice.[4] Japanese justice includes an informal track of confession, repentance, and absolution in the service of new roles for offenders and victims.[5] Current South African discussions point to traditional African notions of community repair as the goal of justice.[6] Some commentators look to therapeutic methods and ideals.[7]

Leading statements of the restorative justice vision focus on responses to ordinary crime.[8] Restorative justice emphasizes the humanity of both offenders and victims. It seeks repair of social connections and peace rather than retribution against the offenders.[9] Building connections and enhancing communication between perpetrators and those they victimized, and forging ties across the community, takes precedence over punishment or law enforcement.[10]

These aims of restorative justice reflect a practical view about human psychology. Unlike retributive approaches, which may reinforce anger and a sense of victimhood, reparative approaches instead aim to help victims move beyond anger and a sense of powerlessness. They also attempt to reintegrate offenders into the community. South Africa's TRC emphasizes truth-telling, public acknowledgment, and actual reparations as crucial elements for restoration of justice and community. The TRC proceeds on the hope that getting as full an account of what happened as possible, and according it public acknowledgment, will lay the foundations for a new, reconciling nation instead of fomenting waves of renewed revenge and divisiveness. Archbishop Desmond Tutu explained the TRC's goals in these terms: "Our nation needs healing. Victims and survivors who bore the brunt of the apartheid system need healing. Perpetrators are, in their own way, victims of the apartheid system and they, too, need healing."[11]

The authorizing legislation directed the TRC reparations committee to assemble requests and proposals from individuals and communities. The TRC in turn has recommended legislation to establish monetary payments, medical treatment, counseling,

information about murdered relatives, and the naming of parks
and schools. The aim of such reparations is "to empower individuals and communities to take control of their own lives."[12]
Other reparation efforts after mass atrocities stress restoring particular stolen properties, paying money damages, or securing
public apologies from governmental authorities.

One danger with any reparations effort is the suggestion that
because some amends have been made, the underlying events
need not be discussed again. Equally troubling to many survivors
are assertions that monetary reparations can remedy nonmone-
tary harms, such as the death of a child, the loss of an arm, the
agony of remembered torture, or the humiliation and shame of
being wrongly detained and interned. The amounts of money
likely to emerge from political processes, especially in economically depressed societies such as South Africa, can offer only
token gestures whose small size underscores their inadequacy.
As statements of actual value, they trivialize the harms. More
basically, money can never bring back what was lost. Even the
suggestion that it can may seem offensive. Restitution of stolen
art, bank accounts, or ancestral bones may return the physical
objects but not the world in which they were taken. Apologies
may restore some dignity, but not the lives as they existed before
the violations.

The process of seeking reparations, and of building communities of support while spreading knowledge of the violations and
their meaning in people's lives, may be more valuable, ultimately,
than any specific victory or offer of a remedy. Being involved in a
struggle for reparations may give survivors a chance to speak
and to tell their stories. If heard and acknowledged, they may
obtain a renewed sense of dignity. The reparations themselves
cannot undo the violence that was done. Yet even inadequate
monetary payments or an apology without any reparations can
afford more opportunities for a sense of recognition and renewal
for survivors, observers, and offenders than would an unsuccess-
ful struggle for an apology, for reparations, or for the restitution
of property, or a relative's bones. When the victimized and their
supporters push for monetary compensation, for restitution of

94   wrongly appropriated artifacts or property, or for official apologies, they also are engaged in obtaining acknowledgment of the
violations and acceptance of responsibility for wrongdoing as
much as they press for a specific remedy.

Reparations and the U.S. Internment of Japanese-Americans

While Karen Korematsu was a high-school student in San Lean-
dro, California, one lesson told of a man who had gone to court
to challenge the internment of Japanese-Americans during
World War II. That man, Karen learned with astonishment, was
her father; Karen had never heard the story from him.[13] *New
York Times* reporter David Margolick explained, "That silence
stemmed in part from humiliation. Like many ethnic Japanese
who spent the war years in the tar paper shacks of Manzanar,
Tule Lake and other 'resettlement camps' scattered through the
West, he wanted little more than to forget the experience."[14]
Yet Fred Korematsu became a crucial figure in the struggle for
restorative justice for survivors of the internment of Japanese-
Americans. An initial effort, shortly after the war, focused
on the restitution of specific property taken from Japanese-
Americans.[15] Yet this remedy did not begin to address the larger
harms and violations involved in the forced evacuation and
confinement.[16]

    In 1941, Korematsu had refused to obey Executive Order No.
9066. That order, signed by President Franklin D. Roosevelt,
authorized military leaders to prescribe military areas from
which any persons could be excluded as protection against espionage and sabotage. General J. L. DeWitt in turn deemed the
entire Pacific Coast such an area, and required relocation of all
persons of Japanese ancestry living along the West Coast to
detention camps in Arkansas and other regions far away from
their homes. Following his unlucky capture enforcing the relocation order, Korematsu was arrested, and sent to a camp.[17] In
1942, he was convicted for violating the military exclusion
order.

    Congress endorsed that order and made it a misdemeanor for

anyone to enter or remain in the restricted zones contrary to military order. Under this authority, in the name of military necessity during World War II the government swiftly removed some 120,000 persons, including about 70,000 United States citizens, from their homes.[18] The exclusion order itself called for returning interned individuals who could demonstrate their loyalty, yet no expeditious or even regular process to permit such demonstrations emerged. Instead, individuals were housed in crude barracks or horse stalls and then shipped to remote relocation centers in compounds guarded by military personnel. As late as the spring of 1945, about 70,000 remained in the camps. The camps themselves were in desolate, dusty places, bounded by barbed-wire fences, and monitored by guard towers, searchlights, and armed military guards. Families were squeezed into small rooms with no privacy.

Fred Korematsu was born a U.S. citizen. No question was ever raised about his loyalty to the United States. He had tried to join the Coast Guard during World War II, but the service would not let him fill out an application.[19] Because of his Japanese ancestry, Korematsu fell under the federal exclusion order. After his conviction for resisting the order to vacate his home and to move to one of the ten relocation centers, Korematsu pursued his challenge on appeal. In 1943 and 1944, Korematsu and others who had been convicted for violating curfew and exclusion orders unsuccessfully challenged their convictions before the U.S. Supreme Court.

A majority of the highest Court declared that any legal restriction curtailing the civil rights of a group defined by race should be "immediately suspect." Nonetheless, the Court reasoned that the war powers of Congress and the Executive justified the exclusion orders in light of real military dangers.[20] In the Court's view, even the military's failure to try to separate loyal individuals from those specifically found to be disloyal did not undermine the constitutionality of the program. Fierce dissents challenged the inference of group disloyalty and the unrestrained military action that so patently discriminated against an entire group. Many scholars and journalists also immediately castigated the decision. In subsequent challenges to the internment and curfew programs, the Court drew the line only against detention of individuals whose loyalty was conceded by the government.[21]

The war ended. The remote camps closed. Gradually, their residents tried to rebuild their lives, although they had lost most of their businesses and homes. Silence surrounded the whole experience. The facts were known mainly only to Japanese-Americans, but they too participated in the silence.[22] School textbooks did not mention the episode. Nor did war memorials. Some camp survivors continued to be afraid; some were broken by the experience. Many felt ashamed. "It was an emasculation. That's why nobody would talk about it. It was rape," recalled Donald Nakahata, who lived in the camp at Tapaz from the time he was twelve until he was fifteen.[23]

The entire Japanese-American evacuation and internment program of World War II breached the legal guarantees of equality, freedom of movement, protections of private property, and presumptions of innocence for individuals not proven guilty. It also expressed and fueled racism and scapegoating. The camps themselves subjected people to brutal, inhuman conditions. The silence that followed the war in the national period of memorializing soldiers, losses, and victories compounded the harms to members of the Japanese-American community.

Some forty years later, a group of fifty volunteer lawyers, including many young Japanese-American lawyers, returned to court to vacate the convictions of Korematsu and others who had resisted the government's orders against Japanese-Americans during the war.[24] In 1983, Fred Korematsu tried to overturn his conviction by filing a petition of *coram nobis*, a rarely used common-law technique for correcting errors in criminal convictions. In the decades intervening since the conviction, lawyers and historians had obtained evidence demonstrating that the government lacked a basis for the assertion of military necessity used to justify the relocation to the camps.[25] Government officials apparently knowingly relied on false rumors of espionage and sabotage by persons of Japanese ancestry.[26] If a

Pacific Coast threat from Japanese forces ever had existed, the
Battle of the Midway in 1942 virtually destroyed the Japanese
fleet and ended any risk of invasion. The exclusion policy and
relocation nonetheless proceeded; indeed, the vast majority of
Japanese-Americans were moved to camps after the Battle of
Midway.[27]

The legal strategy deployed these facts. The lawyers who
reopened Korematsu's conviction and the convictions of other
resisters built upon and in turn helped to strengthen an ongoing
struggle by members of the Japanese-American community to
gain national recognition and redress.

Judge Marilyn Patel granted Korematsu's petition for a writ of
coram nobis.[28] She wiped the conviction off the record books,
and created an occasion for public acknowledgment of the government's egregious violation of basic respect for individual
human rights. The government itself acknowledged that Korematsu was entitled to relief, but urged the court to dismiss the
action and treat it as no longer appropriate given the repeal of
the orders and laws behind the relocation process. "Apparently
the government would like this court to set aside the conviction
without looking at the record in an effort to put this unfortunate episode in our country's history behind us," Judge Patel
observed.[29]

The judge resisted the government's proposal. Instead, she
reviewed in detail the specific evidence proffered to challenge the
conviction; the court's opinion relied in part upon the 1983
report of a Congressional Commission on Wartime Relocation
and Internment of Civilians. The creation of that commission
was the first victory of the larger political movement for recognition and redress for the internment experience. The commission
concluded that military necessity did not warrant the exclusion
and detention of people of Japanese descent in light of evidence
available at the time of the orders in question. Because that evidence was knowingly concealed from the Supreme Court during
Korematsu's original case, there was ample justification for setting aside the conviction, as even the government conceded in

1983. As a district court judge, Judge Patel could not reverse the original Supreme Court decision but only remove its future force, so that it could have virtually no continuing effect.

Judge Patel's opinion details the evidence of concealment and unjustified incursions on individual liberty and equality. By undertaking and publishing an extensive review of the evidence from wartime, the judge self-consciously sought to do more than correct the judicial record. She used the occasion to afford a public acknowledgment of the harm done and a public warning against future similar harms. Thus, the opinion concludes:

> *Korematsu* remains on the pages of our legal and political history. As a legal precedent it is now recognized as having very limited application. As historical precedent it stands as a constant caution that in times of war or declared military necessity our institutions must be vigilant in protecting constitutional guarantees. It stands as a caution that in times of distress the shield of military necessity and national security must not be used to protect governmental actions from close scrutiny and accountability. It stands as a caution that in times of international hostility and antagonisms our institutions, legislative, executive and judicial, must be prepared to exercise their authority to protect all citizens from the petty fears and prejudices that are so easily aroused . . . [30]

Fred Korematsu himself later reflected: "All these years I thought that the Supreme Court decision was wrong. To have the opportunity after 40 years to reopen my case and have a District Court judge rule that I was not a criminal proves that justice in this country is still possible."[31] This decision attracted considerable press attention. It helped garner public support for a political campaign by the Japanese American Citizens' League that was then already underway for congressional action to make official amends for the internment.[32]

Edison Uno, a faculty member at San Francisco State University, had lobbied the league to push for reparations and an official apology throughout the 1970s, but many members resisted. Like Fred Korematsu, they preferred not to talk about their years

in the camps. Some league members felt shame; others dreaded
renewing psychological pain; some feared that they remained
second-class citizens.[33] Yet after nearly a decade of debate, the
league resolved in 1978 to ask Congress for a governmental apology and a financial payment of $25,000 for each individual who
underwent the internment experience.

Four national legislators of Japanese background made that
request a priority. Hawaii's Senator Daniel Inoye had proposed
the creation of the commission that finally in 1983 issued the
report so important to Judge Patel's decision a year later on
behalf of Fred Korematsu. Senator Inoye believed that the commission would be a necessary step for any success in the search
for reparations. "In order to make it succeed, it had to be a
national effort, not just an effort pursued by Americans of Japanese ancestry. So I suggested that the commission be made up not
of Japanese Americans but of a cross-section of distinguished
Americans."[34] The resulting commission, launched in 1981,
included former members of Congress, the Supreme Court, and
the cabinet along with distinguished private citizens. It held
twenty days of public hearings and received testimony from over
750 witnesses. Its 1983 report, entitled *Personal Justice Denied*,
attributed the internment orders to race prejudice, war hysteria,
and failed political leadership, and it described the humiliating
and squalid conditions of the internment camps. Then, in June
1983, the commissioners recommended legislative reparations in
the amount of $20,000 for each survivor, $5,000 less than the
Japanese American Citizens' League had requested.

Five years of legislative lobbying efforts followed. For many of
the participants, the struggle for reparations represented the
search for public acknowledgment of the wrongs done. Some
also sought to correct the public record and to educate the entire
national and even international community about what had happened. The congressional debate itself afforded opportunities for
elected officials to speak out about the experience and to educate
the broader public. California Representative Norman Mineta
tearfully read a letter from an internment camp written by his

father who recalled the forcible removal of the family. Congressman Mineta concluded, "We lost our homes, we lost our businesses, we lost our farms. But worst of all we lost our basic
human rights."[35]

Drama and debate over the proposed reparations heated up
the Senate, where Senator Jesse Helms proposed an amendment
to stipulate that no funds be appropriated until the Japanese government compensated the families of men and women killed at
Pearl Harbor on December 7, 1941. This amendment communi-
cated the same confusion between the nation of Japan and individuals of Japanese ancestry living in the United States that had
fueled the entire evacuation and internment experience. On the
Senate floor, Senator Spark Matsunaga replied, "This amendment is totally unacceptable. It presumes that we Americans of
Japanese ancestry had something to do with the bombing of
Pearl Harbor. That is absolutely false. In this bill we are trying to
distinguish between Japanese-Americans and Japanese."[36] A
motion to table the "Pearl Harbor" amendment passed with only
four dissenting votes. The Civil Liberties Act of 1988 provided
an apology by the government for the internment as well as $1.2
billion for the $20,000 for each surviving individual.[37]

Many called this remedy bittersweet, and the dollar amount
inadequate. As philosopher Jeremy Waldron comments, "The
point of these payments was not to make up for the loss of home,
business, opportunity, and standing in the community which
these people suffered at the hands of their fellow citizens, nor
was it to make up for the discomfort and degradation of their
internment. If that were the aim, much more would be necessary."[38] Instead, the explicit aim, and the actual effects of the
reparations law, illustrate the symbolic significance of official
acknowledgment of wrongdoing, paying respect to living survivors and to a community of memory. The political movement for
reparations and the legal struggle to undo the convictions for
individuals such as Fred Korematsu occasioned national debate
and education. Museums held exhibits and offered days of
remembrance to commemorate the suffering of those who had

been interned. In 1998, President Clinton awarded Fred Korematsu the Presidential Medal of Freedom, the highest civilian
honor.[39] First his *coram nobis* case and then the medal gave Korematsu, who had not talked at home about what had happened,
reason to speak publicly about his experiences. He used speaking
occasions to tell students his life story and to speak about their
equality and rights to speak up.[40]

His case and the larger movement for reparations inspired others within the United States to speak up about group-based injustices and to seek redress. Some African-Americans revived earlier
calls for reparations to African-Americans for slavery.[41] Grassroots groups, such as the National Coalition of Blacks for
Reparations, advanced arguments for monetary payments,
educational scholarships, and other resources as appropriate
remedies for slavery and its legacies in the economy, society, and
politics of the United States. Congressman John Conyers, taking
a page from the struggle for Japanese-American reparations,
introduced a bill to establish a commission to determine if reparations for African-Americans are appropriate.[42] Others have
stressed the irony that legal challenges to affirmative action policies secured judicial approval just as the Congress authorized
reparations for Japanese-Americans.[43] Thus far, none of these
claims on behalf of African-Americans has yielded political or
legal success. Here, and elsewhere, the process of seeking reparations and facing rejection can create new wounds for individuals
affiliated with victimized groups.

Bearing more success, and following the example of the
Japanese-American reparations movement, Native Hawaiians
pressed in the 1990s for redress for the overthrow of the Hawaiian monarchy.[44] Some Japanese-Americans debated whether to
offer an apology and reparations to Native Hawaiians for their
ancestors' involvement in the conquest of Hawaii. Perhaps their
own recent experience taught them the meaning of such acknowledgment and its potential for healing relationships across
strained groups. Asian-American groups in 1993 called for an
Asian-American apology to Native Hawaiians and for repara-

tions for their participation in the overthrow of the Hawaiian monarchy.[45] As Professor Eric Yamamoto described, this motion generated heated, messy debates while also affording an occasion for interracial alliances against subordination by coalitions of nonwhite groups.[46] He explained, "[o]nly when present pain rooted in past harms was addressed and, to the extent appropriate, redressed could there be justice. And only when there was justice could there be reconciliation and a foundation for genuine hope and cooperation."[47]

After emotional meetings and intense discussions, non-Hawaiians began to grasp the depth of pain over the past still experienced by Native Hawaiians. In 1994, the Hawai'i Conference of the United Church of Christ held a solemn apology service and ceremony and supported continuing discussion of reparations. The national board of the church offered Native Hawaiians $1.25 million for an educational trust as a partial reparation.[48] Yamamoto concludes that these events do not close the book on the underlying violations of human rights. Instead, they raise new questions—about the effects of apologies and partial reparations on individual feelings, group relations, public memories, and interracial healing.[49]

This attention to renewed questions, rather than to closure and endings, contrasts with the usual public presentation of public acts of reparation. My account of the struggle for Japanese-American reparations, and of Fred Korematsu's journey in particular, ends with unfinished business. I have not discussed the pain of those denied reparations under the Act, or the basic fact that only survivors became eligible for money payments. The harm to internees does not die when they die. There are no tidy endings following mass atrocity.

Repair for the Irreparable

Monetary payments of the sort offered by Congress to survivors of the Japanese-American internment symbolically substitute for the loss of time, freedom, dignity, privacy, and equality. The offer of money or some other goods at best ends the inaction and silence after the violation. And yet money remains incommensurable with what was lost. Even as an ideal, and certainly in practice, reparations fall short of repairing victims or social relationships after violence.

This inevitable shortfall makes me wonder about the assumption that the most obvious need of victims is for compensation. So asserts Howard Zehr, a theorist of restorative justice in the context of domestic criminal violations. "Financial and material losses may present a real financial burden. Moreover, the symbolic value of losses—their meaning often acknowledged by story-telling and public memory—may be as important or more important than the actual material losses. In either case, repayment can assist recovery."[50] Zehr acknowledges the limitations of restitution; no one can give back an eye destroyed by violence. Yet, he argues, paying for expenses might ease the burdens: "At the same time, it may provide a sense of restoration at a symbolic level."[51]

The return to a symbolic dimension seems crucial because, in fact, most victims of crime rate their needs to know what happened and why more highly than their desires for compensation or restitution.[52] Even those who start with a monetary motivation may find more value in the opportunity to tell their stories and to get help for their trauma. A daughter of a Holocaust survivor explains,

My father is a survivor of Nazi concentration camps. He has been receiving monetary compensation from the German government for many years. A few years ago he heard about the possibility of getting an increase in reparations if he could demonstrate that his experiences caused significant mental trauma. My father pursued that route—interested in money, not healing—and failed to get an increase in reparations. However, in so doing, he had to seek psychological counseling in order to demonstrate his mental trauma. The indirect effect of that process was that he received some very needed counseling—counseling he would not have otherwise sought. He came to realize, after some 50 years, that he had some serious psychological problems that he needed to confront rather than repress. The process was also significantly important to my mother who had to deal with her husband's trauma and who, herself, was a refugee of the War."[53]

Practical, therapeutic benefits from telling their stories and acknowledgment may accrue even for those who seek reparations without consulting a therapist.

The core idea behind reparations stems from the compensatory theory of justice. Injuries can and must be compensated. Wrongdoers should pay victims for losses. Afterward, the slate can be wiped clean. Or at least a kind of justice has been done. This is a commonplace notion of justice in the context of bankruptcy, contracts, and even personal injury law. Extending this idea to victims of mass violence substitutes money or other material benefits—such as insurance, or scholarships—for the devastation inflicted by wrongful incarcerations, or tortures, or murders. This means crossing over differing lexicons of value. Domestic civil justice systems deal with this problem with crude measures of lost earning capacities due to injuries, or random figures to represent the loss of daily contact with a child, a spouse. Some people try to bring rigor to the project of estimating the present value of unjust enrichment from slavery, or from expropriated lands.[54]

Yet no market measures exist for the value of living an ordinary life, without nightmares or survivor guilt. Valuing the losses from torture and murder strains the moral imagination. If a genocide destroys an entire people, the more basic difficulty is knowing whom to compensate. Even if small numbers of a nation survive, compensating them for the loss of their entire world defies computation and comprehension. Symbolic expressions become the only possibilities. German reparations could be directed to the fledgling state of Israel more easily than to disparate fragments of Jewish refugee communities around the globe.[55]

A sense of inappropriateness of putting a value on losses from mass atrocity may lead some to resist the exercise. Consider

what happened when Prime Minister Ryutara Hashimoto of
Japan offered a letter of apology and monetary reparations to
some 500 survivors of the 200,000 "comfort women,"[56] the
euphemism for sexual slaves imprisoned and exploited by the
Imperial Army during World War II.[57] Only six of the women
accepted the offer.[58] Most others rejected it largely because the
fund came from private sources rather than from the government
itself.[59] Even those who accepted the money, however, emphasized that no monetary payment could remedy the horrors and
humiliations they experienced from the rapes, violence, and
destruction of their dignity.[60] Some of the women—from Korea,
Taiwan, China, the Philippines, and Indonesia—found more
gratification when the U.S. Justice Department placed the names
of sixteen Japanese individuals involved in enslaving the women
for sex on a "watch list" of suspected war criminals barred from
entering the United States.[61] Some argued that only prosecutions
by the Japanese government would adequately express governmental contrition and redress the abuse.[62] Others supported
treatment of the "comfort women" in school textbooks as a kind
of reparation through memory.[63]

Some individuals treat an offer of monetary reparations as
affording them the chance to make statements of personal
strength and dignity. But sometimes the harms extend even into
people's abilities to express claims and needs. In South Africa,
observers of the Truth and Reconciliation Commission have
been struck by how most of the victimized who testify express
exceedingly modest requests for reparations. A death certificate
for a relative whose death was denied by the apartheid regime; a
tombstone; these are common requests gathered by the committee on reparations. One woman who was shot repeatedly while
hanging wash on a line asked for removal of the bullets that
remained in her vagina.[64] No less, and no more. Some who
testify ask for subsidies for their children's education, or to
have a park or a school named after victims of torture and
murder.

When are small, modest requests a reflection of the lowered
expectations of the persistently oppressed? When are they,

instead, dignified assertions made by individuals who have no illusions about the possibility of external repair for their losses? When are small requests scrupulous attempts to avoid the implication that torturers can ever remedy the harms that they inflicted? And when are meager requests instead the general expressions of people more committed to building a new collective future—out of what everyone knows to be limited resources—rather than dwelling on an aching past?[65]

These questions recapitulate a debate among feminists over whether an ethic of care reveals women's subordination or instead a vibrant alternative moral perspective. One version of this debate pitted psychologist Carol Gilligan against lawyer Catharine MacKinnon. Gilligan defended an ethic of mutual care and reciprocity over one of individual rights, while MacKinnon argued that an ethic of care emerges when someone has a foot on your neck.[66] I suspect that no abstract resolution of this kind of debate could ever be trustworthy. Only careful judgments embedded in particular historical and personal contexts can illuminate the relationships between moral views and power relationships.

Even so, distinguishing the self-abnegating act from the large-souled gesture may be impossible for an outside observer. This problem highlights the special difficulties in relying on reparations where psychological and political realities push in the direction of modest if not trivial gestures. Yet I do not want to underestimate the power of humble acts of reparations. They can meet burning needs for acknowledgment, closure, vindication, and connection. Reparations provide a specific, narrow invitation for victims and survivors to walk between vengeance and forgiveness. The ultimate quality of that invitation depends on its ability to transform the relationships among victims, bystanders, and perpetrators.

In South Africa, the specific details of reparations for individuals and for the entire society will be decided by the newly constituted government, whose leaders are in so many cases themselves survivors of police brutality and torture. Archbishop Desmond Tutu recently announced a proposal for a one-time grant of money to victims designed to assist access to services such as medical services as one of a five-point proposal for reparation.[67] If voted by the legislature, such payments will not in any immediate or full sense be an instance of perpetrators making reparations, as is the case where an individual criminal offender offers time or money to the victim or victim's family. Indeed, any collective forms of reparations dilute the direct connection an individual offender could make with victims. When Germany made financial contributions to the developing state of Israel after World War II, it provided symbolic expression of national guilt.[68] South Africa's situation makes the process more one of mutual aid than of making amends, although using the instruments of government to respond to the victimized palpably could demonstrate a dramatic shift in the meaning and aims of governmental power in that country.

Two other forms of reparations bypass valuation problems. Restitution, the return of the specific, misappropriated object, and apology, the verbal acknowledgment of responsibility for wrongdoing, deserve attention for this reason, and for their growing use in the contexts of mass atrocities. But restitution and apology raise their own difficulties.

Restitution

In some respects, the demand for returning the actual thing that belonged to the victim would seem the easiest case for reparation. Valuation problems are absent. Restitution returns the very property, bank account, artifact, or work of art wrongly taken from the owner. But securing the return especially after many intervening years can be extremely difficult. Restitution can involve harms to and objections by intervening owners who claim innocence about the underlying harms.

Jeremy Waldron builds a powerful argument against demands for reparation that call for substantial transfers of land, wealth, and resources to rectify past wrongs. His examples include claims by members of the Taranaki Maori tribes to the west coast of New Zealand, and similar claims by native peoples to lands appropriated by colonizing groups.[69] Waldron argues that

regardless of the merits of such claims in terms of historical entitlement, two kinds of intervening events make restitution of the
property unwise solutions. The first—which I find less than
compelling—requires an excursion into counterfactual hypo-
theticals. What if tribal owners of land that was wrongly appropriated in 1865 had actually retained the land? Waldron
speculates that if those owners had free choice, they might have
sold it, or passed it on to children, or lost it in a poker game in the
intervening years.[70] Although this line of inquiry has a quality of
abstract fair-mindedness, it neglects the basic point of wrongdoing: that one group was unjustly enriched by its injury to the original residents of the land. Waldron himself acknowledges that if
the original owners had not lost their lands, and subsequently
made rational choices about it, then their descendants would
have been better off without the colonization than they actually
have been.[71]

Then the second kind of intervening events take center stage.
Some innocent individuals obtain and build their lives around
lands that were wrongly stolen from the original inhabitants.
Waldron objects that restoring the actual property after it has
passed through a chain of ownership, including whole lines of
innocent owners, means committing a current injustice to rectify
a past one. Yet I believe this problem is both overstated and ame-
nable to practical remedy. After the expropriation of native
peoples, none of the subsequent settlers should be described as
wholly innocent. All of them benefited from the expropriation.
Yet it would seem unduly burdensome and accidental to mandate the particular dwellers of plots of land in 1998 return them
to descendants of original owners while leaving intervening owners and sellers untaxed. Taxing a larger group, even the entire
society, to pay monetary compensation to the original owners—
or to help buy out the current owners—would spread the burden
more fairly.

Perhaps imagining just such a social tax, Waldron suggests
that any "[r]eparation of historic injustice really is redistributive:
it moves resources from one person to another." He treats this as

objectionable because it neglects the innocence of intervening
parties.[72] If present-day redistribution is the practical face of restitution for long-ago misappropriations, Waldron argues for a
full-blown estimate of all redistributions needed in light of the
present-day needs of everyone. The narrower redistributions
based solely on claims traced to historic injustice would both
neglect some people with pronounced needs and afford new
resources to some people who currently do not need them.[73] This
argument understates the sheer importance—for the victimized
and for onlookers—of rectifying past wrongs, independent of
people's current needs.

Present-day redistributions, even if they work to redress long-
ago misappropriations, and even if they can be designed to
spread the burden among all intervening owners, still carry a
dilemma. This is a dilemma seen especially clearly in contemporary South Africa and Eastern Europe, where massive patterns of
poverty and inequality present immediate and urgent issues of
injustice. In these contexts, historically oriented restitution
efforts are both too partial and too inadequate to the survival
tasks of rebuilding national economies and civil societies. Yet
even this articulation understates the dilemma. These nations
have embraced protections for individual liberty and property as
well as commitments to address the human rights violations of
the past. For them, restitution presents a potentially impossible
choice. And newly created private markets in Eastern Europe produce fresh patterns of extreme inequality even before rectifying
prior wrongful appropriations of property—lands and goods
held by Jews, dissidents, or out-of-favor politicians.

As Joseph Singer explains, "The new South African Constitution protects the property rights of the white minority while
allowing for, and in some cases, requiring, restitution or reparations for lost property and past violations of human rights . . .
How can South Africa both move ahead, and at the same time,
compensate the victims of *apartheid*, while respecting the property rights of the white minority—a minority whose rights are
founded on an almost unbelievable injustice?"[74] Given the his-

tory of white appropriation of native African lands, as recently as the 1960s, the constitutional project of protecting property rights risks shielding wrongful appropriation of lands in the past.

Once again, it is crucial to return to symbolic dimensions of reparations. Let us bracket the genuinely difficult tensions between compensating past victims without creating new ones, and protecting new regimes of private property without simply entrenching the most recently dealt hand in a crooked game. Instead, restitution can be rooted in perceptions of symbolic meaning. As Waldron notes, a different set of concerns accompany claims by dispossessed groups for the return of burial grounds or lands with religious or symbolic significance.[75] When the realm of meaning takes center stage, the economic calculus and confusions fade in importance. This same recognition of the realm of meaning could accompany property that has no asserted religious significance, but instead marks either the identity of the wronged group or the unrepented advantages of the rest of the society. Restoring such property, or making symbolic gestures in this direction, could revive the dignity of the wronged group, and could express the commitment of the others to acknowledge the violations, to make amends, and to break with the atrocity and its legacy. If the disputed property itself is not returned, some material exchange would lend more meaning to acknowledgments of violations.

Social and religious meanings rather than economic values lie at the heart of reparations. Lands that include burial grounds or religious sites especially become worthy candidates for restitution because of their distinctness. They are unique and nonfungible. Similarly, there are no substitutes for plundered artwork, seized artifacts, and the bones of ancestors. Restitution becomes the proper remedy where there is no other remedy for a distinct and worthy claim. Even when contrasted with arguments made by museums about their comparative advantages in preservation and sharing with a broad public, the claim by an original owner for the return of a painting—and the claim by descendants for the remains of their ancestor—call for restitution as a moral, if not legal, matter.[76] If some of these rightful claimants then make arrangements to lend the objects back to museums, the symbolic dimension of the return will become all the more transparent.[77]

Failures to return the symbols of family and community identities and continuity may inspire revenge. In his novel *Talking God* Tony Hillerman explores a museum's refusal to return human remains to Native American tribes because of the museum's devotion to research and public display.[78] The museum attorney receives a large bulky box, with a letter describing its contents as "a couple of authentic skeletons of ancestors" from the cemetery behind the Episcopal Church of Saint Luke. Enclosed are the disinterred remains of the lawyer's own grandparents. This fictional account captures both the rage and the tit-for-tat exchanges that atrocities can inspire.

The recent saga of Swiss banks, charged with hiding the bank accounts and gold confiscated from European Jews during World War II, reveals the depths of distrust on the part of survivors and their families along with the costs of inattention to symbolic, as well as practical, restitution. Initial refusals by Swiss leaders to respond to inquiries fed claims of cover-ups and wrongdoing. These claims, in turn, helped to inflate survivors' hopes about the scope and extent of hidden bank accounts and assets. At the same time, making property claims became important to Jewish survivors in part to combat anti-Semitic stereotypes of Jews as exploitative moneylenders who cheated others.[79] By seeking restitution, Jewish survivors claim a property right anyone else would claim, and assert roles as any other claimant before a neutral party, not as victims pleading for assistance.[80]

The self-image of the Swiss as neutral actors, free of blame for the Nazi horror, contributed to their current leaders' failures of response. These very failures in turn triggered a spreading disbelief in the possibility of neutrality toward mass atrocity. A preliminary study by the United States government reports that "in the unique circumstances of World War II, neutrality collided with morality; too often being neutral provided a pretext for avoiding moral considerations."[81] The report called for completing the unfinished task of doing justice, and described this as partly a financial task. "But it is also a moral and political task that should compel each nation involved in these tragic events to come to terms with its own history and responsibility."[82]

Under international pressure, Switzerland did create two commissions, one to examine dormant bank accounts and the other to investigate the entire historical relationship between Nazi Germany and Switzerland. Perhaps even more important, private Swiss sources joined with the Swiss government to propose funds for surviving victims, heirs, and other humanitarian causes. Symbolic reparations and negotiated settlements, rather than restitution of preexisting entitlements, offer a path through the political, moral, and legal morass.

Apology

The symbolic dimensions of reparations express implicitly or explicitly an apology for wrongdoing or for failing to do more to resist atrocities. Apologies implicit in acts of reparation acknowledge the fact of harms, accept some degree of responsibility, avow sincere regret, and promise not to repeat the offense. As any parent who has tried to teach a child to apologize knows, however, the problems with apology include insincerity, an absence of clear commitment to change, and incomplete acknowledgment of wrongdoing. A distinct problem in the context of genocide and mass violence arises when an offer of apology comes from persons who have no ability actually to accept or assume responsibility, or who have only remote connections with either the wrongdoers or the victims. Who is in a position to apologize, and apologize to whom? Perhaps most troubling are apologies that are purely symbolic, and carry no concrete shifts in resources or practices to alter the current and future lives of survivors of atrocities.

The U.S. reparations for Japanese-American survivors of the evacuation and internment included a statement of apology. President Ronald Reagan signed into law the bill that expressed the nation's apology as well as authorized financial compensation. Reagan said, "No payment can make up for those lost years. What is most important in this bill has less to do with property than with honor. For here we admit wrong."[83] Two years later President Bush signed letters of apology and checks to individual survivors.[84]

In May 1997, President Clinton offered an apology to survivors of the forty-year study by the U.S. Public Health Service that withheld proven medical treatment from a group of African-American men with syphilis.[85] The study had sought to document the course of the untreated disease. President Clinton acknowledged that the government's behavior was "clearly racist."[86] In that act of public contrition, the president spoke for the government in an effort to restore the faith of the survivors and other witnesses in both government and the medical establishment. Some have called for a similar governmental apology for slavery, while others maintain that an apology for that multicentury, multistate practice would be too trivial or too late.[87] Who is in the proper position to call for, to offer, and to accept such apologies? These questions become especially pronounced in the case of slavery, given its massive evil and the remoteness of current government officials to the events, and the continuing contests over slavery's legacy in America.

Other recent public apologies include Prime Minister Tony Blair's apology for his country's role in the Irish Potato Famine from 1845 to 1851. Although Australian Prime Minister John Howard failed to apologize for his government's long-standing policy of stealing some 100,000 Aboriginal children from their parents to be raised by white families and in orphanages, Australia has now instituted an annual Sorry Day, held on May 26, the anniversary of the release of the best-selling human rights report, *Bring Them Home*.[88] Japanese Prime Minister Tomiichi Murayama apologized for suffering inflicted in World War II; East German lawmakers apologized for the Holocaust after their government had denied responsibility for decades; and Pope John Paul II apologized for violence during the Counter-Reformation[89] and gave a partial apology for the church's role during World War II.[90] The Canadian government apologized to its native Aboriginal population for past governmental actions

that suppressed their languages, cultures, and spiritual practices.[91] President Chirac of France apologized to the descendants
of Alfred Dreyfus, the Jewish army captain who was falsely
arrested, convicted, and degraded for spying in the 1890s.[92]
These public acknowledgments of wrongdoing and statements
of contrition reflect a growing international interest in restorative steps toward justice, and perhaps the mounting influences
of television talk shows on a public culture of private feelings.
Apologies are actual actions officials can take to promote reconciliation and healing in the contexts of political and interpersonal violence. They may also be the most inexpensive and least
difficult actions available to them.

At heart, the apology depends upon a paradox. No matter
how sincere, an apology cannot undo what was done, and yet "in
a mysterious way and according to its own logic, this is precisely
what it manages to do."[93] An apology is inevitably inadequate.[94]
Nevertheless, forgiveness, while not compelled by apology, may
depend upon it. The mystery of apology depends upon the social
relationships it summons and strengthens; the apology is not
merely words.[95] Crucial here is the communal nature of the process of apologizing. An apology is not a soliloquy.[96] Instead, an
apology requires communication between a wrongdoer and a victim; no apology occurs without the involvement of each party.
Moreover, the methods for offering and accepting an apology
both reflect and help to constitute a moral community. The apology reminds the wrongdoer of community norms because the
apology admits to violating them.[97] By retelling the wrong and
seeking acceptance, the apologizer assumes a position of vulnera-
bility before not only the victims but also the larger community
of literal or figurative witnesses.

Expressions of regret and remorse usually are vital to an apology offered by one individual to another. Distinguishing the
superficial from the heartfelt is important to sorting the apology
from the dodge. Nicholas Tavuchis, who has developed a sus-
tained sociology of apology, argues that "[t]o apologize is to
declare voluntarily that one has *no* excuse, defense, justification,
or explanation for an action (or inaction)."[98] He offers in detail

the example of Richard Nixon's resignation speech to illustrate
how a statement of regret can fall short of an apology. Nixon
never mentioned much less acknowledged specific charges.
Instead he tried to explain his decisions in light of lost congressional support for his policies, poor judgment, and errors committed in pursuit of higher national interests.[99] Any diversion
from accepting responsibility is not an apology. Because of this
stringent requirement, an apology may indeed afford victims and
bystanders something that trials, truth-telling, and monetary
reparations or property restitutions cannot. Full acceptance of
responsibility by the wrongdoer is the hallmark of an apology.

Equally important is the adoption of a stance that grants
power to the victims, power to accept, refuse, or ignore the apology. The victims may in addition seek punishment, offer forgiveness, or conclude that the act falls outside domains eligible for
forgiveness.[100] In any of these instances, the survivors secure a
position of strength, respect, and specialness. Although some current Jewish leaders welcomed the Vatican's recent statement on
the Church's responsibilities during World War II, others used
the occasion specifically to reject the statement as insufficient.
Survivors and their families do and should occupy a position of
personal power and social power to articulate the lived meanings
of the values at stake in the acknowledged violation.

All of this renders problematic a statement described as an
apology but neither offered by the wrongdoers nor presented
directly to victims. Again Tavuchis is eloquent: "[A]n authentic
apology cannot be delegated, consigned, exacted, or assumed by
the principals, no less outsiders, without totally altering its meaning and vitiating its moral force."[101] No one can apologize or forgive by proxy. This is what makes the representative apology—
offered by an elected official—so tricky. If the official was not in
power at the time of the atrocity, the apology is at best offered
from the office, not the person. Sorrow is at best offered then in a
formal, official sense.[102] The apology similarly operates in an
official sphere, fixing the record to include acknowledged transgression. An apology by a government actor to a group within
the nation—or by one government to another—necessarily

involves different social relationships than an apology offered by
one individual to another, or even to a group.

When an official apology is made by one nation to another, it
may permit the kind of change in posture that allows diplomatic
thaws or reconciliations. Tavuchis offers as an illustration the
U.S. apology to France for having assisted Nazi war criminal
Klaus Barbie in his escape to Bolivia after World War II. In 1983,
France finally brought Barbie back for trial on charges of
deporting Jews to death camps and committing torture and murder as head of the Gestapo in Lyons. When the United States
issued its report expressing regrets over U.S. behavior that
helped Barbie avoid prosecution in France, relations between
France and the United States improved.

Official apologies can correct a public record, afford public
acknowledgment of a violation, assign responsibility, and reassert the moral baseline to define violations of basic norms. They
are less good at warranting any promise about the future, given
the shifts in officeholders. Unless accompanied by direct and
immediate actions (such as payments of compensation) that manifest responsibility for the violation, the official apology may
seem superficial, insincere, or meaningless. Indeed, in the current
moment, "[a]pologising is now the rage the world over, especially in the US, where it has long been a standard means of win-
ning favour without paying any real price for one's mistakes."[103]
Moreover, individuals who are otherwise insecure may apologize profusely and excessively.[104]

Whether offered by an individual or a public official, an apology does not compel forgiveness. Forgiveness itself is and must
remain unpredictable.[105] Survivors acquire and retain the power
to grant or withhold forgiveness. They, and others, know that
some acts are unforgivable. Albert Speer, the only Nazi leader at
the Nuremberg war crime trials who admitted his guilt, also
wrote, "No apologies are possible."[106] Usually, though, it is survivors who remind the community about what can, and cannot, be
forgiven. The authority to view a violation as beyond forgiveness
marks one of the survivors' contributions to the community's
moral sense.

Reparations offer money or resources in symbolic redress for violations. Restitution returns wrongly appropriated property, artifacts, and human remains. Restitution may be most warranted when the stolen objects themselves carry unique, significant meanings to the victimized. Apologies explicitly acknowledge wrongdoing and afford victims the chance both to forgive or to refuse to forgive. Official apologies following mass atrocities lack the direct connection between perpetrators and victims that help enact the social dimensions of repair. If unaccompanied by direct and immediate action, such as monetary reparations, official apologies risk seeming meaningless.

Reparations, restitution, and apologies present distinct promises and problems as responses to mass atrocity. Each deserves consideration; each belongs in the lexicon of potential responses to collective violence. Yet nothing in this discussion should imply that money payments, returned property, restored religious sites, or apologies seal the wounds, make victims whole, or clean the slate. The aspiration of repair, in each instance, will be defeated by any hint or hope that then it will be as if the violations never occurred. For that very suggestion defeats the required acknowledgment of the enormity of what was done.

6. Facing History

"I can't understand what I'm seeing through the billows of smoke, and at the same time I do understand, but it doesn't connect up with anything I know, either in pictures or in words. I just feel that this is a place where everything ends, not just the embankment and the rails. This is where this world stops being a world at all." —Binjamin Wilkomirski

"not to rake up old coals / but to see with new eyes"
—Nikki Nojima Louis

After mass atrocity, what can and should be faced about the past? World-denying experiences defy description and perhaps even memory; yet refusing to remember even this can risk insulting the victimized and leaving rage to fester. To seek a path between vengeance and forgiveness is also to seek a route between too much memory and too much forgetting. Too much memory is a disease, comments Michael Roth.[1] Charles Maier argues that Americans in particular have "become addicted to memory," making modern American politics "a competition for enshrining grievances."[2] Philosopher Hermann Lubbe argued that suppression of the Nazi past through amnesty and amnesia permitted West Germany in the 1950s to build a stable democracy.[3]

Yet Jean Baudrillard explains that "[f]orgetting the extermination is part of the extermination itself."[4] Journalist Tina Rosenberg concluded from her investigations in Eastern Europe and Latin America that "[n]ations, like individuals, need to face up to and understand traumatic past events before they can put them aside and move on to normal life."[5] Milan Kundera's phrase has come to summarize resistance against totalitarianism: "The struggle against power is the struggle of memory against forgetting."[6] Timothy Garton Ash argues that "victims and their relatives have a moral right to know at whose hands they or their loved ones suffered." In addition, memory becomes a political tool: "Dirty fragments of the past constantly resurface and are used, often dirtily, in current political disputes."[7]

The alternation of forgetting and remembering itself etches the path of power. William Gladstone is said to have commented that "the cause of the problem in Ireland is that the Irish will never forget and the British will never remember."[8] According to historian Patrice Higgonet, French leaders in the nineteenth century conveyed to the nation a commitment to remember and hate the French Revolution and its terror as a form of expiation, while politicians and ordinary citizens in France today treat the Terror as a historical misfortune that one should try to forget.[9]

The double-edged dangers of too much and too little memory lead contemporary figures to make paradoxical calls about remembering the past. Dullah Omar, South Africa's justice minister, exhorts "we want to put the past behind us but we don't want to forget, we want to remember."[10] In his afterword to *Death and the Maiden*, the chilling play of post-terror revenge and justice, Ariel Dorfman writes, "How do we keep the past alive without becoming its prisoner? How do we forget it without risking its repetition in the future?"[11] Even a contemporary children's book tells of a young elephant who must learn to remember what to forget; notably, he must remember to forget another elephant's injurious but accidental assault and violation of rules in order to remember their fundamental brotherhood.[12]

Living after genocide, mass atrocity, totalitarian terror, however, makes remembering and forgetting not just about dealing with the past. The treatment of the past through remembering and forgetting crucially shapes the present and future for individuals and entire societies. Mona Wiessmark, whose parents survived Nazi concentration camps, and Ilona Kuphal, whose father was a Nazi SS officer, organized the first meeting between children of Nazis and children of Holocaust survivors to explore their guilt, anger, resentment. Their intent was not to focus on the past but to change the future.[13] For individuals, and even for communities, traumatic violence becomes part of the current human psyche forged by past oppression.[14] Tina Rosenberg writes, "The first lesson I learned was that many countries are not dealing with the past, because the past is still with them."[15] What's needed, then, is not memory but remembering,[16] not retrieval of some intact picture but instead a dynamic process of both tying together and distinguishing fragments of past and present.[17] What's needed, paradoxically, is a process for reinterpreting what cannot be made sensible, for assembling what cannot be put together, and for separating what cannot be severed from both present and future.

Andrea Barnes, a therapist who became a law student, reflects on the relationships between remembering and forgetting trauma:

> When something happens that is "unthinkable"—so inconsistent with our view of the world that we can't imagine it—we do predictable things to make sense of it. We deny it, assuming we misunderstood or interpreted incorrectly. We find some explanation that helps us feel safer—if we can decide we were responsible for the event, then at least we have some control. We try to push it out of our minds in some kind of voluntary forgetting. The problem is that in our efforts to make this event "logical," we must maintain our role as victim (i.e., there was some reason why this terrible event was supposed to happen).[18]

Therapy is the slow process of reinterpretation.

Crucial for some may be ritualized meetings that emphasize the here and now while also underscoring a combination of personal powerlessness about what has happened and personal responsibility for what will happen. As incongruous as it may seem, precisely this combination of ritualized meetings and emphatic acceptance of both powerlessness and personal responsibility seems to account for the remarkable success of twelve-step mutual aid groups such as Alcoholics Anonymous.[19]

In contrast to individual therapy and mutual aid groups, trials, truth commissions, and reparations each summon official acts to reflect and enable processes of reinterpretation. The focus is not only individuals, but also communities and nation states. The work must be for, but not only for, the victimized; about, but not preoccupied with, the perpetrators; and addressed to but also designed to convert bystanders into actors, agents in their national worlds now and tomorrow.

After mass atrocities, victims, perpetrators, and bystanders each require mutual acknowledgment.[20] Yet there are costs of embracing these three roles as if they are sharply demarcated. Few who survive can fit comfortably into simply one of them. No whites in South Africa have clean hands, notes Alex Boraine at the TRC. Many victims also feel guilt—for their survival, for their failures to do more to help others. And yes, perpetrators too are often victims either of systems of ideology and deceit that led them to believe they acted on principle or, later, of simplistic blame that alleviates everyone else of responsibility or even self-scrutiny. "Hating, blaming and rejecting a group of people does ensure that we do not have to take the risk or responsibility of looking more honestly at the individual members of the group; nor for that matter looking honestly at ourselves and at our deeper feelings."[21]

In the context of ordinary criminal law enforcement, prosecutions and punishments that humiliate and isolate offenders rather than reintegrating them do not reduce crime or make the society more secure.[22] Philosopher Jean Hampton explains that a successful retributive punishment is one that simultaneously inflicts suffering so as to deny the wrongdoer the position of superiority claimed by his or her violence.[23] But such punishment should not itself degrade the wrongdoer so much as render him or her lower than the victim.[24]

Mass violence is different. Torture, kidnappings, and murders —regimes of rape and terror—call for more severe responses than would any ordinary criminal conduct, even the murder of an individual. And yet, there is no punishment that could express the proper scale of outrage. And if the longer-term goals include avoiding cycles of revenge, social reintegration of at least lower-level perpetrators should be pursued. In many circumstances, demonizing all on "that side" means demonizing large segments of the society, including many individuals who believed they were acting for a larger good or who acted out of fear or who rationalize their conduct in other ways. To try to understand those beliefs is not a capitulation to evil nor merely a pragmatic effort to avoid laying the ground for further group conflicts. It is a recognition of the filters of meaning and memory that lead people to view their own conduct and beliefs as justifiable.[25]

Trials, truth commissions, and reparations each hold potential for affording acknowledgment without locking people into roles as victims or trapping them in feelings of unrelenting hatred. Yet, as this book has explored, each response to atrocity also has sharp limitations, in theory and in practice. Here I revisit all three together and consider still further potential responses. Yet perhaps most crucial for individuals and for nations are the processes for deliberating, constructing, disputing, accepting, rejecting, and reconsidering potential responses to mass violence. The victimized who survive must not be treated as objects without ability to participate in those processes. The fact that some perpetrators elude punishment must not excuse everyone else from demanding a process of response. The public staging of official apologies must not silence those who do not accept them. Respect for individuals must pervade the process as well as the results of public and private responses to mass violence.

Trials, Truth Commissions, and Reparations

Trials for war crimes and atrocities convert the impulse for revenge into state-managed truth-seeking and punishment and yet depend for the most part upon symbolism rather than effectuation of the rule of law. At best, tribunals can try a small percentage of those actually involved in collective violence on the scale of recent events in places like Bosnia, Rwanda, Argentina, Cambodia. Prosecutorial decisions at times may seem to create scapegoats; the exercise of discretion not to prosecute may imply a kind of amnesty without any public debate or approval. Especially in the emerging fields of international tribunals, these prosecutorial decisions are deeply influenced by resources and cooperation with other power centers over matters such as arrests and investigations.

There is a stunning juxtaposition of the rhetoric used to justify trials and the discussions of the politics surrounding them. Judge Antonio Cassesse from Italy served as the president of the Appeals Chamber from the inception of the International Tribunal for the former Yugoslavia until November, 1997. He describes how "those who set up the tribunal never intended or expected anything to happen," but the appointed judges and a dedicated staff produced a body of procedural rules even in the absence of a courtroom, defendants, or a culture of legal responses to impunity.[26] After doing so, the immediate participants made the tribunal more of a reality than its funders expected. Now that it, and other tribunals, exist and proceed to address issues of mass atrocity, advocates and journalists claim that trials produce justice, gather truth, and create needed public acknowledgment.

The claim, and the hope, is that trials create official records of the scope of violence and the participants in it, and that guilty verdicts afford public acknowledgment of what happened, and its utter wrongfulness. Justice Jackson argued to the judges in Nuremberg: "If you were to say of these men that they are not guilty, it would be as true to say that there has been no war, there are no slain, there had been no crime."[27] The need for acknowledgment is as likely to come within the group in whose name the violence was done as for any survivors of the victimized. "Serbs and Croats need war crimes trials like the Germans needed Nuremberg—to expose them to the bald, grotesque reality of what political and military leaders did in their name."[28] At the same time, "[i]t is important for the Serbs to know who is a war criminal and who isn't," said one Bosnian Serb this year. "Otherwise, this world will think it is all of us."[29] Hopes for justice and accountability surged recently in Argentina because of the arrest of an individual allegedly involved in the abduction of children "of the disappeared" during the military junta between 1976 and 1983. The Truth Commission reported at least 172 instances in which such children were kidnapped and given to military families. An Argentine newspaper greeted the news of the recent arrest with the headline, "God Exists."[30]

No recent episode better illuminates the hopes and criticisms of prosecutions than the international and domestic trials following the genocidal crimes, killing some 800,000 people during 1994 in Rwanda.[31] The justice system in the nation seemed destroyed; the failure of international intervention became a subject of media discussion; and the UN Security Council created an international criminal tribunal situated in Arusha, Tanzania, to prosecute those responsible for the genocide. The creation of the International Criminal Tribunal for the former Yugoslavia provided a precedent and a goal. Inside Rwanda, the government worked to rebuild its own justice system, training police investigators, prosecutors, and judges. Some 115,000 people were arrested and sent to prisons and detention centers in anticipation of national trials. By 1997, both the international tribunal in Arusha and the Rwanda courts began trials. Defendants in the initial Rwandan trials had no lawyers or opportunities for presenting witnesses or cross-examining prosecution witnesses.[32] Because Rwanda as of 1997 had fewer than fifty practicing lawyers, and most refused to represent defendants charged with genocide, the lack of defense counsel proved a serious obstacle to fair trials.[33]

Tens of thousands of Rwandans came in April, 1998, to watch the executions of twenty-two people convicted by Rwandan courts of genocide.[34] These were the first death penalties ordered for any murders of Tutsi. Included in the group was Froduald Karamira, the primary source of propagandist hate broadcasts that encouraged Hutus to join mass killings of Tutsis in 1994.[35] Rwanda officials justified the trials and convictions as reestablishment of the rule of law and an end to the repeated waves of ethnically motivated violence since the nation's 1962 independence.[36] Instead, according to news reports, the crowd watching the executions at times seemed overtaken with bloodlust. International human rights leaders objected that the underlying trials failed to comport with international standards of justice. Some defendants had no legal representation; others had lawyers without time to prepare. As a result, the Pope, the European Union, the United States, and many human rights organizations unsuccessfully urged stays of execution. Rather than ending the cycles of revenge, the trials themselves were revenge.[37] The more delibera-

tive prosecutions for Rwandan genocide undertaken by the UN
Tribunal—prosecutions focusing on the relatively high-ranking
governmental officials—reached no convictions for three
years.[38] Yet with twenty-two high-ranking officials in custody,
this tribunal actually has a greater chance of successful prosecutions than the tribunal for the former Yugoslavia which has
detained few of the accused.[39]

In a remarkable breakthrough, on May 1, 1998, the former
prime minister of Rwanda pleaded guilty to genocide charges
before the UN Tribunal, and also promised to offer testimony
against others.[40] This high-ranking leader, Jean Kambanda,
thereby fulfilled the vision of a system of accountability for genocide. Kambanda himself led meetings where massacres were
planned, ordered roadblocks to catch escaping Tutsis, and personally refused requests to save Tutsi children who had survived
one massacre, only to die in another one.[41] The guilty plea
involved no exchange for a reduced sentence. The promise of testimony suggested the possibility of a detailed account of the
activities of the interim government that presided over the massacres in 1994.

Where trials do occur, one hope is the creation of transparent
court records that simply speak the truth to the relevant audiences. This hope depends on fairness throughout the proceedings, which seems in jeopardy in the domestic Rwandan trials.
The idea of accessible court records that speak for themselves,
even under much better trial conditions, is problematic. Even the
use of documentary film footage as evidence of mass killings in
the Nazi concentration camps revealed, in Lawrence Douglas's
careful study, the bias of the prosecution toward a story of political terror and war excesses and against an understanding of genocide of Jews.[42]

Who exactly are the intended, and actual, audiences for the
current international tribunals? Judge Cassesse suggests that the
United States and its mass media are major targets, as well as
United Nations leadership. Cassesse speculates that, if only
broadcasts could reach into the former Yugoslavia to portray the
tribunal's work, then the propaganda machines contributing to

the mass violence could be countered and the values expressed by the rule of law could be spread. Yet even were such broadcasts technologically and economically feasible, the lens of interpretation would be shaped by the local leaders. The presence of only one independent newspaper in the region severely impairs the coverage of the tribunal's work. Great hopes for truth-telling to counter distortions and continuing demonization fomented in part by those continuing as leaders in Bosnia thus must be countered by realistic assessment of the remoteness of the region from alternative information and interpretations. Moreover, detailed exposés of what has and what has not been done by the tribunals for the former Yugoslavia and for Bosnia are not likely to inspire great confidence in their capacity to enforce a rule of law or to bring many offenders to account, for they have not yet done so. Contrasting problems arise for Rwanda, where a new government intent on prosecuting may feed a frenzy of revenge. Nothing puts the instruments of justice more at risk in a society struggling for political legitimacy than prosecuting widely known perpetrators of human rights violations and failing to secure convictions or securing them unfairly.

Nongovernmental organizations in this context become crucial in the transmission of information and in creating even the desire for it.[43] It falls to grassroots and international groups of advocates and writers, paradoxically, to create a demand and an appreciation for the ideal of legal responses to mass atrocity. And it is the ideal, not the actual practices, that must be conveyed if the movement for international justice is to build.

Plans to create a permanent international criminal court may transport this movement to a new phase of activity and accomplishment. Most of the world's nations have already participated in designing such a court, which would have jurisdiction over war crimes, genocide, and crimes against humanity, and would operate when national courts are either unavailable or ineffective. Such a court, and the opposition to it from places including the U.S. Senate and the Pentagon, are also likely to generate more of the same dynamics of idealism and cynicism that surround the specific international tribunals.[44]

For actual gathering and broad dissemination of factual materials from large numbers of victims and perpetrators, reports by nongovernmental organizations, and the emerging institutional form of a truth commission, look more useful than trials.[45] When conducted by an official body rather than a nongovernmental group, this truth or investigatory process can also publicize truths that are already known and endow them with official acknowledgment. The Inquiry Commission in the German Bundestag for the Treatment of the Past and Consequences of the SED-Dictatorship in Germany commissioned expert reports, took testimony from hundreds of witnesses, and produced a massive document detailing the role of the secret police, the churches, the courts, and the opposition in East Germany under communism. Timothy Garton Ash suggests, "[f]or students of the East German dictatorship this may yet be what the records of the Nuremberg trials are for the students of the Third Reich."[46] The report's length—15,378 pages—ensures it won't be read by many, but its sheer existence produces a dramatic public acknowledgment of abused power, complicit actors, and the harms to individuals.

Leading participants in the South African Truth and Reconciliation Commission differ over the relationship between its work and prosecutions. Justice Minister Dullah Omar, who helped design the TRC, emphasizes that its work is not inconsistent with domestically conducted criminal prosecutions and instead can build the factual bases for them. Archbishop Desmond Tutu, who heads the commission, in contrast writes that "[t]he purpose of finding out the truth is not in order for people to be prosecuted. It is so that we can use the truth as part of the process of healing our nation."[47]

A truth commission, severed from prosecutions, avoids vengeance and even retribution. It fails to create the potential closure afforded by criminal trials that end in punishment; it does not order victims to forgive perpetrators, although the South African process invites applications for amnesty in exchange for full testimony of perpetrators.[48] Public hearings gathering the testimony of perpetrators and victimized people become important as communal experiences as well as sources of information. "[I]t is the *process* of compiling the commissions' report, as much as the final product, which is important . . . it is the involvement of broad sectors of society in providing information and in being listened to that is crucial," report two observers of investigatory commissions in Latin America.[49] Remarkably, South Africa's commission tries to engage a broad public not only in its business, but also in reflecting on the value and limitations of its work in promoting reconciliation and a new common national identity.[50] Prosecutions, in this context, may be viewed as obstacles to reconciliation and to nation building; prosecutions may solidify the resistance of a particular sector in the society to those projects while feeding a sense of being wronged and misjudged.

Yet ambitious claims that a truth commission can help a nation reconcile and heal after widespread practices of torture, murder, and terror are likely to invite disappointment. A recent cartoon in a leading South African newspaper depicts Archbishop Tutu standing on land labeled as "truth" at the edge of a chasm before other land labeled as "reconciliation;" Tutu scans a map, and the chasm, and says, "oops."[51] The commission's work itself is more a theatrical display of what therapy aims to accomplish much more slowly through intense, personal connections and occasions for not only the telling but the repetition of individual stories of trauma and devastation.[52] To avoid exacerbating trauma, a commission must ensure that participants feel safe, and yet this usually means abandoning the cross-examination and truth-testing techniques normally associated with official fact-finding. Therapist Andrea Barnes suggests that individual victims who testify before a commission should be given a copy of the transcript at least of their own testimony as "further validation that what they experienced was real, was taken seriously, and is part of the historical record."[53] Then, provision of free and accessible therapeutic services, including a forum for further telling of their stories, is crucial if those who testify are actually to receive help in their own healing process.

Because truth commissions so often reject the use of cross-examination and instead seek to validate those who testify about horrors they witnessed or experienced, the "truth" that emerges may be understood as psychological but not historical truth. Dori Laub writes about this contrast in reviewing testimony gathered from Holocaust survivors. One woman's narration told of a powerful visual memory of four chimneys in flames, with people running and stampeding as part of a revolt and escape attempt at Auschwitz in October 1944. When the video testimony was then presented to a group of historians, the historians critiqued the testimony as faulty because in fact, only one chimney, not four, had been blown up during that episode and the revolt itself was a failure. In Laub's analysis, the importance of the testimony, and even its truthfulness, concerned not the number of chimneys nor perceptions about the revolt's success, but instead as a report of the reality of an unimaginable occurrence: a revolt at Auschwitz.[54] Listeners, in this view, are not to abandon judgment about facts that can challenge testimony, but should develop an attentiveness to each person's own grasp of the past. This advice is somewhat disconcerting for truth commissions, whose alleged virtue is the priority given to truth-seeking rather than to prosecution and conviction.

Disappointments with truth commissions are likely to erupt over the reliability and completeness of the reported facts, over interpretations, and over the apparent trade of truth for punishment. A report that recounts the process and makes the underlying testimony available for others to interpret can assist a spirit of open inquiry.[55] Yet the report itself should not jeopardize the moral clarity of firm judgments. Where political and economic constraints set limits on the boundaries of a commission's inquiry, disillusionment only increases. Thus, the international commission to inquire into thirty-six years of terror and disappearances in Guatemala has been castigated as too weak, with a scope too confined to incidents surrounding armed conflict and powers too frail to authorize subpoenas or to name in its final report those individuals responsible for the wrongdoing.[56] South Africa's commission was charged to investigate gross violations of human rights, yet hearings also gathered mountains of evidence of the humiliations of the pass system and the oppressive living and working conditions of black and colored persons under apartheid.

Perhaps reactions to the following story can capture evaluations of truth commissions more generally. The South African Truth and Reconciliation Commission's amnesty committee took testimony from Jeffrey Benzien in conjunction with his application for amnesty for actions committed while he served as a security police officer in the 1980s. Initially, he gave only vague descriptions of his offenses. The commission affords victims the chance to examine amnesty applicants and in that small way reverse their previous roles.[57] Under Ashley Forbes's close questioning, Benzien calmly testified before the committee about how he had developed a particular method for torturing individuals taken into custody, and he demonstrated it through a simulation on a volunteer during the hearing.[58] Called the "wet-bag" technique, the torture method involved forcing the suspect face down on the floor with hands handcuffed behind his or her back; then Benzien would sit on the suspect's back, place a wet cloth bag over the head of the prisoner, and twist it around the neck so the individual would start to suffocate. If the body became slack, Benzien would release the bag, and thus stop short of killing the suspect in time to continue the interrogation.[59]

Benzien, at the time of the hearing, was still working as a policeman. If granted amnesty, he would keep that job and receive no punishment for his acts of torture.[60] During the hearing, Mr. Benzien addressed one of his former victims, Tony Yengeni, who appeared in the audience, as "Sir." Yengeni, who now serves as a member of Parliament for the African National Congress, asked, "What kind of man uses a method like his one of the wet bag, on other human beings, repeatedly listening to those moans and cries and groans, and taking each of those people very near to their deaths?"[61] Benzien replied, "With hindsight, sir, I realise that it was wrong," but that at the time he thought he was working to rescue South Africa from a communist movement and to fight for his and his family's right to live as they had in their country.[62] After apologizing for his wrongdoing, Benzien concluded that the new regime made him "extremely amazed and very happy to still be in South Africa today—and I am still a patriot of the country."[63]

What should one make of this? The contrition and apology may be as welcome as the factual details confirmed for the victimized, but the setting—a hearing to request amnesty—casts doubts on Benzien's sincerity or depth of motivation. Moreover, that such a person would still serve as a police officer in the new regime seems an abomination, but also a reminder of how widespread are the networks of agents for the apartheid regime, perhaps too widespread to eliminate in a peaceful transition process. Yet, reporters in South Africa repeatedly announce that many of the victimized do not seem vengeful, but want to rebuild a shared nation much the same as does Benzien himself. That shared nation depends upon a new, fledgling culture of human rights, itself not likely to advance through vengeance against the thugs of the old regime.

Instead, to build that culture, the fact gathering about hundreds and thousands of encounters between individuals like Benzien and Yengeni turns the finger back at a silent white minority, and demands a different commitment by all South Africans for the future. The truth sought by a truth commission includes not just who did what but also asks, for the nation, What was done in our name, our nationhood?[64] The asking and the telling unwind something more than complicity; a complicated process of identification and implication in the past must be confronted as part of building a new relationship between all the citizens and the state. This tall order could easily founder in the face of short-term disillusionment and frustration with practical difficulties—such as less adequate and more expensive legal assistance for testifying victims than for testifying perpetrators.[65]

In contrast, concrete reparations—whether in the form of monetary compensation, restitution of misappropriated property or even apologies—may seem more appealing. The danger here is that reparations elevate things over persons, commodities over lives, money over dignity. "The salvation and redemption of the graters, kettles, and chairs, even if it were to happen, has bearing on the course of human events only if we humans have also been turned into objects."[66] Symbolic reparations such as the creation of peace parks for children or schools named for individuals murdered during the atrocity challenge this equation of persons and things and potentially speak to the individuality and dignity of those who were victimized. Even with such efforts to avoid trivializing and reducing mass atrocities to material harms, the palpable insufficiency of reparations could stoke fires of revenge or further victimize the victimized as trivializing their harms or suggesting a payoff for silence.[67] Dullah Omar argues that it is best to leave the acceptability of reparations in the hands of the victimized. Albie Sachs, now a constitutional court judge in South Africa, whose missing arm is a daily reminder of the bomb sent by the old regime to destroy him, declares that "[t]he real reparation we want lies with the constitution, the vote, with dignity, land, jobs and education."[68] Yet he also urges people not to underestimate the "role of apology, shame and humanising the relationship between perpetrator and victim."[69]

Eric Yamamoto, law professor and advocate for Japanese-Americans after the World War II internment, and for Native Hawaiians, offers this useful guide to the appropriate use of reparations following atrocity: 1) don't assume we know their effect in each situation; 2) consider whether reparations will promote reconciliation or instead perpetuate or deepen social divisions; 3) ask whether the reparations would really improve material conditions of survivors; and 4) ask if reparations and the process for securing them would in fact alter attitudes toward people at the margins.[70] The truth-telling surrounding the struggles for reparations can alter attitudes more than the reparations themselves, yet the palpable symbolism of actual reparations will redeem those struggles in ways that all the narration and fact-gathering never could.

Similar contextual concerns should inform the pursuit of prosecutions and truth commissions. Hans-Jörg Geiger, who directed the federal office opening access to the files of the East German secret police, put the case for contextual considerations.[71] "Every system, every time has its own special situation—even as far as the reasons for human rights violations are concerned. . . . it's more important to look for the correct way to reckon with each past separately rather than to develop a theoretical system."[72] By context, I mean to identify six kinds of inquiries into particular historical and political circumstances.

1. Does the project of nation building or reconstituting a new national community have real promise? Then efforts to reconcile—and most likely truth commissions rather than prosecutions—should be pursued. Some may even argue that putting aside the past and avoiding even fact-finding inquiries would serve nation building.[73] Yet "the return of the repressed," or the potentially virulent resurfacing of unacknowledged horrors, counsel against that tactic.

2. What is the distribution of minority and majority groups; how many survivors of the victimized groups remain compared with perpetrators and bystanders; how many of the different groups remain as conationalists or instead are dispersed across political borders? Some of South Africa's unique approach embodied in the TRC is traceable to the fact of a black majority, now launched to control the democracy. The victimized now can rule, but in partnership with others who still control resources, international bond ratings, and other crucial elements of the new nation. The destruction of European Jewry during World War II produced a diametrically contrasting circumstance of nations with none or very few of the victimized group left. The creation of Israel could be viewed as a kind of international reparation effort; the prosecutions of Nuremberg, and later, the Eichmann trial in Israel itself, became both memorials to the dead and justifications for the reparation of new nationhood. Then, as Timothy Garton Ash puts it, "[w]hereas Poles and Hungarians are, so to speak, alone with their own pasts, East and West Germans have to work it out together."[74] And in Latin America, clearly identifiable victims were tortured, murdered, or made to disappear by another group of also identifiable people, while in

Eastern Europe, totalitarian regimes depended on much larger numbers of people who used less violence and more surveillance, with no sharp line between "us" and "them."[75]

3. How involved, or potentially involved, are international institutions and nongovernmental organizations? Such involvement can be a resource to support prosecutions and truth commissions but also can conflict with or dilute efforts at nation building; in contrast, participation by people from different groups within the affected society can promote the perceived and real legitimacy of the response.

4. How much time has passed since the atrocity? How many, if any, generations have intervened? Some truths cannot be recaptured when much time has passed, but other truths cannot be heard when little time has elapsed. There are foreseeable openings for renewed attention to fact-finding, reparations, and sometimes prosecutions, when a second or third generation comes of age and wants to know and not forget.

5. Were the atrocities part of war, with human rights violations committed by all sides? Then some process of even-handed response would be crucial to the movement for international respect for human rights. Did peace or a new regime emerge from political compromise instead of total victory? Then certain restrictions, such as promises of amnesty, will constrain responses to atrocity. Yet such constraints can be well justified if the compromise produces a genuine democracy. "Victory sometimes substitutes for final justice, as in countries where winners of democratic elections have chosen not to punish their former oppressors."[76]

6. Is the response to genocide or collective violence addressed by a successor regime or by members of the very regime that presided over the wrongs? How many members of the military and police force are still the same as when the atrocities occurred? How many of the judges? The answers to these questions are not only relevant to assessments of the practicality of any proposed strategy, but are also germane to remedial capacities of prosecutions compared with truth commissions, and of each compared with reparations. Playwright Ariel

Dorfman asks in his afterword to *Death and the Maiden*: "How to heal a country that has been traumatized by repression if the fear to speak out is still omnipresent everywhere? And how do you reach the truth if lying has become a habit?"[77] If these indeed are the conditions, strategies both more drastic and more subtle than prosecutions, truth commissions, or reparations are required.

It is the responsibility of private groups, national stages, and international bodies to devise responses in light of such contextual inquiries. Although individual survivors may lack the power to design the response they most want, it is their prerogative, as individuals, to accept, or to reject, specific offers of reparations or apologies directed to them.

Survivors differ remarkably in their desires for revenge, for granting forgiveness, for remembering, and for moving on. Family members of murdered individuals in this country clash over the death penalty. Anne Coleman, a mother whose daughter was murdered, joined Murder Victims Families, a group opposed to capital punishment, and then reflected, "A lot of people used to say to me, 'You're not a normal victim's family member' because I didn't want revenge. Now, I know I am not alone."[78] Another family member of a murder victim explains how "[t]he emotions that family members experience in losing loved ones to violent crime ran the gamut in my family. I had aunts and uncles who wanted to personally wreak havoc and vengeance on the perpetrators. But my grandmother's response to the anger and outrage of other family members was that no human being had a right to determine who should live or die."[79] Restoring dignity to victims after atrocity should at minimum involve respecting their own responses; at the same time, the repertoire of any person's responses will be powerfully shaped by the rhetorics and institutions available in the larger society. Expanding avenues between vengeance and forgiveness can assist survivors. Vengeance should be tamed by state control over the apparatus of punishment; survivors' attitudes about prosecutions are relevant but not determinative here because the society as a whole has been wronged as well. Yet it must remain the choice of survivors whether to grant forgiveness, or to accept apologies or reparations. The role to accept or reject such avenues is uniquely theirs.

Other Possibilities

Where a government countenanced or committed atrocities, one alternative remedy is to remove from government offices and pensions those individuals who were directly involved in the offenses. The continued presence and exercise of power by people who participated in the regime of atrocity ironically provides both constant reminders and routinized forgetting of what happened. Sometimes called a purge, and sometimes "lustration," the removal of categories of people from public office or benefits can have a purification effect, but can also sweep in too many people, unfairly.[80]

The case of Jeffrey Benzien, the security police officer in South Africa who invented a particularly cruel and painful technique of torture, seems especially troubling because he still works as a police officer, and will retain that post if he secures amnesty. Some process of removing from power and privilege the very perpetrators who wielded it to torture others would permit a new beginning for the government and the citizenry.

Eastern European countries that have turned to this kind of response encounter the difficulty of identifying accurately who should be removed or barred from government posts, and what should count as unacceptable levels of commission, omission, or complicity. Tina Rosenberg recounts the painful story of Rudolf Zukal, a noted dissenter under the Czechoslovak Socialist Republic, who was fired from his academic post and forced to work as a bulldozer driver cleaning mud from lakes for twenty years, after he refused to sign a statement endorsing the 1968 Soviet invasion of Prague.[81] One triumph of the "Velvet Revolution" was Zukal's resurrection as a national hero and parliamentary leader—under the application of the resolution to screen out of public office all collaborators with the old regime. Zukal had voted for that resolution. Yet his own name then surfaced on the unacceptable list. His name, and the assertion that he was an

informer, appeared in secret police files because of conversations
he had had, while on a nine-month fellowship during his academic years, with a Czech undercover security agent who posed
as his friend while they both participated in the international
community in Vienna.[82] Forced to step down from Parliament,
Zukal's case illustrates difficulties with a purge practice in a
regime of secret spies and subtle collaborators.

Amnesty across the board for government actors, insurgents,
and dissidents is another potential response to mass violence.
Sometimes justified in the name of getting on with the future,
amnesties can be constructive acknowledgments of the past.
Yet amnesty is cowardice if it grows out of fear of the continuing
power of the wrongdoers, or even fear of the costs of naming
the wrongs. As one observer puts it, "[a]n amnesty is credible
only as a humane means to remember, not as a legislation of
forgetfulness."[83]

For those societies recovering from governmentally sponsored
totalitarianism, granting each citizen a right to inspect his or her
own state espionage file can restore a sense of control, or at least
help the individual understand the scope of invasion under the
regime.[84] As painful as it may be to discover that a friend or family member was an informant, such knowledge enables victims to
shatter the patterns of power enabled by secrecy. Opening secret
internal security records for use in public criminal and civil investigations and the work of private historians affords a more general public exposure to particular hidden information, as well as
to the scale and methods of secrecy and threat. The decision to
open the Stasi (secret police) files in East Germany is a contribution to victims and to the possibility of reckoning with the past.
Yet nothing in this process invites or requires informers to come
forward to confess or repent. Initial signs indicate that "[t]he line
of demarcation between perpetrators and victims seems to be
stronger now than shortly after the fall of the Wall."[85]

A very different sort of response, but one that still looks to the
future, is to build new institutions. Domestically, building democratic institutions and a culture of human rights may be the crucial task. The adoption of the Fourteenth and Fifteenth Amend-

ments to the United States Constitution after the Civil War, for example, marked a project of commemoration, "an effort to fix the meaning and purpose of the war in an enduring form. The conquering nation sought through the means of law to construct some tangible proofs that the war had achieved a moral reformation justifying its cataclysmic violence."[86] Beyond individual nations, however, individuals, nongovernmental organizations, and collections of nations try to create international institutions —from the United Nations to the permanent international criminal court—as living memorials to atrocities and vital vows for change.[87]

More literal and concrete forms of commemoration and monuments use sculptures and paintings, museums, plays, and poems. Shared spaces and experiences enabled by public art do not produce singular or coherent memories, but they can enable ways to hold and reveal, in common, competing memories.[88] Memorials can name those who were killed; they can depict those who resisted and those who rescued. They can accord honor and confer heroic status; they can express shame, remorse, warning, shock. Devoting public spaces to memories of atrocities means devoting time and energy to decisions about what kinds of memories, images, and messages to embrace, critique, and resist.

Again, the period after the United States Civil War offers examples. Hundreds of towns and cities in both the North and the South engaged in vigorous debates and then plans for soldier monuments.[89] Some advocates of such public art argued "that people are forgetful and need their social memory bolstered by powerful mnemonic aids," while others instead maintained "that memory is safe in the present but monuments are needed to transmit it across generations," and still others advanced "a startling counterargument—that the memory of heroism is undying and will outlast the monuments, which are therefore built simply as proof of memory's reality and strength."[90] Whether anxious or celebratory, people arguing over those and similar monuments tend to assume that a common memory, secured by tangible presences in public spaces, is vital to people's strength and independence. Indeed, more dangerous than disputes over memory

would be complacent divestment of the obligation of memory
once memorials are mounted.[91]

Whose story and whose interests are served by the design of
particular monuments? Historian Kirk Savage argues that the
post–Civil War monuments afforded whites a chance to reconcile after the war while excluding or subordinating the freed
slaves. Yet once proposed, and even once constructed, public art
permits debates over memory, and potentially conflicting and
multiple meanings and perspectives on the underlying events.
The memorial erected in Boston to Robert Gould Shaw, for example, depicts the white leader of black soldiers as a hero, although
he was one of hundreds of men killed in a hopelessly outmatched
battle at Fort Wagner, South Carolina, 1863. In recent years,
African-American activists have protested the lack of individuality in the faces of the black soldiers and the elevation of Gould as
hero in the war over slavery without even naming the members
of the 54th Regiment, the Union army's first African-American
regiment.[92] Yet competing claims about what to memorialize—
and what the war meant for race relations—started with the
initial discussions concerning the 54th Regiment memorial
after the war.

Shaw's own family vetoed the proposal for a sculpture of
Shaw alone on a horse set on a pedestal of soldiers.[93] The
resulting design places Shaw at the center of a relief but not as
leader of the troops, who themselves can be seen by viewers as
either brave or confused, in solidarity or subordinated.[94] Racial
power relations persisted; only the words of whites who spoke at
the dedication ceremony were carved in the memorial, even
though several African-Americans also spoke there.[95] The names
of the African-American soldiers killed in the 1863 battle were
not added to the memorial until sufficient protests mounted in
1982. Yet, precisely at that time, the monument itself helped to
unite members of the Boston community after bitter conflicts
over school desegregation.[96] On the hundredth anniversary of
the monument, the city held a public symposium and series of
events to revisit the history and meanings it commemorates. The
entire cover of the current informational brochure about the

memorial is a closely cropped photograph of the face of one of the African-American soldiers, inset with a small photo depicting Shaw.

Public disputes over proposed and existing memorials may occasion the productive if painful kind of struggle for memory as do fights over reparations. Again, the U.S. Civil War provides examples. Some 120 years after Southern communities mounted tributes to Confederate leaders, African-Americans and some white critics called for tearing them down, much as French and Russian Revolutionaries dismantled royal monuments—and the post–Soviet Russians toppled massive sculptures of communism's demigods. Vividly capturing and recasting memory, fights over monuments in the streets and in debates usefully disturb congealed memories and mark important junctions between the past and a newly invented present. Historian Eric Foner has urged such struggles to make room for new, or countermemorials, rather than destruction of the old; and the juxtaposition of old and new would itself render new meanings to memories. Thus, he argues, "[r]ather than tear down the statues of Confederate generals or Monument Avenue in Richmond, Va., why not add a marble likeness of Gabriel, who in 1800 plotted to liberate Virginia's slaves" or one of African-Americans who fought in the Union army, or the seventeen African-Americans elected to Congress during Reconstruction.[97]

Maya Lin's Vietnam Memorial also evoked vigorous and even angry debate, while inspiring the addition of more memorials and art responding to the U.S. involvement in Vietnam. Designed initially in response to a class project, Lin's plan called for a simple, polished wall engraved with the names of the 58,196 Americans who died in the Vietnam War. Lin also intended the memorial to work with the land, and to be placed in a space that would draw visitors down a sloping path alongside the wall that itself gradually rises in height. The experience of walking alongside the wall, then, would catch visitors by surprise as they noticed how the gradual descent leads downward to an encounter with mounting lists of names, rising in the air.

The image of a gash in the land offended many who sought

a more heroic and conventional tribute to those who served in
that socially divisive war. Veterans groups organized to finance
a representational sculpture of men in combat. Then a group of
women veterans organized to fund a similarly realistic sculpture.
Now the three sit in close proximity on the Mall in Washington,
D.C., and provide the most frequently visited site in that city of
frequently visited sites. The wall has become a familiar image in
film, television shows, and popular culture. Perhaps to the surprise of some, the literal and figurative reflections offered by its
gleaming wall of names afford a dignified and moving tribute to
those who died and to the nation that struggled over its involvement in the war. The competing memorials include not only the
additional sculptures but also offerings of distinctive personal
objects, at times gathered in their own exhibitions as further art
commemorating the war and the war dead.[98] The failure to
acknowledge the Vietnamese citizens who died occasions further
debates over the memorials, and calls for additions or alternative
commemorations.[99]

Pained and extended discussions have transpired in Europe, in
Japan, and in the United States over potential and actual memorials and monuments commemorating World War II, the Holocaust, and the atomic bomb.[100] Should such memorials be literal
or abstract? Should they honor the dead or disturb the very possibility of honor in atrocity? Should they be monumental, or
instead disavow the monumental image, itself so associated with
Nazism? Preserve memories or challenge as pretense the notion
that memories ever exist outside the process of constructing
them? James Young, historian and critic of Holocaust memorials, writes of a large cube of black stones placed "like a black cof-
fin" in Münster, Germany, and dedicated to "the missing Jews of
Münster."[101] Some opposed it on aesthetic grounds, others
because it hampered limousine drop-offs. It was demolished in
March, 1988. Young comments: "An absent people would not be
commemorated by an absent monument." More debate and dis-
sent followed. The artist built a new version of the monument for
a new home in another German city.[102]

Although that example did not involve preplanned elimination of the monument, other recent tributes do, as artists and communities struggle for forms of commemoration that in and of themselves shock complacency and settled categories for remembering. Can the art itself express inexpressibility, and disrupt the consignment of memory to a settled physical space, outside the responsibility of those currently alive to struggle for memory? Jochen and Esther Gerz designed what they designated as a countermonument in response to an invitation by the city of Harburg, Germany, to create a "Monument Against Fascism, War, and Violence—and for Peace and Human Rights." A twelve-meter-high pillar positioned in a pedestrian shopping mall, the Harburg Monument Against Fascism called for citizens and visitors to add their names on the monument and thereby "commit ourselves to remain vigilant."[103] The monument was designed then to descend gradually into the ground, and eventually completely disappear. Its inscription offered this prediction of the monument's future: "One day it will have disappeared completely, and the site of the Harburg monument against fascism will be empty. In the end, it is only we ourselves who can rise up against injustice."[104] Indeed, after a series of lowerings over five years, this never beautiful or restful monument entirely disappeared, returning the burden of memory to tourists. Provocation, not consolation, is the goal of such countermonuments.[105]

In addition to monuments, other artistic responses to mass atrocity explore the possibilities of provocation and disturbance. Historian Lawrence Langer emphasizes that art by survivors themselves can afflict "our desire to redesign hope from the shards of despair with the vision of an anguish that is recordable but not redeemable."[106] Art of the unthinkable should disturb as well as commemorate.[107] Similarly, critic David Roskies explains how art of the Holocaust makes readers "partners in poetic resurrection with specific names"[108] and yet other works recall ancient archetypes, remote from specific events and persons.[109] Holocaust art so often avoids human figures and shocks with disharmony and disorientation. "Though in the past, enormous evil could be dealt with figuratively, these artists seem to be arguing that the new order of atrocity—the transformation of humans into things, the utter anonymity of their death, the total denial of choice—precludes a recognizable human landscape."[110]

Commemoration could work with time rather than space. Thus, some seek to build new rituals, such as days of remembrance. Copying the techniques of established religions, states and private groups create liturgies of remembrance, mourning, and collective reconstruction.[111] Australia created Sorry Day as a national day of apology for the misappropriation of native children.[112] Yom Hashoah has become a day of remembrance for the Holocaust, with public events held globally each year for a day in April.

The production of new historical narratives and accounts that build bridges between past and present and resist the temptations of victors' justice while maintaining a moral stance is one more response to genocide and collective violence. "Catastrophe, in fact, has always been a part of the process of rethinking the past."[113] History is never one story, and the telling of history involves a certain settling of accounts.[114] No telling can fully escape the preoccupations of the moment or the political concerns of the authors. For generations after an atrocity, the historical project poses the difficulty of wresting the past from fictions and legends.[115] Moreover, narratives that imply closure and mastery almost certainly distort genocide and torture.[116] Yet work by journalists and historians, rather than political figures and government officials, can collect and connect seemingly disparate accounts of the violence, its causes, and its consequences. Historians can, and should, combine distance and empathy with all involved, even the perpetrators, in order to pursue the aspiration of truthfulness.[117]

In addition, specific historical work addressing shifting responses to atrocity can help set in relief the choices made in different settings at different times. International law scholar Theodor Meron has worked to recover responses to atrocity long predating the contemporary scene by a fresh consideration of the military law of Europe in the Middle Ages and then in the nineteenth-century law of war.[118] Meron suggests that contemporary international human rights law, such as recognition of the crime against humanity, should be understood as an expansion of the parameters of chivalric rules, to apply not just within but between tribes, religions, and ethnicities.[119] By focusing on the history of responses to atrocity rather than atrocity alone, scholars can underscore the continuing human project of dealing with—and preventing—mass inhumanity.

Deliberate programs of education, teaching materials, books, exhibits, and events, for adults and for children—all of these are vital responses to mass violence. Margot Strom founded the educational group, Facing History and Ourselves, to develop curricular materials and to build teachers' capacities to teach about the conditions that led to the Holocaust and about the human potential for responding to early signs of intergroup violence and abuse. Demonstrating the crucial role of dehumanization of particular groups of people before genocide or mass violence occurs can alert young people to the dangers of group exclusions and degradations in their own worlds.[120] Strom emphasizes that such educational efforts should avoid freezing the events in a museum of the past and also resist preoccupation with perpetrators. Instead, the education efforts should teach "that history is largely the result of human decisions, that prevention is possible, and that education must have a moral component if it is to make a difference."[121] Rather than substituting one propaganda for another, education about genocide and mass violence should help young people think critically and independently, or, as one school administrator puts it, "to know the past as fact and to confront its implications in ways that make us all seek to change the future for better. If there are no simple answers to the hatred and violence from the past or in the present, there are the countering forces of intellectual honesty, integrity, justice, and empathy."[122]

Carol Gilligan, who is herself involved with Facing History and Ourselves, warns that "education is too often teaching, not knowing; teaching cannot be just about facts, but must be about empathy, participation, finding common humanity, asking kids where does the hate come from, relevance."[123] Effective education must connect the histories of mass atrocities with students' own lives and personal experiences. Such education programs are likely to clash at times with other messages the school, parents, and the community give about particular histories, the significance of remembering, and duties to respond to violence. Here Margot Stern Strom responds: "by denying our students access to this history, we fail to honor their potential to confront, to cope, and to make a difference today and in their futures."[124]

One intriguing response to the Holocaust was the Thanks to Scandinavia scholarship fund, founded "in gratitude for the humanity and bravery of people throughout Scandinavia who protected persons of the Jewish faith during and after the Second World War."[125] The fund combines this tribute to rescuers with education by financing fellowships for American and Scandinavian students to join together to explore Scandinavian democracy, culture, resistance to Nazism, and contemporary human rights issues.

Reflections

Much of the talk and work responding to mass atrocities claims, or hopes, to deter future violations of human dignity and rights. Despite my own invocation of the future and education of new generations as a focus for responses to past instances of mass violence, deterrence has not been my motivation in this book. Deterrence may require very different kinds of actions. One author proposes practical restrictions on the mass media used to promote propaganda, such as jamming the semiprivate radio used to incite mass violence in Rwanda.[126] Yet such restrictions would violate the commitment to a free and open society that others believe would itself be the best guard against large-scale violence. No one, of course, knows how to deter genocide or mass violence. Oppression, hatred, slaughters, and torture unfortunately are constants in human history. Pumla Gobodo-Madikizela paused during a conference discussion of her work on the South African Truth and Reconciliation Commission to comment on the stunning juxtaposition, occurring as they did at the same time, of the first free and democratic South African election and the Rwandan massacre.[127]

No one really knows how to deter those individuals who become potential dictators or leaders of mass destruction, although much hard work has been spent on this question.[128] One hopes that current-day prosecutions would make a future Hitler, or Pol Pot, or Radovan Karadzic change course, but we have no evidence of this. Perhaps those who say evil will always be with us are right, and genocide and mass violence are their case in chief. Even if this view is right, and even if no deterrence can be secured, societies, and international communities, must respond to mass atrocities. For the victimized deserve the acknowledgment of their humanity and the reaffirmation of the utter wrongness of its violation. And bystanders must see a response, and face their own choices about action and inaction, for these, too, are significant. The response should do more than reiterate the boundaries between groups that helped give rise to the atrocities and instead enlarge a sense of community and membership. The response should resist the temptation to dehumanize perpetrators and instead seek to confirm the humanity of everyone—whether by holding all to account under basic norms of human rights, by including all in a process of truth-telling and healing, or by forging connections through rituals and monuments of commemoration, shared resources, or offers of apology and forgiveness. Affirming common humanity does not mean turning the other cheek or forgetting what happened.

Perhaps the challenge is to meet a basic need for balance and wholeness.[129] Apparently pervasive processes for making amends within communities of nonhuman primates should interest those who look to evolution to assess human capacities.[130] A leading scholar in this field notes, in contrast, the inadequate studies of reconciliation behavior among humans.[131] Although chimpanzees apparently do keep negative acts of their peers in mind, a system of revenge has not yet been observed in any animal but humans.[132] Nor have devastations like genocide.

Genocide, mass murders, torture, and rapes defy comprehension and escape human conventions for making sense and meaning of life. Visual artist Samuel Bak, a survivor of the destruction of the Vilna Ghetto and the Holocaust, explains that as a survivor he constantly experiences "[t]he absurdity of looking for any kind of moral logic in the horrific events taking place around me" and the greatest absurdity of all, is "the fact of my survival."[133] Responses to collective violence lurch among rhetorics of history (truth), theology (forgiveness), justice (punishment, compensation, and deterrence), therapy (healing), art (commemoration and disturbance), and education (learning lessons). None is adequate. Yet, invoking any of these rhetorics, through collective steps such as prosecutions, truth commissions, memorials, and education, people wager that social responses can alter the emotional experiences of individuals and societies living after mass violence. Perhaps rather than seeking revenge, people can come to desire to rebuild. The wager is that social and political frameworks can make a difference to how individuals emerge from devastating atrocities.

The wager is based at least in part on the recognition that some past responses seem linked to subsequent horrors. Tina Rosenberg comments, "For too many governments, dealing with past injustice has been not a way to break free of it, but the first step in its recurrence."[134] Repression of the facts of the violence may inspire its resurgence in a later generation; but so can immersion in a narrative of victimization. War crime prosecutions, truth commissions, reparations—each can reflect and invigorate cycles of high expectations and cynical disappointment.

Ultimately, perhaps, responses to collective violence bear witness: to it, and to the human beings destroyed by it.[135] The obligations of witnessing include enabling the practice of "re-memory," which is Toni Morrison's term for practices that concretely encourage people to affirm life in the face of death, "to hold onto feelings of both connection and disconnection, and to stay wide enough awake to attend to the requirements of just recollection and the work of transforming the future."[136] Between vengeance and forgiveness lies the path of recollection and affirmation and the path of facing who we are, and what we could become.

Notes

1. Introduction

First epigraph: Moderator, panel on "Healing the Victims: Possibilities and Impossibilities," Yale University Conference, "Searching for Memory and Justice: The Holocaust and Apartheid," 9 February 1998. Second epigraph: Introduction, "Darkness Visible," in *Holocaust Remembrance: The Shapes of Memory*, ed. Geoffrey H. Hartman (Oxford: Blackwell, 1994), 1, 16.

1. Raphael Lemkin offered the term "genocide" to mean "a coordinated plan of different actions aiming at the destruction of essential foundations of the life of the national groups, with the aim of annihilating the groups themselves." Raphael Lemkin, *Axis Rule in Occupied Europe* (Washington, D.C.: Carnegie Endowment for International Peace, 1944; reprint, New York: Howard Fertig, 1973), 79. The United Nations later formulated genocide to mean actions "committed with intent to destroy in whole or in part a national, ethnic, racial, or religious group as such." United Nations, *Yearbook of the United Nations, 1948–49* (New York: Columbia University Press, 1949), 959–60. The term, "genocide" has triggered debate among scholars. See David Rieff, "An Age of Genocide," *New Republic*, 29 January 1996, 27. The term has also filtered into common usage with a wide range of meanings. I will for the most part instead talk of mass murders, torture, mass violence, and massacres.

2. It is hard not to be aware, but also hard to comprehend fully, this moment in time to be writing on this subject: more than fifty years after Nuremberg; more than a decade after Latin American transitions; less than a decade since the beginning of Eastern European transitions; and still in the midst of those in South Africa; with reverberations in the United States through reparations for Japanese-American World War II

internment; proposals for U.S. governmental apologies for slavery; and growing fights in Hawaii over land claims.

3. Hannah Arendt, *The Human Condition* (Chicago: University of Chicago Press, 1958), 241.

4. Lawrence L. Langer, *Admitting the Holocaust* (New York: Oxford University Press, 1995), 171.

5. Gayle Kirshenbaum, "Women of the Year: Jadranka Cigelj and Nusreta Sivac," *Ms. Magazine*, January/February 1997, 64–68.

6. The identification of rape as a political harm was also an accomplishment of the antilynching campaign in nineteenth-century United States, see Bettina Aptheker, *Women's Legacy: Essays on Race, Sex, and Class in American History* (Amherst, Mass.: University of Massachusetts Press, 1982), 63; and second-wave feminism in the late twentieth century, see Linda Gordon and Ellen DuBois, "Seeking Ecstasy on the Battlefield: Danger and Pleasure in Nineteenth-Century Feminist Thought," *Feminist Studies* (spring 1983): 7–25. See also Rhonda Copeland, "Gendered War Crimes: Reconceptualizing Rape in Time of War," in *Women's Rights, Human Rights: International Feminist Perspectives* (New York: Routledge, 1995), 197; Catharine A. MacKinnon, "Rape, Genocide, and Women's Human Rights," *Harvard Women's Law Journal* 17 (1994): 5; Dorothy Q. Thomas and Regan E. Ralph, "Rape in War: Challenging the Tradition of Impunity," [Johns Hopkins University] *School of Advanced International Studies Review* (winter/spring 1994): 81.

7. Elizabeth Neuffer, "Justice at Hague Moves Slowly for Bosnia Rape Victims," *Boston Globe*, Sunday, 11 January 1998, sec. A, p. 10.

8. Quoted in Neuffer, "Justice at Hague," sec. A, p. 10.

9. Kirshenbaum, "Women of the Year," 67. Similar efforts to will a separation from the perpetrators can take different forms.

10. Ibid., 67–68. Pumla Gobodo-Madikizela, a psychologist serving on South Africa's Truth and Reconciliation Commission, reported the testimony of one woman about the police who shot her family members: "I cannot honor them by keeping them in my thoughts." Comments at "Collective Violence and Memory: Judgment, Reconciliation, Education, Facing History and Ourselves," 12th Annual Human Rights and Justice Conference, 10 April 1997, cosponsored by Harvard Law School Graduate Program, Cambridge, Massachusetts.

11. Lynn V. Andrews, *Crystal Woman: The Sisters of Dreamtime* (New York: Warner Books, 1987). Ruby Plenty Chiefs is a Native American medicine women, or shaman, of the Cree band in Canada.

2. Vengeance and Forgiveness

First epigraph: Chesire Calhoun, "Changing One's Heart," *Ethics* 103 (October 1992): 76, 84. Second epigraph: Susan Jacoby, *Wild Justice: The Evolution of Revenge* (New York: Harper & Row, 1983), 362.

1. For example, Stanley Cohen, "State Crimes of Previous Regimes: Knowledge, Accountability, and the Policing of the Past," *Law and Social Inquiry* 20 (1995): 7.

2. Ibid., 43.

3. Ibid., attributing it to José Zalaquett. See Kate Millett, *The Politics of Cruelty: An Essay on the Literature of Political Imprisonment* (New York: W. W. Norton, 1994).

4. Diane F. Orentlicher, "Settling Accounts: The Duty to Prosecute Human Rights Violations of a Prior Regime," *Yale Law Journal* 100 (1991): 2539.

5. Jeffrie G. Murphy, introduction to Jeffrie G. Murphy and Jean Hampton, *Forgiveness and Mercy* (New York: Cambridge University Press, 1988), 16.

6. See Wai Chee Dimock, *Residues of Justice: Literature, Law, Philosophy* (Berkeley: University of California Press, 1996), 11.

7. Webster's definition for vicious; see also vindictive. "1. disposed to seek revenge: vengeful . . . 2. vicious, spiteful." *Webster's Third New International Dictionary of the English Language* (Springfield, Mass.: G. & C. Merriam Co., 1968).

8. See Geiko Müller-Fahernholz, *The Art of Forgiveness: Theological Reflections on Healing and Reconciliation* (Geneva: World Council of Churches Publications, 1997), 19. Revenge is about maintaining an equity of horror; "revenge is also about maintaining an equity of suffering. There must be a gruesome compatibility of guilt and suffering on both sides. The scales must be balanced. Each party in a vendetta must share the same suffering. The perpetrator must be made into a victim while the victim becomes a perpetrator . . . Moreover, it turns into a cult of violence because no attempt is made to heal or in any way transcend the suffering, only to replicate it."

9. John R. Reed, *Dickens and Thackery: Punishment and Forgiveness* (Athens, Ohio: Ohio University Press, 1995).

10. Robert Littell, *The Amateur* (New York: Dell, 1982), 54.

11. Quoted in Lawrence Weschler, "A Reporter at Large," *New Yorker*, 10 December 1990, 127.

12. Jacoby, *Wild Justice*, 115. See also page 5: "Establishment of a balance between the restraint that enables people to live with one another and the ineradicable impulse to retaliate when harm is inflicted has always been one of the essential tasks of civilization. The attainment of such a balance depends in large measure on the confidence of the victimized that someone else will act on their behalf against the victimizers."

13. I do not join those who equate vengeance and retribution. See, for example, *Furman v. Georgia*, 408 U.S. 238, 304 (1972). Retribution is "naked vengeance" arising from the needs of our "baser selves"; J. L. Mackie, "Morality and the Retributive Emotions," *Criminal Justice Ethics* 1 (1982): 3; Jacoby, *Wild Justice*, 4; and Jeffrie G. Murphy, "Retributive Hatred: An Essay on Criminal Liability and the Emotions," in *Liability and Responsibility*, ed. R. G. Frey and Christopher W. Morris (Cambridge: Cambridge University Press, 1991), 351. Instead, let us distinguish the vengeful, self-help response of tit-for-tat from the deliberate, retributive use of governmentally administered punishment to vindicate the victim's value. Jean Hampton, "The Retributive Idea," in Jeffrie G. Murphy and Jean Hampton, *Forgiveness and Mercy* (New York: Cambridge University Press, 1988), 111, 135, 137.

14. Kurt Baier, "The Strengths and Limits of the Retributive Theory of Punishment," *Philosophy Exchange* 2 (1977): 37, 39; and Jeffrie G. Murphy, "Hatred: A Qualified Defense," in Jeffrie G. Murphy and Jean Hampton, *Forgiveness and Mercy* (New York: Cambridge University Press, 1988), 95.

15. See Andrew von Hirsch, "Deservedness and Dangerousness in Sentencing Policy," *Criminal Law Review* 1986 (February 1986): 79; Herbert Pacer, "Making the Punishment Fit the Crime," *Harvard Law Review* 77 (1964): 1071; Lawrence Crocker, "The Upper Limit of Just Punishment," *Emory Law Journal* 41 (1992): 1059; and David F. Parlett, "Punitive Damages: Legal Hot Zones," *Louisiana Law Review* 56 (1996): 781, 803.

16. Hampton, "Retributive Idea," 137. She acknowledges, however, that many people slide between revenge and retribution because both involve seeking to inflict pain as a way of mastering another.

17. Ibid., 138–43.

18. Ibid., 135–37.

19. Ibid., 145.

20. For example, Murphy, "Hatred: A Qualified Defense," 92; Adam Smith, *The Theory of Moral Sentiments* (1759; Indianapolis: Liberty Press, 1982), 38.

21. Jean Hampton, "Forgiveness, Resentment and Hatred," in Jeffrie G. Murphy and Jean Hampton, *Forgiveness and Mercy* (New York: Cambridge University Press, 1988), 78.

22. Judith Herman, *Trauma and Recovery* (New York: Basic Books, 1992), 189.

23. See Murphy, "Hatred," 92–94.

24. Ibid., 104, 107.

25. Michael Ignatieff, "The Elusive Goal of War Trials," *Harper's*, March 1996, reprinted in "Articles of Faith, Index on Censorship," *Harper's*, September/October 1997, 15, 16–17.

26. Ibid., 17.

27. Geoffrey H. Hartman, Introduction, "Darkness Visible," in *Holocaust Remembrance: The Shapes of Memory*, ed. Geoffrey H. Hartman (Oxford: Blackwell, 1994), 1, 14.

28. Robert Grams Hunter, *Shakespeare and the Comedy of Forgiveness* (New York: Columbia University Press, 1965), 243.

29. See Müller-Fahernholz, *Art of Forgiveness*, 24–48.

30. José Zalaquett, "Conference Proceedings," in *Dealing with the Past: Truth and Reconciliation in South Africa*, ed. Alex Moraine, Janet Levy, and Ronel Scheffer (Capetown: IDASA, 1994).

31. Müller-Fahrenholz, *Art of Forgiveness*, viii: "Auschwitz makes it abundantly clear that *forgiveness can never replace justice.* Human codes of law establish indispensable rules of life together and standards of relationships . . . Any attempt to weaken the supremacy of the law thus entails the erosion of the humane. Forgiveness is about renouncing unjustified power, not about weakening the pursuit of justice." See also Murphy, introduction to *Forgiveness and Mercy*, 22, 33.

32. Jeffrie G. Murphy, "Mercy and Legal Justice," in Jeffrie G. Murphy and Jean Hampton, *Forgiveness and Mercy* (New York: Cambridge University Press, 1988), 162, 167. See generally David W. Augsburger, *Helping People Forgive* (Louisville, Ky.: Westminster John Knox Press, 1996), 165–68. This book connects forgiveness and reparations with an ethical context that includes facing guilt and responsibility. Accordingly, forgiveness as "not a moral victory for the offended; it is not a self-serving mercy that controls, obligates, or morally judges the offender; rather it transforms the relationship." Id., 166.

33. Jeffrie G. Murphy, "Forgiveness and Resentment," in Jeffrie G. Murphy and Jean Hampton, *Forgiveness and Mercy* (New York: Cambridge University Press, 1988), 33.

34. For the last alternative, see Jules L. Coleman, "Adding Institutional Insult to Personal Injury," *Yale Journal on Regulation* 8 (1990): 223, 225.

35. Jacoby, *Wild Justice*, 5. Of course, the central Christian concern is forgiveness and reconciliation with God. See Vincent Taylor, *Forgiveness and Reconciliation: A Study in New Testament Theology* (London: Macmillan, 1960).

36. Elizabeth Neuffer, "Justice at Hague Moves Slowly for Bosnia Rape Victims," *Boston Globe*, Sunday, 11 January 1998, sec. A, p. 10.

37. Calhoun, "Changing One's Heart," 76, 84.

38. See Aurel Kolnai, "Forgiveness," *Proceedings of the Aristotelian Society* 74 (1973–74): 91, 99.

39. Justice Albie Sacks, "Conceptions of Justice," Yale University Conference, "Searching for Memory and Justice: The Holocaust and Apartheid," 8 February 1998.

40. Müller-Fahrenholz, *Art of Forgiveness*, ix.

41. Donald Shriver, *An Ethic for Enemies: Forgiveness in Politics* (New York: Oxford University Press, 1995), 119.

42. Quoted in Jacoby, *Wild Justice*, 117. See also Murphy, introduction to *Forgiveness and Mercy*, 1, 21. "I do not have *standing to resent or forgive you unless I have myself been the victim of your wrongdoing.*" Some victims, in turn, may forgive, or seem to forgive, in order to appear strong and not hurt. If this involves denying or minimizing the harm, though, it is not truly forgiveness, which instead requires full acknowledgment of the harm.

43. Comments of Justice Pius Langa, Yale University Conference, "Searching for Memory and Justice: The Holocaust and Apartheid," 8 February 1998.

44. Ibid.

45. See responses of Moshe Bejski, in Simon Wiesenthal, *The Sunflower: On the Possibilities and Limits of Forgiveness*, rev. and enl. ed. (New York: Schocken Books, 1998), 111, 115. "According to Jewish tradition, even God Himself can only forgive sins committed against Himself, not against man." See also page 171 (Response of Abraham Joshua Heschel).

46. Women in Western fiction are often associated with forgiving

natures. See Reed, *Dickens and Thackery*, 475. Does this reflect social pressures to doubt their own self-worth, or a sense of personal value insulated against insult?

47. Murphy, introduction to *Forgiveness and Mercy*, 14–16.

48. See Aaron Lazare, "The Healing Process of Apology," unpublished lecture, 10. Some people do not want to reestablish relationships, for example, many Holocaust survivors seek no relationships with Nazis.

49. Hampton, "Forgiveness, Resentment and Hatred," 80–81.

50. Some argue that if the contrition and apology are sincere and matched by behavior, at a certain point, the burden of response shifts from the wrongdoer to one who has the capacity to forgive. Conversation with Rabbi Jonathan Kraus, Belmont, Massachusetts, 24 June 1998 (discussing Talmudic sources). It is difficult to apply this traditional view to perpetrators of mass violence. Hannah Arendt said about the crimes of the Holocaust: "[A]ll we know is that we can neither punish nor forgive such offenses and that they therefore transcend the realm of human affairs and the potentialities of human power." Hannah Arendt, *The Human Condition* (Chicago: University of Chicago Press, 1958), 241.

51. See Hampton, "Forgiveness, Resentment and Hatred," 84.

52. See, for example, Joanna North, "Wrongdoing and Forgiveness," *Philosophy* 62 (1987): 499, 502.

53. Reed, *Dickens and Thackeray*, 17.

54. See Lazare, "Healing Process of Apology," 11 (describing these benefits from apology).

55. Harold S. Kushner, *How Good Do We Have to Be: A New Understanding of Guilt and Forgiveness* (Boston: Little Brown, 1996), 107.

56. Ibid.

57. Comments of Commissioner Dumisa Ntsebeza, Yale University Conference, "Searching for Memory and Justice: The Holocaust and Apartheid," 9 February 1998. See also response of the Dalai Lama, in Wiesenthal, *Limits of Forgiveness*, 129, 130 (recounting his conversation with a Tibetan monk who found the biggest danger in eighteen years of imprisonment in China to be the risk of losing his compassion for the Chinese).

58. Müller-Fahrenolz, *Art of Forgiveness*, 21.

59. Comments of Dumisa Ntsebeza, "Searching for Memory."

60. Jacoby, *Wild Justice*, 352. Similarly, cautions Jacoby, the across-

the-board critique of retribution on therapeutic grounds confuses specific acts of retaliation with vengefulness as a way of life. Forgiveness on occasion may be as inappropriate, and even self-destructive, as vindictiveness.

61. See Murphy, "Forgiveness and Resentment," 23. Turning to therapy to deal with resentment reflects selfish motives for mental health, not forgiveness. See also response of Cynthia Ozick, in Wiesenthal, *Limits of Forgiveness*, 213, 215. Ozick argues against mercy to the cruel because it can lead to indifference toward the innocent.

62. See North, "Wrongdoing and Forgiveness," 499, 502.

63. Hartman, Introduction, "Darkness Visible," 15.

64. See chapter 4 for a discussion of conditional amnesty in the South African Truth and Reconciliation Commission.

65. Perhaps a society infused with Christianity would especially support a notion of forgiveness that celebrates the virtue of charity with a rich sense of common humanity, common evil, and original sin. See Hunter, *Comedy of Forgiveness*, 243. He notes that Shakespeare's comedies of forgiveness depend on the ability of the audience to participate in such a celebration. In a more secular, diverse community, charity follows more the making of allowances, with pity and tolerance for one more unfortunate, more constrained, more inferior than oneself. But no one can be made to forgive.

66. Jacoby, *Wild Justice*, 362. Vengeance and forgiveness *can* converge. Forgiveness does not entail refraining from punishment; vengeance can animate a bounded retributive punishment authorized by law. But forgiveness can also be offered with no call for punishment, and vengeance can press for more than lawful punishment would permit.

67. Ibid.

68. See Margaret Atwood, *Handmaid's Tale* (Toronto: McClelland and Stewart, 1985), 173–74 (forgiveness is a power); Lazare, "Healing Process of Apology," 10 (a victim who nurses a grudge retains a sense of control and power by refusing to forgive).

69. See Reed, *Dickens and Thackeray*, 478 (discussing *Lord Jim*).

70. Jacoby, *Wild Justice*, 64.

71. Saul Friedlander, "Trauma, Memory, and Transference," in *Holocaust Remembrance: The Shapes of Memory*, ed. Geoffrey H. Hartman (Oxford: Blackwell, 1994), 252, 261.

72. Ibid., 262.

3. *Trials*

First epigraph: Justice Robert Jackson, opening statement to Nuremberg tribunal, The Trial of German Major War Criminals, by the International Military Tribunal Sitting at Nuremberg, Germany (commencing 20th November 1945) (International Military Tribunal, under the authority of H. M. [Her majesty] attorney general by H. M. Stationery Office: London 1946). Second epigraph: Tina Rosenberg, *The Haunted Land: Facing Europe's Ghosts after Communism* (New York: Vintage, 1995), 350.

1. See Margaret Jane Radin, "Reconsidering the Rule of Law," *Boston University Law Review* 69 (1989): 781, 792. As Margaret Radin has summarized, that aspiration includes the ideas that: "(1) law consists of rules; (2) rules are prior to particular cases, more general than particular cases, and applied to particular cases; (3) law is instrumental (the rules are applied to achieve ends); (4) there is a radical separation between government and citizens (there are rule-givers and appliers, versus rule-takers and compliers); (5) the person is a rational chooser ordering her affairs instrumentally . . ." Ruti Teitel has questioned whether the rule of law thus stated can be compatible with periods of revolution, disorder, and legal and political instability. See Ruti Teitel, "Transitional Jurisprudence: The Role of Law in Political Transformation," *Yale Law Journal* 106 (1997): 2009, 2017.

2. Civil trials could also be pursued. For example, some federal courts have permitted civil actions to proceed under the Alien Tort Claims Act in the United States. Thus, in *Filartiga v. Pena-Irala*, 630 F. 2d 876 (2d Cir. 1980), two Paraguayan nationals who had applied for political asylum in the United States successfully invoked the jurisdiction of a federal court to sue the alleged torturer of Dr. Filartiga's son in Paraguay for damages. Other courts have rejected similar claims, however. See, for example, *Tel-Oren v. Libyan Arab Republic*, 517 F. Supp. 542 (1981), aff'd 726 F. 2d 774 (D.C. Cir. 1984), cert. denied, 470 U.S. 1003 (1985).

3. Comments, panel on "Due Process in the Pursuit of Truth," Truth and Reconciliation Commission meeting (sponsored by the World Peace Foundation, Cape Town, 30 May 1998).

4. See generally, Jay A. Baird, introduction to *From Nuremberg to My Lai* (Lexington, Mass.: D. C. Heath, 1972), vii–xvii.

5. There was a brief effort at the United Nations to draft an international convention on the suppression and punishment of apartheid, but

it did not culminate in any action. See Paul D. Marquardt, "Law Without Borders: The Constitutionality of an International Criminal Court," *Columbia Journal of Transnational Law* 33 (1995): 73, 89.

6. See John Duffett, ed., *Against the Crime of Silence* [Proceedings of the Russell International War Crimes Tribunal] (Stockholm, Copenhagen; New York: Bertrand Russell Peace Foundation, 1968).

7. See Telford Taylor, *Nuremberg and Vietnam: An American Tragedy* (Chicago: Quadrangle, 1970).

8. Compare Teitel, "Transitional Jurisprudence," with Diane Orentlicher, "Settling Accounts: The Duty to Prosecute Human Rights Violations of Prior Regime," *Yale Law Journal* 100 (1993): 2537; and Naomi Rhot-Arriaza, "State Responsibility to Investigate and Prosecute Grave Human Rights Violations in International Law," *California Law Review* 78 (1990): 451.

9. See Carlos Nino, *Radical Evil on Trial* (New Haven, Conn.: Yale University Press, 1995), 5, 6; and Baird, *Nuremberg to My Lai*, viii.

10. Nino, *Radical Evil*, 6.

11. Good summaries of these arguments appear in Baird, *Nuremberg to My Lai*, vii, vx; "Motion Adopted by All Defense Counsel," 19 November 1945 (submitted by Dr. Stahmer), in Baird, *Nuremberg to My Lai*, 81–83; Dr. Hermann Jahreiss, "Statement Before the Nuremberg Tribunal," in Baird, *Nuremberg to My Lai*, 84–91. See also Bernard Meltzer, "Remembering Nuremberg," (occasional paper, University of Chicago Law School, no. 34, 1995); and Steven Fogelson, "The Nuremberg Legacy: An Unfulfilled Promise," *Southern California Law Review* 63 (1990): 833, 858–67.

12. Quoted in Denis J. Hutchinson, *Justice Jackson and the Nuremberg Trials* (forthcoming) (quoted in Meltzer, "Remembering Nuremberg," 34). Telford Taylor, a key American member of the Nuremberg prosecutorial team, acknowledges "lingering unease about the fact that the aggressive war charge raised fundamental ex post facto issues." See James Rodgers, "Remembering Nuremberg," *ABA Journal* (October 1983): 88, 91.

13. Meltzer, "Remembering Nuremberg," 8. See also Richard A. Falk, "Nuremberg: Past, Present, and Future," *Yale Law Journal* 80 (1971): 1501. The fact that leaders of defeated nations also faced no charges for conduct—such as air attacks on civilian cities that the Allies widely used—also sharply limited the trials' value in moral education.

14. "I should be the last to deny that the case may well suffer from incomplete researches and quite likely will not be the example of professional work which any of the prosecuting nations would normally wish to sponsor." Robert H. Jackson, "Opening Statement for the United States Before the International Military Tribunal," 21 November 1945, reprinted in Baird, *Nuremberg to My Lai*, 19, 22.

15. Ibid., 23–24.

16. See comment on the Nuremberg trials, in Henry J. Steiner and Philip Alston, eds., *International Human Rights in Context: Law, Politics, Morals* (Oxford: Clarendon Press, 1996), 99.

17. This is the London Agreement of August 8, 1945, 59 Stat. 1544, E.A.S. No. 472 (Articles 6 [crimes against peace, war crimes, crimes against humanity], 7 [no excuse for heads of State or other responsible government officials], 8 [no excuse in acting under governmental orders]).

18. See generally Nino, *Radical Evil*, 6–8. The defense also challenged conspiracy charges related to anything but crimes against peace, and prevailed on this theory. See also Knut Ipsen, "A Review of the Main Legal Aspects of the Tokyo Trial and Their Influence on the Development of International Law," in Chihiro Hosoya, Nisuke Ando, Yaskuaki Onuma, and Richard H. Minear, eds., *The Tokyo War Crimes Trial* (Tokyo: Kodansha, 1986), 37, 44–45.

19. See International Military Tribunal (Nuremberg), 1946, "Judgment of Nuremberg Tribunal," *American Journal of International Law* 41 (1947): 172.

20. Herbert Wechsler, "The Issues of the Nuremberg Trial," *Political Science Quarterly* 62 (1941): 11, 23.

21. See Francis Biddle, "The Nuremberg Trial," *Virginia Law Review* 33 (1947): 679, 694.

22. Debate did persist, though, over whether law or instead rough justice had been applied in Nuremberg. See Hans Kelsen, "Will the Judgment in the Nuremberg Trial Constitute a Precedent in International Law?" *International Law Quarterly* 1 (1947): 153.

23. Thomas F. Lambert Jr., "Recalling the War Crimes Trials of World War II," *Military Law Register* 149 (1995): 15, 23.

24. Marquardt, "Law without Borders," 82.

25. Ibid.

26. Stephen Breyer, "Crimes against Humanity: Nuremberg, 1946," *New York University Law Review* 71 (1996): 1161, 1163.

27. Theodor Meron, "America and the World," National Public Radio, 15 April 1993, transcript #9315.

28. Security Council Res. 780 (1992); S.C. Res. 808 (1993); and S.C. Res. 827 (1993). The tribunal's official name is the International Tribunal for the Prosecution of Persons Responsible for Serious Violations of International Humanitarian Law Committed in the Territory of Former Yugoslavia since 1991.

29. See UN Charter, Articles 39–42.

30. Steiner and Alston, *International Human Rights in Context*, 1071.

31. See Payam Akhavan, "Justice in the Hague, Peace in the Former Yugoslavia? A Commentary on the United Nations War Crimes Tribunal," *Human Rights Quarterly* 20 (November 1998): 66–69.

32. Quoted in *Prosecutor v. Dražen Erdemović*, Judgment, in the appeals chamber, 7 October 1997, 4.

33. *Prosecutor v. Dražen Erdemović*, Judgment, 17; *Prosecutor v. Dražen Erdemović*, Joint Separate Opinion of Judge Gabrielle Kirk McDonald and Judge Lal Chand Vohrah, 1.2.

34. *Prosecutor v. Dražen Erdemović*, Judgment, 17.

35. It exposes in a particular light the difficulties posed by individual responsibility in "administrative massacres." See later in this chapter the discussion of administrative massacres.

36. See James O'Brien, "The International Tribunal for Violations of International Humanitarian Law in the Former Yugoslavia," *American Journal of International Law* 87 (1993): 639; Steiner and Alston, *International Human Rights in Context*, 1070.

37. Quoted in Meron, "America and the World." See also Justice Richard Goldstone, "Prosecuting War Criminals," (occasional paper, David Dawes Memorial Institute of International Studies, no. 10, August 1996), 6 (no ex post facto issues for the International Tribunals for the former Yugoslavia and Rwanda).

38. See Keith R. Chaney, "Pitfalls and Imperatives: Applying the Lessons of Nuremberg to the Yugoslav War Crimes Trial," *Dickinson Journal of International Law* 14 (1995): 57, 85.

39. Nino, *Radical Evil*, 23.

40. Ibid., 24. See also Gabor Halmi and Kim Lane Schepple, "Living Well Is the Best Revenge: The Hungarian Approach to Judging the Past," in A. James McAdams, ed., *Transitional Justice and the Rule of Law in New Democracies* (Notre Dame, Ind.: University of Notre Dame Press, 1997): 155–84. Halmi and Schepple defend the Hungarian

assertion of constitutional restrictions against democratic power directed against members of the former regime.

41. Nino, *Radical Evil*, 24.

42. Although the Yugoslavia conflict initially occurred within one nation, the breakup of that nation quickly ensured the international features of that conflict and ensured the possibility of international jurisdiction. See Meron, "America and the World."

43. Kenneth Anderson, "Nuremberg Sensibility: Telford Taylor's Memoir of the Nuremberg Trials," *Harvard Human Rights Journal* 7 (1994): 281. See also Hartley Shawcross, "Let the Tribunal Do Its Job," *New York Times*, 22 May 1996, sec. A, p. 11 (Britain's chief prosecutor at Nuremberg argues that the Yugoslavia tribunal would fail without NATO arrests of those indicted for the most serious crimes in the former Yugoslavia).

44. Branko Milinkovic and Guido de Bruin, "Yugoslavia: Divisions Emerge Over War Crimes Tribunal," *Inter Press Service*, 15 February 1994; see Goldstone, "Prosecuting War Criminals" (discussing dangers to the peace process).

45. Samantha Power, "The Stages of Justice," review of *Mass Atrocity, Collective Memory, and the Law*, by Mark Osiel, *New Republic*, 2 March 1998, 32.

46. See Judith Shklar, *Legalism: Law, Morals, and Political Trials* (Cambridge, Mass.: Harvard University Press, 1986); Morton J. Horwitz, *Transformation of American Law*, 2 vols. (New York: Oxford University Press, 1992); Morton Horwitz, "Law and Economics: Science or Politics?" *Hofstra Law Review* 8 (1981): 905.

47. See Power, "Stages of Justice," 32.

48. Between December 9, 1946, and April 11, 1949, 185 concentration camp guards, doctors, members of the secret police killing squads, and directors of major corporations supplying war materials faced charges. Of these, 25 received death sentences, 20 received life sentences, 97 faced shorter terms, and 35 were acquitted. See Donald W. Shriver, Jr., *An Ethic for Enemies: Forgiveness in Politics* (New York: Oxford University Press, 1995), 248 n. 21 (citing United States Holocaust Memorial sources).

49. Ipsen, "Main Legal Aspects of Tokyo Trial," 42; Rosenberg, *Haunted Land*, 350 (describing Telford Taylor's critique of the collective guilt theory before indictments of SS members who stayed after knowing of its prior deeds).

50. B. V. A. Roling, introduction to *The Tokyo War Crimes Trial: An International Symposium* (Tokyo: Kodansha, 1986), 15, 17.

51. Mark Osiel, "Ever Again: Legal Remembrance of Administrative Massacre," *University of Pennsylvania Law Review* 144 (1995): 463, 468.

52. Ibid., 507.

53. Rosenberg, *Haunted Land*, 261–305, 340–51.

54. Ibid., 265–66.

55. See ibid., 269–70.

56. Ibid., 287.

57. Ibid., 269.

58. Ibid., 344.

59. Ibid., 344.

60. Ibid., 346.

61. Ibid., 271.

62. Ibid., 280, 284.

63. Ibid., 285, 287.

64. Ibid., 344.

65. Judgment of Judge Theodor Seidel, quoted in Rosenberg, *Haunted Land*, 345. The judge did not specifically invoke international law, but instead maintained that the guards should have realized that their conduct violated national values of East Germany. Rosenberg faults him for failing to understand the context and patterns of indoctrination in East Germany. Id., 349.

66. Ibid., 346.

67. Ibid., 348.

68. Ibid.

69. Ibid., 349.

70. Carlos H. Acuna and Catalina Smulovitz, "Guarding the Guardians in Argentina: Some Lessons about Risks and Benefits of Empowering Courts," in A. James McAdams, ed., *Transitional Justice and the Rule of Law in New Democracies* (Notre Dame, Ind.: University of Notre Dame Press, 1997), 93, 103; Nino, *Radical Evil*, 41–104.

71. Acuna and Smulovitz, "Guarding the Guardians," 108.

72. Nino, *Radical Evil*, 13–14.

73. Otto Krazbuhler, "Nuremberg Eighteen Years Afterward," *DePaul Law Review* 14 (1964): 334, 348. See also Herbert Kraus, "The Nuremberg Trial of the Major War Criminals: Reflections After Seventeen Years," *DePaul Law Review* 13 (1964): 233.

74. Comments of Paik Choong-Hyun, in Roling, *Tokyo War Crimes Trial*, 52, 54.

75. Quoted in Milinkovic and de Bruin, "Yugoslavia: Divisions Emerge Over War Crimes Tribunal."

76. See Allan Ryan, "The Search for Justice," *Boston Globe*, 9 December 1995, 11. "There are not enough lawyers, judges, courtrooms; even if these could be imported there are not enough witnesses, evidence or time." There is not even electricity within the Ministry of Justice in Rwanda.

77. Mark Osiel, *Mass Atrocity, Collective Memory and the Law* (New Brunswick, N.J.: Transaction Publishers, 1997), 6. Osiel, "Legal Remembrance of Administrative Massacre," 463, 466.

78. Osiel, "Legal Remembrance of Administrative Massacre," 510.

79. Ibid., 467, 652–71.

80. Osiel, *Mass Atrocity*, 69.

81. Osiel emphasizes the legal fiction that people exercise an inalienable capacity for autonomous choice when breaking the law, and the law thereby seeks to make people choosers. Ibid., 72–73. It is a curious sort of "making," as the trials occur after the fact of the deeds in question. Osiel's elaborated argument in the book defends trials as "monumental spectacles" to forge social solidarity after mass atrocity.

82. Cf. Hannah Arendt, *Eichmann in Jerusalem: A Report on the Banality of Evil*, rev. and enl. ed. (1963; New York: Penguin Books 1977), 9 (describing how show trials require individual defendants to serve as central, heroic characters).

83. An eloquent defender of trials as vehicles for constructing a truth of individual liability for crimes, Payam Akhavan nonetheless acknowledges that trials do not produce a comprehensive record, and do not focus on victims' suffering. See Akhavan, "Justice in the Hague," 6. Akhavan is legal advisor in the Office of the Prosecutor of the International Tribunal of the Former Yugoslavia.

84. International Military Tribunal, *Trial of the Major War Criminals Before the International Military Tribunal, Nuremberg, 14 Nov. 1945 – 1 Oct. 1946*, vol. 3 (Nuremberg: International Military Tribunal, 1947), 92.

85. See Michael Marrus, "History and the Holocaust in the Courtroom," January 1998, 15. Paper prepared for "Searching for Memory and Justice: The Holocaust and Apartheid."

86. Arendt to Karl Jaspers, 17 August 1946, *Hannah Arendt–Karl*

Jaspers Correspondence, 1926–1969, ed. Lotte Kohler and Hans Saner (New York: Harcourt Brace Jovanovich, 1992), 51, 54.

87. See Elisabeth Young-Bruehl, *Hannah Arendt: For Love of the World* (New Haven, Conn.: Yale University Press, 1982), 257.

88. Meron, "America and the World."

89. Breyer, "Crimes against Humanity."

90. Ibid., 1161.

91. Ibid.

92. Ibid.

93. Ibid.

94. Ibid., 1164.

95. Richard H. Minear, "The Individual, The State, and the Tokyo Trial," in Chihiro Hosoya, Nisuke Ando, Yaskuaki Onuma, and Richard H. Minear, eds., *The Tokyo War Crimes Trials* (Tokyo: Kodansha, 1986), 159, 160.

96. Jackson, opening statement to Nuremberg tribunal, 28. (See first epigraph note for full citation, p. 156.)

97. See Nino, *Radical Evil,* x.

98. Jackson, opening statement to Nuremberg tribunal.

99. Thus the International Criminal Tribunal for the former Yugoslavia carefully justified Dusko Tadic's liability for crimes against humanity rather than only war crimes because of his enthusiastic support for attacking non-Serbs, while treating as a mitigating factor the propaganda that exacerbated ethnic tensions. *Prosecutor v. Tadic,* Sentencing Judgment, Case No. IT-94-1-T (14 July 1997), 36, paragraphs 66–67.

100. Quoted in Rosenberg, *Haunted Land,* 351.

101. Ibid.

4. *Truth Commissions*

First epigraph: Zbigniew Herbert, "Report" in *Besieged City and Other Poems,* trans. John Carpenter and Bogdana Carpenter (New York: Ecco Press, 1985), 67. Second epigraph: Michael Ignatieff, "The Elusive Goal of War Trials," *Harper's,* March 1996, reprinted in "Articles of Faith, Index on Censorship," *Harper's,* September/October 1997, 15, 16–17.

1. See Geiko Müller-Frahrenholz, *The Art of Forgiveness: Theological Reflections on Healing and Reconciliation* (Geneva: World Council of Churches Publications, 1997), 85–101.

2. See The National Unity and Reconciliation Act, Act No. 34, 1995, Republic of South Africa, Government Gazette, vol. 361, No. 16579 (Cape Town, July 26, 1995).

3. The German Parliament founded a human rights commission to study abuses in East Germany; the Uruguayan Parliament established an investigatory commission on the situation of "disappeared" people. Priscilla B. Hayner, "Fifteen Truth Commissions—1974–1994: A Comparative Study," *Human Rights Quarterly* 16 (1994): 600.

4. Ibid., 600 n. 102; and Address of Dullah Omar, to the National University Forum on 2 March 1995 on the Truth and Reconciliation Commission.

5. See Thomas Buergenthal, "The United Nations Truth Commission for El Salvador," 27 *Vanderbilt Journal of Transitional Law,* 27 (1994): 497.

6. See Aryeh Neier, "What Should Be Done about the Guilty?" *New York Review of Books,* 1 February 1990, 32, 34; Carlos Nino, "The Duty to Punish Past Abuses of Human Rights Put into Context: The Case of Argentina," *Yale Law Journal* 100 (1991): 2619. Similarly, the National Commission for Truth and Reconciliation in Chile was created by President Patricio Aylwin Azocar. It has been credited with creating an official record of human rights abuses that were committed by the Pinochet regime, and spurring reparations to victims, and stimulating further investigation into the cases of "disappeared" persons. See Carnegie Commission on Preventing Deadly Conflict, *Preventing Deadly Conflict* (New York: Carnegie Corporation, 1997), 97. See also Priscilla B. Hayner, "Commissioning the Truth: Further Research Questions," *Third World Quarterly* 17 (1996): 19 (describing nineteen commissions).

7. See Hayner, "Fifteen Truth Commissions," 600.

8. Ibid., 629.

9. Ibid., 239–40, 244–45.

10. Lawrence Weschler, *A Miracle, A Universe: Settling Accounts with Torturers* (New York: Pantheon, 1990), 24. Weschler's riveting account of the undertaking is a testament to human courage and ingenuity in the face of terror.

11. See Nino, "Duty to Punish," 34. A private group, named Memorial, organized in the Soviet Union before the change in government and worked to gather information on the victims of Stalinism. Neier, "What Should Be Done about the Guilty?"

12. Nino, "Duty to Punish," 75.

13. See Timothy Garton Ash, "True Confessions," New York Review of Books, 17 July 1997, 33; Explanatory Memorandum to the Parliamentary Bill (establishing the Truth and Reconciliation Commission) (1995).

14. André Du Toit, in "Human Rights Program," Harvard Law School and World Peace Foundation, *Truth Commissions: A Comparative Assessment* (Cambridge, Mass.: Harvard Law School Human Rights Program and World Peace Foundation, 1997), 20.

15. Dr. Abdullah M. Omar, The South African Truth and Reconciliation Commission (written remarks of the justice minister, presented to the Facing History and Ourselves, 12th National Human Rights and Justice Conference, Harvard University, 10 April 1997), 3.

16. Ibid., 5.

17. Explanatory Memorandum to the Parliamentary Bill (1995).

18. Ash, "True Confessions," 33.

19. See *Azanian Peoples Organization v. President of the Republic of South Africa*, Case CCt 17. 96, Constitutional Court of South Africa, July 25, 1996; see also Daniel F. Wilhelm, "Note," *American Journal of International Law* 91 (1997): 360 (Constitutional Court of South Africa refused challenge to the Promotion of National Unity and Reconciliation Act).

20. Neier, "What Should Be Done about the Guilty?" 33.

21. Naomi Roht-Arriaza, ed., *Impunity and Human Rights in International Law and Practice* (Oxford: Oxford University Press, 1995), 22.

22. The Act states the objectives this way:

3. (1) The objectives of the Commission shall be to promote national unity and reconciliation in a spirit of understanding which transcends the conflicts and divisions of the past by—

(a) establishing as complete a picture as possible of the causes, nature and extent of the gross violations of human rights which were committed during the period from 1 March 1960 to the cut-off date, including the antecedents, circumstances, factors and context of such violations, as well as the perspectives of the victims and the motive and perspectives of the persons responsible for the commission of the violations, by conducting investigations and holding hearings;

(b) facilitating the granting of amnesty to persons who make full disclosure of all the relevant facts relating to acts associated with a political objective. . . . ;

(c) establishing and making known the fate or whereabouts of victims and by restoring the human and civil dignity of such victims by granting them an opportunity to relate their own accounts of the violations of which they are victims, and by recommending reparation measures in respect of them;

(d) compiling a report providing as comprehensive an account as possible of the activities and findings of the commission . . . which contains recommendations of measures to prevent the future violation of human rights. (*Government Gazette*, 6; c. 2.)

23. See Wai Chee Dimock, *The Residues of Justice: Literature, Law, Philosophy* (Berkeley: University of California Press, 1996).

24. Stephan Landsman, "Alternative Responses to Serious Human Rights Abuses—Of Prosecutions and Truth Commissions," 4, presented to the Law and Society Annual Meeting, May–June 1997; to appear in *Law and Contemporary Problems*.

25. Ibid., 5. Landsman also identifies the role of prosecution in educating the citizenry about the nature and extent of wrongdoing, which could help deter future abuses; and prosecution can help identify the basis for compensating victims. Id., 4. See also Hannah Arendt, *The Human Condition* (Chicago: University of Chicago Press, 1958).

26. See Margaret Popkin and Naomi Roht-Arriaza, "Truth as Justice: Investigatory Commissions in Latin America," in Neil J. Kritz, ed., *Transitional Justice: How Emerging Democracies Reckon with Former Regimes*, vol. 1 (Washington, D.C.: U.S. Institute of Peace Press, 1995), 262, 289.

27. For example, Mary Albon, "Truth and Justice: The Delicate Balance—Documentation of Prior Regimes and Individual Rights," in Neil J. Kritz, ed., *Transitional Justice: How Emerging Democracies Reckon with Former Regimes*, vol. 1 (Washington, D.C.: U.S. Institute of Peace Press, 1995), 290; Douglass W. Cassell, Jr., "International Truth Commissions and Justice," in Neil J. Kritz, ed., *Transitional Justice: How Emerging Democracies Reckon with Former Regimes*, vol. 1 (Washington, D.C.: U.S. Institute of Peace Press, 1995), 326, 333.

28. See John Dugard, "Retrospective Justice: International Law and the South African Model," in A. James McAdams, ed., *Transitional Justice and the Rule of Law in New Democracies* (Notre Dame, Ind.: Notre Dame University Press, 1997), 269–90 (attributing disadvantages of the TRC to the underlying political compromise). Actually, South Africa's truth commission legislation does not preclude prosecutions, and several have already been pursued.

29. Herbert Mayes, ed., An Editor's Treasury: A Continuing An-

thology of Prose, Verse, and Literary Curiosa (New York, Atheneum, 1968), 1032.

30. See Tina Rosenberg, "A Reporter at Large: Recovering from Apartheid," *New Yorker*, 18 November 1996, 86, 87.

31. See ibid. Rosenberg discusses the ANC decision prior to the transition of power to provide care for Dirk Coetzee, a white police officer from a counterinsurgency unit, who corroborated the ANC's claims of government-sponsored murder and torture.

32. Suzanne Daley, "Bitter Medicine: Settling for Truth in the Quest for Justice," *New York Times*, 27 October 1996, sec. 4, p. 1., col. 1.

33. The National Unity and Reconciliation Act provided that the commission "shall within a period of 18 months from its constitution or the further period, not exceeding six months, as the President may determine, complete its work." National Unity and Reconciliation Act *supra* note 4, at chapter 7, section 43(1). Work initially was supposed to be completed by July 1997, but Parliament formally extended the life of the commission until April 1998, and the final report is slated to go to the state president by July 31, 1998 (Promotion of National Unity and Reconciliation Second Amendment Bill No. 109, 1997).

34. Du Toit, "Human Rights Program," 36. Julie Mertus argues that survivors need to feel a part of whatever record is created after an atrocity, and forums for the telling of stories by survivors should not take the form of courts, requiring compression and translation into legal language. See Julie Mertus, "Only a War Crimes Tribunal: Triumph of the 'International Community,' Pain of the Survivors" (chapter of a forthcoming book).

35. Pumla Gobodo-Madikizela comments at conference.

36. The Act also permits extension of this year. See chapter 4, para 18(1), *Government Gazette*, 16, an extended period beyond that time announced by the Commission. Amnesty committee members initially were told to expect 200 applicants, but received some 7,000. Antji Krog, *Country of My Skull* (Johannesburg: Random House, 1998), 121.

37. Ash, "True Confessions," 34.

38. Tina Rosenberg, *The Haunted Land: Facing Europe's Ghosts after Communism* (New York: Vintage, 1995), 26.

39. Ibid., 24.

40. Ibid. See also Rosenberg, "Reporter at Large," 86, 95. "The purpose of the Truth Commission's public hearings is to help all South Africans recognize their complicity in apartheid—group therapy for forty-one million people."

41. Charles Maier notes that "I certainly believe that a person's victimhood should be recognized and repaired, but should the victim's status as victim be a constitutive pillar of a new political order? I'm uncertain about that. Maybe the book has to be closed at some point." Harvard Law School and World Peace Foundation, "Human Rights Program," 17.

42. Saul Friedlander, Keynote Address, Yale University Conference, "Searching for Memory and Justice: The Holocaust and Apartheid," 8 February 1998.

43. Harvard Law School and World Peace Foundation, "Human Rights Program," 15 (comments of Lawrence Weschler, quoting W. S. Merwin, "Unchopping a Tree," in *The Miner's Pale Children* [New York: Atheneum, 1970], 85–88).

44. Lawrence Langer, panel on "Hearing the Victims," Yale University Conference, "Searching for Memory and Justice: The Holocaust and Apartheid," 8 February 1998.

45. Ignatieff, "Elusive Goal of War Trials," 16.

46. After watching the South African police harass his family weekly, Donovan "Faried" Ferhelst dropped out of high school at age seventeen to join Umkhonto We Sizwe, the banned military wing of the African National Congress. He was arrested and tortured in prison, and Ferhelst emerged a "war machine," making pipe bombs and seeking revenge. *Hearts and Minds: The Burden of Truth* (SoundPrint Media Center, 1997) (broadcast on National Public Radio). He and his mother later testified before the TRC regarding his torture. His mother described her pain at picking up her son's clothes from prison and discovering bloodstains on them.

47. Tina Rosenberg, *Children of Cain: Violence and the Violent in Latin America* (New York: Penguin Books, 1991), 83–95.

48. For example, Judith Herman, *Trauma and Recovery* (New York: Basic Books, 1992), 72–73.

49. Eric L. Santner, "History Beyond the Pleasure Principle: Some Thoughts on the Representation of Trauma," in Saul Friedlander, ed., *Probing the Limits of Representation: Nazism and the "Final Solution,"* (Cambridge, Mass.: Harvard University Press, 1992), 143, 147–48, 153–54. Santner also applies a psychoanalytic framework to the debate among historians about how to treat or represent the Holocaust. Id., 145, Santner discusses the dynamics of transference implicating the historians in labors of psychic mastery.

50. Ibid., 151.

51. Ibid., 153.

52. Robert Jay Lifton, *The Broken Connection: On Death and the Continuity of Life* (New York: Simon and Schuster, 1979), 176.

53. Herman, *Trauma and Recovery*, 32.

54. Ibid., 84–85. Also see page 121 which provides diagnostic characterization of complex post-traumatic stress disorder.

55. David Becker, Elizabeth Lira, Maria Isabel Castillo, Elana Gomez, and Juana Kovaksys, "Therapy with Victims of Political Oppression in Chile: The Challenge of Social Reparation," in Neil J. Kritz, ed., *Transitional Justice: How Emerging Democracies Reckon with Former Regimes*, vol. 1 (Washington, D.C.: U.S. Institute of Peace Press, 1995), 583, 586. See also Ervin Staub, "Breaking the Cycle of Violence: Helping Victims of Genocidal Violence Heal," *Journal of Personal and Interpersonal Loss* 1 (1996): 191.

56. Herman, *Trauma and Recovery*, 121.

57. Ibid., 2.

58. See ibid., at 137–38, 229–31.

59. Ibid., 92.

60. Ibid., 93.

61. For example, ibid., 157.

62. These themes are powerfully explored in the documentary film by Margaret Lazarus and Renner Wunderlich, *Strong at the Broken Places: Turning Trauma into Recovery*. 60 min., Cambridge Documentary Films, Cambridge, Mass., 1998.

63. Herman, *Trauma and Recovery*, 207–11.

64. Ibid., 9.

65. Becker et al., "Therapy with Victims," 587.

66. Herman, *Trauma and Recovery*, 181.

67. Comments of James Gilligan, Facing History and Ourselves, 12th National Human Rights and Justice Conference, 10 April 1997.

68. See Inger Agger and Soren B. Jensen, "Testimony as Ritual and Evidence in Psychotherapy for Political Refugees," *Journal of Traumatic Stress* 3 (1990): 115.

69. Richard Mollica, "The Trauma Story: The Psychiatric Care of Refugee Survivors of Violence and Torture," in F. Ochberg, ed., *Post-Traumatic Therapy and Victims of Violence* (New York: Brunner/Mazel, 1988), 295, 312.

70. Herman, *Trauma and Recovery*, 182.

71. Becker et al., "Therapy with Victims," 587.

72. Ibid.

73. Herman, *Trauma and Recovery*, 195.

74. Becker et al., "Therapy with Victims," 586–87. Herman reports that a mental health team counseled survivors of a capsized offshore oil rig and gave them each a one-page fact sheet describing post-traumatic stress disorder. The sheet recommended talking with others despite the predictable temptation to withdraw and avoiding the use of alcohol to deal with symptoms. A year after the disaster, many of the men still carried the fact sheets, tattered from rereadings. Herman, *Trauma and Recovery*, 158.

75. Testimony to South African Truth and Reconciliation Commission Human Rights Committee, quoted in Krog, *Country of My Skull*, 31 (testimony of Lucas Baba Sikwepere).

76. Quoted in "Human Rights Program," Harvard Law School and World Peace Foundation, *Truth Commissions: A Comparative Assessment* (1997), 16. For some people, testifying at a criminal trial can afford a similar opportunity. Yet the central rules of examination and cross-examination alter that kind of testimony and potentially interfere with the narrative and the chance for validation.

77. Rosenberg, "Reporter at Large," 92.

78. Buergenthal, "United Nations Truth Commission for El Salvador," 292, 321.

79. Agger and Jensen, "Testimony as Ritual," 115, 124.

80. Ibid.

81. See Herman, *Trauma and Recovery*, 159 (noting that a therapist may need to treat the traumatized patient's search for help as an act of courage and strength rather than weakness and defeat).

82. Comments by André Du Toit, *Truth Commissions: A Comparative Assessment*, 28.

83. Becker et al., "Therapy with Victims," 588.

84. Herman, *Trauma and Recovery*, 177.

85. Ibid., 179.

86. See remarks of Tina Rosenberg, *Truth Commissions: A Comparative Assessment*, 26.

87. For example, Joyce Mtimkhulu brought the TRC a handful of the hair of her then-twenty-one-year-old son, imprisoned, poisoned, and then murdered by security police officers. " 'This is Siphiwe's hair. I want the commission to witness what I've brought here today so that they should know the effects of the poison that was used on my son. I thought I would make burial of my son through his hair, but by God's

will I didn't, as if I knew I would be here today.' " Quoted in Mark Gevisser, "The Witnesses," *New York Times Magazine*, 27 June 1997, 32, 34.

88. See Herman, *Trauma and Recovery*, 178–80.

89. Becker et al., "Therapy with Victims," 586.

90. Ibid., 587.

91. Ibid.

92. Staub, "Breaking the Cycle of Violence," 193–94.

93. Herman, *Trauma and Recovery*, 135.

94. Ibid. (Describing Yael Danieli's work with Holocaust survivors.)

95. Justice Pius Langa, "Hearing the Victims," Yale University Conference, "Searching for Memory and Justice: The Holocaust and Apartheid," 8 February 1998.

96. See ibid.

97. Du Toit, *Truth Commissions*, 28; Justice Pius Langa, comments, Yale University Conference.

98. Commissioner Dumisa Ntsebeza of the TRC recounted how the widow of Mapetla Mohapi, a man found hanged with a suicide note in an apartheid jail cell in 1977, had demanded an inquest, which yielded inconclusive results. She then sued the government, with no success, at enormous cost to herself. In 1996 she testified before the TRC and afterward reported that for the first time, there, she felt she was treated with belief rather than hostility. She concluded that she no longer needed to know the details about what happened to her husband. If the TRC's investigative unit found out the information, that would be a bonus on top of the benefit she had already received. Dumisa Ntsebeza, "Healing the Victims: Possibilities and Impossibilities," at Yale University Conference, "Searching for Memory and Justice: The Holocaust and Apartheid," 9 February 1998.

99. A written account appears in Gevisser, "The Witnesses," 32, 34.

100. Comments at Yale University Conference.

101. Herman, *Trauma and Recovery*, 114 (discussing therapists with Holocaust survivors, Indochinese refugees, and other victims of violence).

102. Ibid.

103. Ibid., 144–45. (Describing this as one aspect of countertransference.)

104. Ibid.

105. Ibid., 153–54.

106. Becker et al., "Therapy with Victims," 589.

107. See Gevisser, "The Witnesses," 38. De Klerk's view that the commission is biased toward the liberation movement is "emblematic of most white South Africans, who have been shocked by the evidence ("We never knew!") but have neither taken responsibility nor displayed remorse for the acts committed in their name."

108. Editorial, "The Truth About Steve Biko," *New York Times*, 4 February 1997, sec. A, p. 22, col. 1.

109. This appears on the TRC home page, www.truth.org.za (visited on March 19, 1998).

110. Paul Harris, "Tutu Asks Whites to Support Work of His Reconciliation Panel," *Boston Globe*, Feb. 19, 1998, sec. A, p. 8, col. 3.

111. Sachs, Yale University Conference.

112. Rosenberg, "Reporter at Large," 95 (quoting Brandom Hamber).

113. Buergenthal, "United Nations Truth Commission for El Salvador," 321.

114. Ibid.

115. Staub, "Breaking the Cycle of Violence," 193.

116. Gevisser, "The Witnesses," 32.

117. Ibid.

118. Daley, "Bitter Medicine," sec. 4, p. 1, col. 1.

119. Ibid.

120. Gevisser, "The Witnesses," 38.

121. Dr. Abdullah M. Omar, The South African Truth and Reconciliation Commission (written remarks of the justice minister, presented to the Facing History and Ourselves, 12th Annual Human Rights and Justice Conference, Harvard University, 10 April 1997), 22–23.

122. Ntsebeza, Yale University Conference.

123. To an American audience, Archbishop Desmond Tutu explained, "To get justice, we must strive to undo the top dog/underdog reversals that make human horror endure." Archbishop Tutu, by Colin Greer, *Parade Magazine*, 11 January 1998, 6.

124. See comments of José Zalaquett, *Truth Commissions*, 29–31.

125. See generally Ervin Staub, *The Roots of Evil: The Origins of Genocide and Other Group Violence* (Cambridge: Cambridge University Press, 1989). See also particular commission reports, reprinted in Kritz, *Transitional Justice*.

126. *Truth Commissions: A Comparative Assessment*, 24 (comments of Father Hehir).

127. See also Buergenthal, "United Nations Truth Commission for El Salvador," 325: "A nation has to confront its past by acknowledging the wrongs that have been committed in its name before it can successfully embark on the arduous task of cementing the trust between former adversaries and their respective sympathizers, which is a prerequisite for national reconciliation. One cannot hope to achieve this objective by sweeping the truth under the rug of national consciousness, by telling the victims or their next of kin that nothing happened, or by asking them not to tell their particular story. The wounds begin to heal with the telling of the story and the national acknowledgment of its authenticity.

How that story is told is less important than that it be told truthfully. Hence, whether the names of the perpetrators are revealed, whether trials are held, sanctions imposed, compensation awarded, or amnesties granted, these are all considerations that may well depend upon the nature of the conflict, the national character of the country, the political realities, and compromises that produced the end of the conflict. But if the basic truth about the past is suppressed, it will prove very difficult to achieve national reconciliation."

128. Deputy President Thabo Mbeki testified as part of the ANC's amnesty application: "We should avoid the danger whereby concentrating on these particular and exceptional acts of the liberation movement, which could be deemed as constituting gross human rights violations, we convey the impression that the struggle for liberation was itself a gross violation of human rights." Quoted in Krog, *Country of My Skull*, 124.

129. See Gevisser, "The Witnesses," 38. One remarkable individual, Father Michael Lapsley, lost both hands and an eye, and suffered enormous pain after opening a letter bomb while relocated by the ANC to Zimbabwe. He explained to the TRC: "I do not see myself as a victim, but as a survivor of Apartheid . . . this is part of my triumph of returning to South Africa and living my life as meaningfully and joyfully as possible . . . I am not captured by hatred, because then they would not only have destroyed my body, but also my soul . . . Ironically, even without hands and an eye, I am much more free than the person who did this to me . . . I say to everyone who supported Apartheid, your freedom is waiting for you . . . but you will have to go through the whole process." Quoted in Krog, *Country of My Skull*, 133.

130. Gevisser, "The Witnesses," 38.

131. Du Toit, quoted in *Truth Commissions*, 28.

132. Comments of Dennis Thompson, in *Truth Commissions*, 37–38.

133. Yael Tamir, in *Truth Commissions*, 34. She continues: "Again, the Israeli nation has experienced both the trauma of surviving the Holocaust and the trauma of acknowledging its capability of heaping suffering upon others."

134. Rosenberg, "Reporter at Large," 88.

135. Ibid. Samantha Power, "The Stages of Justice," review of *Mass Atrocity, Collective Memory, and the Law,* by Mark Osiel, *New Republic,* 2 March 1998, 32, 34, describes the inadequacy of TRC treatment of Steven Biko's interrogators who offered one of many circulating accounts of his death in application for amnesty. "[A]ll that the widow takes away from the proceeding is the image of her husband dying of a brain hemorrhage, chained to a bedpost and frothing at the mouth."

136. Rosenberg, "Reporter at Large," 90. Tutu apparently also referred to *ubuntu*, a traditional African notion of interconnection and as Rosenberg explains it, "the idea that no one can be healthy when the community is sick." Id. Critical observers suggest that this notion of *ubuntu* may be as much a current invention as a recovery of past practices. Richard A. Wilson, "The Sizwe Will Not Go Away: The Truth and Reconciliation Commission, Human Rights and Nation-Building in South Africa," *African Studies* 55, no. 2 (1996): 1, 11–13. In any case, Archbishop Tutu is explicit in rooting his conception of restorative justice in Christianity. Id.

137. Omar, written remarks, 23: "To the majority of victims, . . . the knowledge and full disclosure of what happened to their loved ones has been extremely relieving and satisfying. Indeed, we have had occasions where victims have embraced perpetrators and clearly indicated a commitment to work for reconciliation."

138. Quoted in Krog, *Country of My Skull*, 109.

139. During a panel discussion on the subject of reconciliation at the University of Cape Town, organized by the TRC and the Department of African Studies, Father Mxolisi Mpambani told this story that has become a touchstone in conversations about the interdependence between reconciliation and economic transformation in South Africa: "Once, there were two boys. Tom and Bernard. Tom lived right opposite Bernard. One day Tom stole Bernard's bicycle and every day Bernard saw Tom cycling to school on it. After a year, Tom went up to Bernard, stretched out his hand and said, 'Let us reconcile and put the

past behind us.' Bernard looked at Tom's hand. 'And what about the bicycle?' 'No,' said Tom, 'I'm not talking about the bicycle—I'm talking about reconciliation.' " Quoted in Krog, *Country of My Skull*, 109.

140. The TRC, unlike most previous commissions, has subpoena power. Nonetheless, local police departments often respond to requests by saying the materials do not exist, or were housed in a building that was destroyed. The TRC did use its subpoena power to trigger a contempt hearing after former President P. W. Botha refused to appear before the commission. Suzanne Daley, "South African Trial Hears the Questions Botha Won't Answer," *New York Times*, 2 June 1998, sec. A, p. 3, col. 1. See also Buergenthal, "The United Nations Truth Commission for El Salvador," 292.

141. Gevisser, "The Witnesses," 38; Suzanne Daley, "Divisions Deepen on Apartheid Crimes Inquiry," *New York Times*, 8 June 1997, p. 6, col. 1.

142. It will take some time to sort out the effects of Winnie Mandela's appearances at the TRC. In the short term, in refusing to give a full account of her conduct she lost the public support necessary to secure elected office.

143. Buergenthal, "United Nations Truth Commission for El Salvador," 301. He recounts that walls of silence began to crumble after a commission issued a report relevant to the dismissal, demotion, or retention of military officers, based on their human rights records, professional competence, and capacities to function in a democratic society. Id., 302–3.

144. For example, Du Toit, in *Truth Commissions*, 28.

145. Bronwen Manby, "South Africa Violence Against Women and the Medico-Legal System," *Human Rights Watch* (August 1997): 9.

146. Dr. Wendy Orr, "Trauma and Catharsis, The Psychology of Testimony" (prepared for World Peace Foundation South African Truth and Reconciliation Commission Meeting, 28–30 May 1998), 5 (discussing testimony of Mrs. Yvonne Khutwane).

147. This is Tina Rosenberg's speculation. Comments in *Truth Commissions*, 28–29. Also she suggests that those seeking answers about what happened to their loved ones are more likely to come forward than those who were direct victims and know what happened to themselves. Id., 29. Antji Krog notes that very few women have testified about rape before the TRC in South Africa, and yet, "[a]pparently high-profile women, among them Cabinet ministers, parliamentarians and businesswomen, were raped ansd sexually abused under the previous

dispensation—and not only by the regime, but by their own comrades in the townships and liberation camps. But no one will utter an audible word about it." Krog, *Country of My Skull*, 182. Cultural traditions, political ambiguity, and desires not to be identified publicly with this humiliation could explain the silence.

148. Robert Lowell, epilogue to *Day by Day by Robert Lowell* (New York: Farrar, Straus & Giroux: 1977).

149. Quoted in *Truth Commissions*, 17 ("They should concentrate largely on facts, which may be proved, whereas differences about historical interpretation will always exist.") Zalaquett further distinguishes efforts to reveal the truth of secret crimes and efforts to interpret the political processes leading up to such crimes. Id. See also id., 21 (a commission should also "analyze evidence and present facts in a coherent framework while avoiding the most contentious aspects of historical interpretation, and arrive at substantiated conclusions").

150. Ibid., 23 (Dennis Thompson).

151. Quoted in Glenn Frankel, "For Apartheid's Victims, a Denial of Justice?" *Washington Post*, Weekly Ed., 25 September–1 October 1995, p. 18, col. 1.

152. Natalie Zeman Davis, *The Return of Martin Guerre* (Cambridge, Mass.: Harvard University Press, 1983); Natalie Zeman Davis, *Fiction in the Archives: Pardon Tales and Their Tellers in Sixteenth-Century France* (Stanford, Calif.: Stanford University Press, 1987).

153. See Hannah Arendt, "Truth and Politics," in *Between Past and Future: Eight Exercises in Political Thought* (New York: Penguin Books, 1977), 227, (perplexities inherent in historical sciences "are no argument against the existence of factual matter, nor can they serve as a justification for blurring the dividing lines between fact, opinion, and interpretation").

154. Buergenthal, "United Nations Truth Commission for El Salvador," 306–7.

155. Ibid. Quoted on page 308.

156. For example, Stanley Cohen, "State Crimes of Previous Regimes: Knowledge, Accountability, and the Policing of the Past," *Law and Social Inquiry* 20 (1995): 7.

157. Ibid.

158. Ibid. (attributing the point to José Zalaquett). See Kate Millett, *The Politics of Cruelty: An Essay on the Literature of Political Imprisonment* (New York: W. W. Norton, 1994).

159. Diane F. Orentlicher, "Settling Accounts: The Duty to Prose-

cute Human Rights Violations of a Prior Regime," *Yale Law Journal* 100 (1991): 2539.

160. See Suzanne Daley, "Apartheid-Era Defense Chief Defends Role in Ordering Raids on Neighboring Countries," *New York Times*, 8 May 1997, p. 16, col. 1. Malan said: "I come here to tell you my story and to face your judgment . . . I shall be content if what I am saying may spur the slightest understanding of former adversaries. I shall rejoice if my efforts can contribute in the minutest sense toward reconciliation and if all soldiers may obtain moral amnesty . . . It is understanding and forgiveness we really seek, not legal pardons." Id.

5. Reparations

First epigraph: Nicholas Tavuchis, *Mea Culpa: A Sociology of Apology and Reconciliation* (Stanford, Calif.: Stanford University Press, 1991), 7. Second epigraph: Joseph W. Singer, "Reparation," in *Entitlement: The Paradoxes of Property* (draft, 26 May 1998), 252.

1. Howard Zehr, *Changing Lenses: A New Focus for Crime and Justice* (Scottsdale, Pa.: Herald Press, 1990), 211–14.

2. Many advocates of mediation emphasize dimensions of restorative justice; critics suggest that mediation assumes the presence of a community of interest that may not exist. See, for example, John Paul Lederach and Ron Kraybill, "The Paradox of Popular Justice: A Practitioner's View," in Sally Engle Merry and Neal Milner, eds., *The Possibilities of Popular Justice: A Case Study of Community Mediation in the United States* (Ann Arbor, Mich.: University of Michigan, 1993), 357, 376.

3. See, for example, Baba Kamma 94b. For an English translation, see E. W. Kirzner, trans., Baba Kamma 94b, 547–50, in the series *The Babylonian Talmud: Seder Nezikin*, trans. Rabbi Dr. I. Epstein (London: Soncino Press, 1935).

4. See Jim Consedine, *Restorative Justice: Healing the Effects of Crime* (Lyttelton, New Zealand: Ploughshares Publications, 1993).

5. John O. Haley, "Confession, Repentance and Absolution," in Martin Wright and Burt Galaway, eds., *Mediation and Criminal Justice* (London: Sage Publications, 1989).

6. See chapter 4, n. 136 for a discussion of *ubuntu*.

7. See generally David B. Wexler and Bruce J. Winick, *Law in a Therapeutic Key: Developments in Therapeutic Jurisprudence* (Durham, N.C.: Carolina Academic Press, 1996).

8. See, for example, Consedine, *Restorative Justice*; Burt Galaway and Joe Hudson, eds., *Criminal Justice, Restitution, and Reconciliation* (Monsey, N.Y.: Criminal Justice Press, 1990); Zehr, *Changing Lenses*.

9. See Consedine, *Restorative Justice*, 157–58. See also Albert English, "Beyond Restitution," in Joe Hudson and Burt Galaway, eds., *Restitution in Criminal Justice* (Lexington, Mass.: Lexington Books, 1977), 91; Daniel W. Van Ness, "New Wine in Old Wineskins: Four Challenges to Restorative Justice," *Criminal Law Forum* 4 (1993): 251.

10. See Mark S. Umbreit, "Holding Juvenile Offenders Accountable: A Restorative Justice Perspective," *Family Court Journal* 46 (1995): 31.

11. Archbishop Desmond Mpilo Tutu, foreword, H. Russell Botman and Robin M. Petersen, eds., *To Remember and To Heal: Theological and Psychological Reflections on Truth and Reconciliation* (Cape Town: Human & Rousseau, 1996).

12. Truth and Reconciliation Commission, "Truth Commission Announces Reparation Plan," *African News*, 24 October 1997.

13. David Margolick, "Legal Legend Urges Victims to Speak Out," *New York Times*, 24 November 1984, p. 25, col. 5.

14. Ibid.

15. American-Japanese Evacuation Claims Act of 1948, 50 U.S.C. 1981–1987 (1994) (providing for compensation for specified property losses). Similarly, the United States Indian Claims Commission, established in 1946, heard claims concerning abrogation of tribal or other Indian property occurring prior to 1940. See Robert N. Clinton, Nell Jessup Newton, and Monroe E. Price, *American Indian Law*, 3d ed. (Charlottesville, Va.: Michie, 1991), 721–24.

16. For an extended treatment of the relocation and internment, and their links to the treatment of Native Americans in the United States, see Richard Drinnon, *Keeper of Concentration Camps: Dillon S. Myer and American Racism* (Berkeley, Calif.: University of California Press, 1987). See also Yasuko I. Takezawa, *Breaking the Silence: Redress and Japanese American Ethnicity* (Ithaca, N.Y.: Cornell University Press, 1995); Jeanne Wakatsuki Houston, *Farewell to Manzanar* (New York: Bantam Books, 1974); Jacobus tenBroek, Jacob N. Barnhard, and Floyd W. Matson, *Prejudice, War and the Constitution: Causes and Consequences of the Evacuation of the Japanese Americans in World War II* (Berkeley, Calif.: University of California Press, 1954).

17. Korematsu apparently had not intended to create a test case; he wanted to stay with his girlfriend, who was Italian-American. Margolick, "Legal Legend Urges Victims to Speak Out." His wife described his

motivations as reflecting his nonconformity, even in having a Caucasian girlfriend. Caitlin Rother, "Rebel with a Medal Talks to UCSD Students," *San Diego Union-Tribune*, 5 February 1998, sec. B, p. 8. See also Peter Irons, *Justice at War* (New York: Oxford University Press, 1983), 93–99. Korematsu had undergone plastic surgery; he explained he had done so in order to avoid ostracism when he and his Italian girlfriend traveled to the Middle West. Id., 95. Often portrayed as motivated solely by personal, romantic concerns rather than political resistance, by the time he met with a lawyer in jail, Korematsu showed a willingness to participate in a test case challenging the constitutionality of the evacuation program and statute. Id., 97–98. Proceeding with the resistance and the case certainly required remarkable courage and personal conviction.

18. A novel depicts how white Americans could view this as natural and necessary. See Ella Lefland, *Rumors of Peace* (New York: Harper & Row, 1979).

19. Rother, "Rebel with a Medal," sec. B, p. 8.

20. 323 U.S. 214 (1944).

21. Ex parte Endo, 323 U.S. 283 (1944).

22. See Takezawa, *Breaking the Silence*, 54 (quoting reading used at 1986 Seattle Day of Remembrance: "We could not find the voice within ourselves to tell others, often even our own children, about what happened to us personally. And so we the victims exiled ourselves to a silence that lasted forty years.").

23. Donald Nakahata, in John Tateishi, ed., *And Justice for All: An Oral History of the Japanese American Detention Camps* (New York: Random House, 1984), 32, 37 (hereinafter cited as *And Justice for All*). See also Paul Shinoda, in *And Justice for All*, 51, 58: "I lost about five years—I just lost them. If I'd gone into the Army, I'd have lost about the same, though. The sad part of it is, there's no glory in being evacuated, you can't say I'm an evacuee—veteran of the evacuation"; and Garrett Hongo, "HR:442: Redress," in Susan Richards Shreve and Porter Shreve, eds., *Outside the Law* (Boston: Beacon Press, 1997), 82. "Japanese Americans themselves had to overcome their own powerful feelings of shame and fear that had remained from those times."

24. Another strategy unsuccessfully sought 27.5 billion dollars through a lawsuit for redress. See William Minoru Hohri, *Repairing America: An Account of the Movement for Japanese-American Redress* (Pullman, Wash.: Washington State University Press, 1988); *William Hohri et al. v. United States*, 586 F. Supp. 769 (D.D.C. 1984), aff'd in

part, rev'd in part, 782 F. 2d 227 (D.C. Cir. 1986), vacated, 482 U.S. 64 (1987).

25. See Irons, *Justice at War.*

26. See Kenneth Karst, review of *Justice at War,* by Peter Irons, *Texas Law Review* 72 (1984): 1147, 1150–51.

27. John Tateishi, introduction, to *And Justice for All,* xx.

28. *Korematsu v. United States,* 584 F. Supp. 1406 (N.D. Cal. 1984). A few years later, another court granted a writ of *coram nobis* in *United States v. Hirabayashi,* a similar 1942 Supreme Court decision. *Hirabayashi v. United States,* 627 F. Supp. 1445 (W.D. Wash. 1986).

29. 584 F. Supp. 1406, 1413.

30. 584 F. Supp. 1406, 1420.

31. Margolick, "Legal Legend Urges Victims to Speak Out," 25.

32. See Hongo, "HR:442: Redress," 82.

33. Ibid., 82. The Japanese American Citizens' League also fought successfully for repeal of the Cold War–era Emergency Detention Act that authorized the president to detain persons involved in espionage or sabotage during war or domestic insurrection. Takezawa, *Breaking the Silence,* 34.

34. Quoted in Hongo, "HR:442: Redress," 87–88.

35. Quoted in Hongo, "HR:442: Redress," 89.

36. Quoted in Hongo, "HR:442: Redress," 91.

37. 38 U.S.C. section 4214 (1988). The Act was upheld in the face of legal challenge. *Jacobs v. Barr,* 959 F. 2d 313 (D.C. Cir. 1992).

38. Jeremy Waldron, "Superseding Historic Injustice," *Ethics* 103 (October 1992): 2, 607.

39. Rother, "Rebel with a Medal," sec. B, p. 8.

40. Ibid.

41. Alex M. Johnson, Jr., Symposium on Race Consciousness and Legal Scholarship, "Defending the Use of Quotas in Affirmative Action: Attacking Racism in the Nineties," *University of Illinois Law Review* 1992 (1992): 1043, 1073; Mari Matsuda, "Looking to the Bottom: Critical Legal Studies and Reparations," *Harvard Civil Rights–Civil Liberties Law Review* 22 (1987): 323; Vincene Verdun, "If the Shoe Fits, Wear It: An Analysis of Reparations to African Americans," *Tulane Law Review* 67 (1993): 597; and Rhonda V. Magee, "The Master's Tools, from the Bottom Up: Responses to African-American Reparations Theory in Mainstream and Outsider Remedies Discourse," *Virginia Law Review* 79 (1993): 863. See also Boris L. Bitker, *The Case for Black Reparations* (New York: Random House, 1973). This is an ear-

lier extensive legal treatment of the reparations claim for African-Americans.

42. Commission to Study Reparation Proposals for African Americans Act, H.R. 1684, 102d Cong., 1st Sess. (1991).

43. See Reggie Oh and Frank Wu, "The Evolution of Race in the Law: The Supreme Court Moves from Approving Internment of Japanese Americans to Disapproving Affirmative Action for African-Americans," *Michigan Journal of Race Law* 1 (1996): 165.

44. See Jennifer M. L. Chock, "One Hundred Years of Illegitimacy: International Legal Analysis of the Illegal Overthrow of the Hawaiian Monarchy, Hawaii's Annexation, and Possible Reparations," *Hawaii Law Review* 17 (1995): 473.

45. See Eric K. Yamamoto, "Rethinking Alliances: Agency, Responsibility and Interracial Justice," *UCLA Asian Pacific American Law Journal* 3 (1995): 33, 39, 71–74 (describing Motion 5 at the 171st annual meeting of the Hawai'i Conference of the United Church of Christ).

46. See ibid.

47. Ibid., 73.

48. Ibid., 74.

49. Ibid.

50. Zehr, *Changing Lenses*, 26.

51. Ibid.

52. Ibid.

53. Helena Silverstein, e-mail to author, 6 June 1997.

54. See, for example, Richard F. America, ed. *African Development and Reparations: Redistributive Justice and the Restitution Principle* (forthcoming).

55. West Germany's initial offer of reparations to Israel triggered domestic opposition, but did establish a framework for acknowledging crimes of racial, religious, and political persecution committed in the name of the German people. See Robert G. Moeller, "War Stories: The Search for a Usable Past in the Federal Republic of Germany," *American Historical Review* (October 1996): 1008, 1016–18.

56. An important and difficult legal and moral issue arises when a government claims that individual claims for reparation can be disposed by treaties or accords between nations. Japan so claimed pointing to its postwar accords with the home countries of "comfort women." In the absence of a fair process representing such claimants, this kind of nation-to-nation resolution seems painfully inadequate.

57. Seth Mydans, "WWII Victim Accepts Japanese Reparation," *Dallas Morning News*, 13 December 1996, sec. A, p. 61.

58. Ibid.

59. Ibid.

60. Ibid. In contrast, one letter writer argued that reparations would be more important than apologies. C. Suzkuki, "Concentrate on Reparations," *South Morning Post*, 13 September 1995.

61. Sonni Efron, "Justice Delayed 50 Years," *Los Angeles Times*, 13 December 1996, sec. A, p. 1, col. 1.

62. Ibid. (quoting Kim Yoon Sim).

63. Ibid.

64. Remarks of Dr. Pumla Gobodo-Madikizela, Human Rights Violation Committee member, at the 12th Annual Human Rights and Justice Conference, sponsored by Facing History and Ourselves and the Harvard Law School Graduate Program, 10 April 1997.

65. See text at note 12 (noting the TRC chief reparations principle to promote the abilities of individuals and communities to take control of their own lives). Finding a way to rebuild a society deformed by apartheid seems to defy simple notions of compensation. A lawyer for the Mfengu clan, who were forcibly removed by the regime from their land in 1977 and sent to untillable homelands, recently asked: "How do you compensate for some 18 million honest people who went to town to search for work in attempts to escape poverty and destitution in the homelands, and were imprisoned because of pass law offenses . . . How do you compensate for the results of Bantu education, a system designed to make African children inferior so that they are only trained to minister to the needs of the white man? How do you compensate for the regional destabilization war, the land mines? How do you compensate for 3.5 million people who were forcibly removed and had their lives destroyed?" Quoted in Dele Olojede, "Building a Better South Africa: Far to Go on Its Long Road," *Newsday*, 1 June 1997, sec. A, p. 4.

66. See, for example, Ellen C. Dubois, Mary C. Dunlap, Carol J. Gilligan, Catharine A. MacKinnon, and Carrie J. Menkel-Meadow, "Feminist Discourse, Moral Values, and Law—A Conversation," *Buffalo Law Review* 34 (1985): 11, 74–75. Catharine MacKinnon called for a change in the power structure that would allow a woman to define power in ways that she cannot currently articulate, "because his foot is on her throat." Carol Gilligan argued that women articulate values of care and connection that have value independent of women's social and

political status. MacKinnon responded that it is "infuriating" to call
those values women's "because we have never had the power to develop
what ours really would be."

67. Message from Archbishop Desmond Tutu, 31 March 1998,
TRC Web site, www.truth.org.za.

68. See Nicholas Balabkins, *West German Reparations to Israel*
(New Brunswick, N.J.: Rutgers University Press, 1971).

69. See also Paul Brodeur, *Restitution: The Land Claims of the
Mashpee, Passamaquoddy, and Penobscot Indians of New England*
(Boston: Northeastern University Press, 1985); Anthony DePalma,
"Canadian Court Ruling Broadens Indian Land Claims," *New York
Times*, 12 December 1997, sec. A, p. 3, col. 1 (based on oral evidence of
traditional ceremonies and oral histories, Canadian Supreme Court
rules that native peoples have broad claims to land they once occupied
and natural resources and therefore deserve compensation or rights to
resources).

70. Waldron, "Superseding Historic Injustice," 9.

71. Ibid., 11.

72. Ibid., 13.

73. Ironically, some of the very claimants for restitution have thrived
and no longer place the use of the lost property at the center of their
lives. Id., 18–19. "I may of course yearn for the lost resource and spend
a lot of time wishing that I had it back. I may even organize my life
around the campaign for its restoration. But that is not the same thing
as the basis for the original claim. The original entitlement is based on
the idea that I have organized my life around the use of this object." Id.,
19. Here Waldron is directly addressing theories of property entitlement based on autonomy and showing their insufficiency in establishing violable rights. A separate line of critique of Waldron's own
approach would question any link between entitlement claims and failures of resilience. In his analysis, those who had failed to move onto
new ways of life arguably would have more viable claims to the misappropriated resource. Those who are more adaptable would have lesser
claims. This seems to create perverse incentives as well as relying on a
needs-based rather than a fairness-based view of justice, contrary to
Waldron's general approach.

74. Singer, "Reparations," 248.

75. Waldron, "Superseding Historic Injustice," 19.

76. See The Native American Graves Protection and Repatriation
Act, 25 U.S.C.A. sections 3001–3013, 18 U.S.C.A. section 1170 (1990)

(American Indian and Native Hawaiian human remains and burial objects found on tribal or federal lands belong to the legal descendants or else to the relevant tribe); and Jane Perlez, "Austria Is Set to Return Artworks That Nazis Plundered from Jews," *New York Times*, 7 March 1998, sec. A, p. 1, col. 1. Perlez quotes the director of an Austrian museum on the promised return of artworks to the Rothschild family: "We are open to the restitution of everything given to the museum in an immoral trade. This should have been done 30 or 40 years ago. We have to fulfill a specific moral debt." Id., sec. A, p. 27, col. 2.

77. See Perlez, "Austria Is Set to Return Artworks," sec. A, p. 27 (reporting that Baroness Bettina der Rothschild reports bitter feelings but also a sense of noblesse oblige that may prompt the family to agree to some loans).

78. Tony Hillerman, *Talking God* (New York: Harper & Row, 1989), 1–6.

79. Singer, "Reparations."

80. Ibid.

81. "U.S. and Allied Efforts to Recover and Restore Gold and Other Assets Stolen or Hidden by Germany During World War II: Preliminary Study" (coordinated by Stuart E. Eizenstat, prepared by William Slaney, n.p., May 1997), v.

82. Ibid., x.

83. Tavuchis, *Mea Culpa* (citing Reagan).

84. Ibid., 108.

85. See Editorial, "Apology Now; Vigilance, Too," *Plain Dealer*, 26 May 1997, sec. B, p. 8.

86. Editorial, "The Tuskegee Apology," *St. Louis Post-Dispatch*, 21 May 1997, sec. C, p. 6; Joan Beck, "Apology Can't Erase Tuskegee Horror," *St. Louis Post-Dispatch*, 30 May 1997, sec. B, p. 7. The president's apology occurred after a widely acclaimed television documentary on the subject entitled *Miss Evers' Boys*. See John Carman, "The Emmy Nominees Are—What, You Again?" *San Francisco Chronicle*, 12 September 1997, sec. C, p. 1.

87. Compare DeWayne Wickham, "Why Clinton Must Stop Dodging Slavery Apology," *USA Today*, 16 December 1997, sec. A, p. 15, with Bill Nichols, "Should the Nation Apologize? Critics Argue Substance is Need, Not Symbolism," *USA Today*, 18 June 1997, sec. A, p. 1.

88. "A World Apart," *Sydney Morning Herald*, 10 March 1998, 13.

89. See Nichols, "Should the Nation Apologize?" sec. A, p. 1.

90. Vatican's Statement on Holocaust 1998, reported in "New Catholic Line on the Holocaust," *Jerusalem Post*, 17 March 1998, 3; "The Vatican and the Holocaust: the Overview; Vatican Repents Failure to Save Jews from Nazis," *New York Times*, 17 March 1998, sec. A, p. 1, col. 6; "Act of Repentance: Vatican Issues Statement on the Holocaust," *Newsday*, 17 March 1998, sec. A, p. 7.

91. Alexander Chancellor, foreword to "Pride and Prejudice: Easier Said Than Done," *The Guardian*, London, 17 January 1998, 8.

92. Ibid.

93. Tavuchis, *Mea Culpa*, 5

94. Some harms, though, can only be repaired by an apology, such as "defamation, insult, degradation, loss of status, and the emotional distress and dislocation that accompany conflict." Hiroshi Wagatsuma and Arthur Rosett, "The Implication of Apology: Law and Culture in Japan and the United States," *Law and Society Review* 20 (1986): 461, 487–88.

95. Tavuchis, *Mea Culpa*, 115.

96. Ibid., 121.

97. Ibid., 8.

98. Ibid., 17.

99. Ibid., 55.

100. Ibid., 20.

101. Ibid., 49.

102. Ibid., 104.

103. Chancellor, "Pride and Prejudice," 8.

104. Tavuchis, *Mea Culpa*, 40.

105. See Hannah Arendt, *The Human Condition* (Chicago: University of Chicago Press, 1958), 241: "In contrast to revenge, which is the natural, automatic reaction to transgression and which because of the irreversibility of the action process can be expected and even calculated, the act of forgiving can never be predicted; it is the only reaction that acts in an unexpected way and thus retains, though being a reaction, something of the original character of action. Forgiving, in other words, is the only reaction which does not merely re-act but acts anew and unexpectedly, unconditioned by the act which provoked it and therefore freeing from its consequences both the one who forgives and the one who is forgiven."

106. Paul L. Montgomery, "Albert Speer, 76, Architect of Hitler's Nazism Is Dead," *International Herald Tribune*, 13 September 1981, 13.

6. Facing History

First epigraph: Binjamin Wilkomirski, *Fragments: Memories of a Wartime Childhood*, trans. Carol Brown Janeway (New York: Schocken Books, 1996), 94. Second epigraph: Nikki Nojima Louis, "Breaking the Silence," reprinted in Yasuko I. Takezawa, *Breaking the Silence: Redress and Japanese American Ethnicity* (Ithaca, N.Y.: Cornell University Press, 1995), viii.

1. Michael S. Roth, "Remembering Forgetting: Maladies de la Memoire in Nineteenth-Century France," *Representations* 26 (spring 1989): 49–86.

2. Charles Maier, "A Surfeit of Memory? Reflections on History, Melancholy and Denial," History and Memory 5, no. 2 (fall/winter 1993): 136. He continues: "The surfeit of memory is a sign not of historical confidence but a retreat from transformative politics."

3. See Timothy Garton Ash, "The Truth about Dictatorship," *New York Review of Books*, 19 February 1998, 36.

4. James E. Young, *The Texture of Memory: Holocaust Memorials and Meaning* (New Haven, Conn.: Yale University Press, 1993), 1 (quoting Baudrillard).

5. Tina Rosenberg, *The Haunted Land: Facing Europe's Ghosts after Communism* (New York: Vintage, 1995), xviii. She offers similar comments in a review of a recent book on Argentina. Rosenberg, "The Land of the Disappeared," *New York Times*, Sunday, 26 April 1998, sec. 7, p. 19, col. 1.

6. Milan Kundera, *The Book of Laughter and Forgetting* (New York: Knopf, 1980), pt. i, sec. ii.

7. Ash, "Truth about Dictatorship," 36. For an insightful discussion of the complex relationships between politics and memory, history, and tradition, see Aviam Soifer, *Law and the Company We Keep* (Cambridge, Mass.: Harvard University Press, 1995): 104–11.

8. Henry J. Steiner, introduction, in Harvard Law School Harvard Human Rights Program and World Peace Foundation, *Truth Commissions: A Comparative Assessment* (Cambridge, Mass.: Harvard Law School Human Rights Program, 1991), 7 (quoting Gladstone).

9. Comments at Harvard Law School Human Rights Program, "Remembering and Forgetting Gross Human Rights Violations," 5 April 1997.

10. Comments at Collective Violence and Memory: Judgment, Reconciliation, Education, Facing History and Ourselves, 12th Annual

Human Rights and Justice Conference, 10 April 1997, Cambridge,
Massachusetts.

11. Ariel Dorfman, afterword to *Death and the Maiden* (New York: Penguin Books, 1992).

12. Faith McNulty, *The Elephant Who Couldn't Forget* (New York: Harper and Row, 1980). See page 58, wise grandmother teaches that "Sometimes, in order to remember something important you have to forget something that isn't important."

13. See Mona S. Weissmark, Daniel A. Giacomo, and Ilona Kuphal, "Psychosocial Themes in the Lives of Children of Survivors and Nazis," *Journal of Narrative and Life History* 3 (1983): 319; see also Daniel Bar-On, *Legacy of Silence: Encounters with Children of the Third Reich* (Cambridge, Mass.: Harvard University Press, 1989).

14. Comments of Walter Robinson, Facing History and Ourselves conference planning session, January 1997.

15. Rosenberg, introduction to *Haunted Land*.

16. This is the formulation offered by psychiatrist and law professor Alan Stone. Stone also objects to common talk of memory and forgetting surrounding human rights violations especially when the notion of repression surfaces to refer to forgetting. He explains it is not really repression in the sense of keeping trauma out of the consciousness. Instead, the failure to remember stems from disassociation; the memory is there but not accessible; it is split off from the self, not underneath awareness but separate. Alan Stone, panel, Harvard Law School Human Rights Program, 5 April 1997.

17. "The memory of a past event is not even stored in one location in the brain. Rather, the sights, sounds, smells, thoughts and emotions of a memory are each stored in different sites. Retrieving a memory is the process of tying these fragments back together, which [Daniel] Schacter analogizes to assembling a jigsaw puzzle. The process is subject to influences present at the time the memory is retrieved, such as one's mood or the setting. Schacter argues that memory is therefore 'not a literal replaying of the present but a dynamic interaction between past and present.'" Joseph Glenmuller, "Memory Lanes," review of *Searching for Memory*, by Daniel Schacter, *Boston Globe*, 23 June 1996, sec. B, pp. 35, 38.

18. Andrea Barnes, reflection paper, 29 January 1998 (unpublished seminar paper, Boston College Law School).

19. Klause Mäkelä, Ilkka Arminen, Kim Bloomfield, Irmgard Eisenbach-Stangl, Karin Helmersson Bergmark, Noriko Kurube, Nico-

letta Mariolini, Hildigunnur Ólafsdóttir, John H. Peterson, Mary Phillips, Jürgen Rehm, Robin Room, Pia Rosenqvist, Haydée Rosovsky, Kerstin Stenius, Grażyna Światkiewicz, Bohdan Woronowicz, and Antoni Zieliński, *Alcoholics Anonymous as Mutual-Help Movement: A Study in Eight Societies* (Madison, Wis.: University of Wisconsin Press, 1996), 118, 133–34. The crucial steps involve admitting one's powerlessness, and building belief in a power greater than oneself, while also taking personal responsibility for actions. In twelve-step programs, meetings serve as quasi-ritualized speech events that allow people to report personal experience in the here and now.

20. Payam Akhavan, "Justice and Reconciliation in the Great Lakes Region of Africa: The Contribution of the International Criminal Tribunal for Rwanda," *Duke Journal of Comparative and International Law* 7 (1997): 325, 348. "[J]ustice and reconciliation cannot be relegated to the preserve of the victim and perpetrator alone, because our shared humanity dictates that those who were mere spectators in the face of humanity are also part of the equation."

21. Richard Lowell Nygaard, "On the Role of Forgiveness in Criminal Sentencing," *Seton Hall Law Review* 27 (1997): 980, 996. Nygaard is a federal appellate court judge in the United States. His article urges exploration of forgiveness for most criminal defendants, but he excludes from this argument "offenders who have committed such unspeakable atrocities, acts of war, and terrorist cowardice, that regardless of how contrite they later become, neither their guilt nor their acts can be diminished by light treatment. The public would wretch at the sight of injustice and imbalance, and any concept of justice would suffer." See pages 995–96. He does not address what should happen when large numbers in a society participated in terror and torture.

22. Toni M. Massaro, "The Meanings of Shame: Implications for Legal Reform," *Psychology, Public Policy and Law* 1997 (1997): 645, 648 (reviewing literature).

23. Hampton, "An Expressive Theory of Retribution," in Wesley Cragg, ed., *Retributivism and Its Critics* (International Association for Philosophy of Law and Social Philosophy, Nordic Conference held at the University of Toronto, 25–27 June 1990), 1, 14.

24. Ibid.

25. In contrast, realpolitik arguments against prosecutions for war crimes include the prediction that war criminals are also war lords whose cooperation is needed to bring about peace. See "An End to

Impunity," *Financial Times*, London, 8 April 1998, 20. These are the kinds of arguments that have appropriately given ground with the growing strength of international human rights and prosecutorial efforts. Id.

26. Judge Antonio Cassesse, interview by author, The Hague, November 1996.

27. John H. Phillips, "Practical Advocacy," *The Australian Law Journal* 69 (August 1995): 596 (quoting Robert Jackson at Nuremberg).

28. Indira R. Lakshmanan, "To Forgive Thy Neighbor," *Boston Globe*, 18 February 1996, 83. Toward this end, Muslims need to be prosecuted just as vigorously for atrocities. Id.

29. Elizabeth Neuffer, "Elusive Justice: It Will Take an International Court to Deter War Criminals," *Boston Globe*, 29 December 1996, sec. D, pp. 1–2.

30. Editorial, "An Enemy of Argentina's People," *Boston Globe*, Sunday, 14 June 1998, sec. F, p. 6, col. 1.

31. See, generally, Payam Akhavan, "The International Criminal Tribunal for Rwanda: The Politics and Pragmatics of Punishment," *American Journal of International Law* 90 (1996): 501.

32. Lawyers Committee for Human Rights, "Prosecuting Genocide in Rwanda: The ICTR and National Trials," July 1997, 59 (hereinafter cited as "Prosecuting Genocide in Rwanda").

33. Ibid., 61 (identifying only sixteen lawyers in Rwanda). Another source reported forty-four lawyers admitted to the bar in August, 1997. At that time, the country adopted a law establishing a bar society and also helped to create a corps of judicial defenders who did not have a law degree but obtained a six-month training certificate. See Stef Vandeginste, "Justice for Rwanda and International Cooperation" (Center for the Study of the Great Lakes Region of Africa, Universiteit Antwerpen, September 1997), 4.

34. James C. McKinley, Jr., "As Crowds Vent Rage, Rwanda Executes 22 for '94 Massacres," *New York Times*, 25 April 1998, sec. A, p. 1.

35. Ibid., sec. A, p. 6, col. 3.

36. Ibid.

37. Ibid., "'Revenge is not justice,' Marc Saghi of Amnesty International told The Associated Press."

38. Ibid. Also, the international tribunal has no death penalty, in line with international accords.

39. "Prosecuting Genocide in Rwanda," 2.

40. James C. McKinley, Jr., "Ex-Premier Admits He Led Massacres in Rwanda in 1994," *New York Times*, 2 May 1998, sec. A, p. 1, col. 6.

41. Ibid., sec. A, p. 7, cols. 5–6.

42. Lawrence Douglas, "Film as Witness: Screening Nazi Concentration Camps Before the Nuremberg Tribunal," *Yale Law Journal* 105 (1995): 449, 451.

43. Payam Akhavan, "Justice in the Hague, Peace in the Former Yugoslavia? A Commentary on the United Nations War Crimes Tribunal," *Human Rights Quarterly* 20 (November 1998): 66–69.

44. See Eric Schmitt, "Pentagon Battles Plans for International War Crimes Tribunal," *New York Times*, 14 April 1998, sec. A, p. 11, col. 1. Pentagon leadership warned that such a court could subject even peace-keeping soldiers to politically motivated investigations, although draft language for the court specifically excludes soldiers from nations with functioning judicial systems. Senator Jesse Helms is also an outspoken opponent of such a court on grounds that it would jeopardize U.S. sovereignty. Id. Even supporters of the court acknowledge the difficulties in working out precisely how to assure the court's independence while pre-serving the idea of state responsibility for crimes where committed.

45. See Ford Foundation Report, winter 1998, 22 (emphasizing the TRC's importance in making the facts in South Africa broadly available).

46. Ash, "Truth about Dictatorship," 38–39.

47. Ford Foundation Report, winter 1998 (quoting *New York Times*, October 1997), 22. Potentially constructive interaction between trials and the truth commission process in South Africa has emerged recently. Colonel Eugene de Kock, head of the Vlakplaas police unit, was prosecuted successfully for murder and fraud. He then offered testi-mony in the contempt hearing following former President P. W. Botha's refusal to respond to subpoenas issued by the TRC. Mr. de Kock testi-fied that he was rewarded with a medal, requiring the approval of Botha, for his involvement in blowing up buildings belonging to the ANC in London in 1981. He also indicated that violent covert operations were approved by Botha and his inner circle, who then left low-level opera-tives like himself "hung out to dry." Suzanne Daley, "Killer Tells of Rewards for Defending Apartheid," *New York Times*, 4 June 1998, p. 11, col. 1.

48. Many argue that truth-seeking is a prerequisite for forgiveness.

"To be able to forgive, we must have the guts to look hard at the wrongness, the horridness, the sheer wickedness of what somebody did to us. We cannot camouflage; we cannot excuse; we cannot ignore. We must eye the evil face to face and we call it what it is. Only realists can be forgivers." Lewis B. Smedes, *Forgive and Forget: Healing the Hurts We Don't Deserve* (San Francisco: Harper & Row, 1984), 141. See also Nygaard, "On the Role of Forgiveness," 980, 984. Forgiveness is not pardon, or mercy, "Forgiveness looks evil in the eye, condemns it, but still permits one who meets *the forgiver's* criteria, to start anew."

49. Margaret Popkin and Naomi Roht-Arriaza, "Truth as Justice: Investigatory Commissions in Latin America," *Law and Social Inquiry* 20 (1995): 99.

50. See, for example, Statement from the Truth and Reconciliation Commission, 9 March 1998. It announces a meeting to discuss process of reconciliation and whether "the reams of data produced by the Truth Commission from victims, and perpetrators, will on their own, help us realise the vision of a commonly shared identity as a nation." This inquiry has parallels to the invocation to transformation offered by Rev. John Stendahl when addressing the legacies of anti-Semitism within the work of Luther: "[C]an we face the truth with a grace that will transform it, that will make such reality not a source for more violence, but for truer reconciliation?" John Stendahl, "With Luther, Against Luther," in Howard Clark Kee and Irvin J. Borosky, eds., *Removing the Anti-Judaism from the New Testament* (Philadelphia: American Interfaith Institute, 1998), 165–70 (addressing the legacies of anti-Semitism within Lutheranism).

51. Cartoon by Zapiro, *Mail and Guardian*, 27 May 1997.

52. Barnes, reflection paper.

53. Ibid.

54. Dori Laub and Shoshana Felman, *Testimony: Crises of Witnessing in Literature, Psychoanalysis, and History* (New York: Routledge, 1992), 59–60.

55. Admirable humility and commitment to transparency accompanies the writing of the TRC report. Charles Villa-Vicencio, head of the TRC research department, described the place for the report this way: "I see it as a road map that will lead investigative journalists and scholars and politicians and critics and—I hope—poets and musicians and everyone else into that body of material, so that they in turn will be able to critique it and address many of those issues that we in the commission simply do not have time to do." Leon Muller, "Moment of Truth

Ahead for the TRC: Final Report Proves Nightmare for Staff," (Cape Town) *Argus*, 4 February 1998, 7 (quoting Charles Villa-Vicencio).

56. Richard Wilson, "Violent Truths: The Politics of Memory in Guatemala," *Accord: An International Review of Peace Initiatives* 2 (1997): 18. The same evaluation finds the subsequent Recovery of Historic Memory project of the Catholic Archbishop's Human Rights office more substantial, and especially commends its efforts to work with local communities. Id., 21.

57. One observer suggests that Benzien actually replayed the role of torturer even while answering the questions posed by his former victims during the TRC hearing. "Within the first few minutes he manages to manipulate most of his victims back into the roles of their previous relationship—where he has the power and they the fragility." Antji Krog, *Country of My Skull* (Johannesburg: Random House, 1998), 74 (describing Benzien amnesty hearing). Even though the interaction made the voices of his questioners shake, their questions made Benzien supply detailed information that he initially dodged. Benzien himself had a nervous breakdown in 1994. Id., 76.

58. "Burying South Africa's Past: Of Memory and Forgiveness," *Economist*, 1 November 1997, 21.

59. Benzien tried unsuccessfully, and strangely, to suggest that he and his victim Ashley Forbes developed a rapport by sharing food and conversations. Krog, *Country of My Skull*, 74; Dr. Wendy Orr, "Trauma and Catharsis: The Psychology of Testimony" (prepared for the World Peace Foundation South African Truth and Reconciliation Commission meeting, 28–30 May 1998), 12. Benzien asserted that he acted from patriotism. He apparently experienced psychological difficulties when he learned that his prior political bosses described him as an extremist acting beyond his orders.

60. Graeme Simpson, executive director of the Centre for the Study of Violence and Reconciliation, predicts that people like Benzien will remain in the police force or else join private security forces, aimed especially at controlling youth. Simpson also suggests that many young people, currently charged with criminal activity in South Africa, grew up viewing antiapartheid outlaws and heroes and have yet to find a place in the new social order. Comments, World Peace Foundation South African Truth and Reconciliation Commission meeting, 28–30 May 1998.

61. "Burying South Africa's Past," 21 (quoting Tony Yengeni).

62. Ibid., 23.

63. Ibid.

64. This is Kwame Anthony Appiah's formulation, expressed in a planning meeting for the Facing History and Ourselves conference.

65. Lizeka Mda, "Victims Get the Short Straw at Hearings," *Mail and Guardian*, 17–23 October 1997, 12.

66. David G. Roskies, *Against the Apocalypse: Response to Catastrophe in Modern Jewish Culture* (Cambridge, Mass.: Harvard University Press, 1984), 310.

67. Alex Boraine, Janet Levy, and Ronel Scheffer, eds., *Dealing with the Past: Truth and Reconciliation in South Africa* (Cape Town: IDASA, 1994) (comments of José Zalaquett).

68. Judge Albie Sachs, "Human Rights: Good or Bad for South Africa," Harvard Law School Human Rights Program, 21 January 1998.

69. Albie Sachs, letter to author, 17 July 1997.

70. Comments at Harvard Facing History and Ourselves conference, 10 April 1997.

71. See Hans-Jörg Geiger, "Consequences of Past Human Rights Violations: The Significance of the Stasi Files for Dealing with the East German Past," in Menard R. Rwelamira and Gerhard Werle, eds., *Confronting Past Injustices: Approaches to Amnesty, Punishment, Reparation and Restitution in South Africa and Germany* (Durban, South Africa: Butterworth, 1996), 41.

72. Ibid.

73. "Forgetfulness, and I shall even say historical error, form an essential factor in the creation of a nation." Ernest Renan, "What Is a Nation?" in *The Poetry of the Celtic Races, and Other Studies,* trans. William G. Hutchison (1896; reprint, Port Washington/London: Kennikat Press, 1970), 66, quoted in Gary Smith, "Work on Forgetting" (April 1996, draft).

74. Ash, "Truth about Dictatorship," 36.

75. Ibid.

76. Lakshmanan, "To Forgive Thy Neighbor," 83.

77. Dorfman, afterword to *Death and the Maiden*, 73.

78. Don Terry, "Victims' Families Fight for Mercy," *New York Times*, 1 February 1996, sec. A, p. 10, col. 1 (quoting Anne Coleman). Coleman's adult son said "he could understand the people on the other side of the fence [awaiting an execution] calling for blood because he had wanted vengeance after his sister was killed. 'I'm glad I realized that wasn't the way to go,' he said. 'Over time, I learned to let it go.' " Id.

Another one of Coleman's children fought anger and depression over his sister's death, and expressed desire for revenge; he died at the age of twenty-five of cardiac arrest after taking antidepressant medications. See "Murder Victims Families for Reconciliation, Not In Our Name" (1997 pamphlet).

79. "Not in Our Name" (quoting Pat Clark).

80. See Rosenberg, *Haunted Land*, 67–121.

81. Ibid., 3.

82. Ibid., 35–39.

83. Smith, "Work on Forgetting," 10.

84. See Geiger, "Consequences of Past Human Rights Violations," 46 (describing The Stasi Record Act and its purposes).

85. Ibid., 52.

86. Kirk Savage, "The Politics of Memory: Black Emancipation and the Civil War Monument," in John R. Gillis, ed., *Commemorations: The Politics of National Identity* (Princeton, N.J.: Princeton University Press, 1994): 127.

87. The complex positioning of domestic politicians and global leaders in the international arena is well illustrated in the debate over the international criminal court. See John R. Bolton, "Why an International Criminal Court Won't Work," *Wall Street Journal*, 30 March 1998, sec. A, p. 19, col. 3 (describing support from Clinton administration and objections raised by others within and beyond the United States); Barbara Crossette, "Helms Vows to Make War on U.N. Court," *New York Times*, 27 March 1998, sec. A, p. 9, col. 1.; Farhan Haq, "Rights: Progress Slow on Formation of Intl. Criminal Court," *Inter Press Service*, 2 April 1998 (some in United States will resist international criminal court on grounds it would erode U.S. sovereignty).

88. See James E. Young, *Texture of Memory*, 6. Public art can "create shared spaces that lend a common spatial frame to otherwise disparate experiences and understanding . . . the public monument attempts to create an architectonic ideal by which even competing memories may be figured." For a thoughtful inquiry into the nature of public monuments and the political debates they can trigger, see Sanford Levinson, *Written in Stone: Public Monuments in Changing Societies* (Durham, N.C.: Duke University Press, 1998).

89. Savage, "Politics of Memory," 129.

90. Ibid., 130.

91. "Once we assign monumental form to memory, we have to some degree divested ourselves of the obligation to remember." Introduction,

"Darkness Visible," in Geoffrey H. Hartman, ed., *Holocaust Remembrance: The Shapes of Memory* (Oxford: Blackwell, 1994), quoting James Young.

92. Michael Kenney, "Historic Mistakes Carved in Stone," review of *Standing Soldiers, Kneeling Slaves: Race, War, and Monument in Nineteenth-Century America*, by Kirk Savage, *Boston Globe*, 5 December 1997, sec. E, p. 12; Christine Temin, "Boston's Conscience Turns 100," *Boston Globe*, 25 May 1997, sec. N, p. 1.

93. Savage, "Politics of Memory," 136; Facing History and Ourselves, "The New England Holocaust Memorial Study Guide" (Brookline, Mass.: Facing History and Ourselves, 1996), 10–13.

94. Savage, "Politics of Memory," 136–39.

95. "New England Holocaust Memorial Study Guide," 11. Booker T. Washington was among the speakers at the dedication ceremony.

96. Ibid., 12.

97. Eric Foner, "The South's Hidden Heritage," *New York Times*, 22 February 1997, sec. 1, p. 21, col. 3.

98. See Freida Lee Mock, *Maya Lin: Strong Clear Vision* (1995 Oscar-winning documentary film about Maya Lin); Robert Atkins, "When the Art Is Public, the Making Is, Too," *New York Times*, 23 July 1995, p.1, col. 1; Edward Guthman, "Freida Lee Mock's Strong Clear Vision Director Says Lin Stands on Its Own," *San Francisco Chronicle*, 8 November 1995, sec. D, p. 1; Jay Pridmore, "Revealing Displays Make Vietnam Museum Noteworthy," *Chicago Tribune*, 9 September 1994, p. 14.

99. See Todd Gitlin, "The Fabric of Memory," review of *Tangled Memories: The Vietnam War, the AIDS Epidemic, and the Politics of Remembering*, by Marita Sturken, *New York Times*, 2 March 1997, sec. 7, p. 16. "National myth-making is full of selective memory, and memory can be a way of forgetting. Thus, as Ms. Sturken points out, Maya Lin's brilliant Vietnam Memorial in Washington, recording the names of 58,196 dead Americans, writes off at least two million Vietnamese dead and converts the war into solely an American tragedy."

100. See Young, *Texture of Memory*, 8–15, 17–25 (documenting disputes over Holocaust memorials); Alan Cowell, "A Memorial to Gay Pain of Nazi Era Stirs Debate," *New York Times*, 29 December 1996, p. 11; Alan Cowell, "In Berlin, Wartime Ghosts Hinder Projects Memorializing Past," *New York Times*, 15 January 1997, 11.

101. Young, *Texture of Memory*, 17.

102. Ibid., 18–19.

103. Ibid., 30 (quoting Harburg monument).

104. Ibid.

105. Ibid., 30–31. See also Sara R. Horowitz, *Voicing the Void: Muteness and Memory in Holocaust Fiction* (Albany, N.Y.: SUNY Press, 1997). She explores narratives and fictions that depict or express "enforced muteness" as both the source of atrocity and its effects.

106. Lawrence L. Langer, *Admitting the Holocaust* (New York: Oxford University Press, 1995), 52.

107. Ibid., 107. See also Hartman, *Holocaust Remembrance*, 17–19.

108. Roskies, *Against the Apocalypse*, 257.

109. Ibid., 289.

110. Ibid., 303.

111. Rabbi J. B. Soloveichich argued that the traditional mourning period in Judaism, between the seventeenth day of the Hebrew month of Tammuz to the ninth of Av, include the chanting of Lamentations, an extremely bleak text. The process of mourning was designed to bring individuals into the collective memory of historical destructions of the two sacred temples and to ease people back into everyday routine. Roskies, *Against the Apocalypse*, 36–39.

112. "A Day to Honour the Stolen Generations," *Canberra Times*, 7 April 1998, sec. A, p. 12.

113. Roskies, *Against the Apocalypse*, 310.

114. Boraine, Levy, and Schefer, *Dealing with the Past.*

115. Hartman, *Holocaust Remembrance*, 10.

116. Ibid., 5.

117. Ash, "Truth about Dictatorship," 40. See also Hannah Arendt, *The Human Condition* (Chicago: University of Chicago Press, 1958), 279: "[E]ven if there is no truth, man can be truthful, and even if there is no reliable certainty, man can be reliable."

118. See Theodor Meron, *Henry's Wars and Shakespeare's Laws: Perspectives on the Law of War in the Later Middle Ages* (Oxford: Clarendon Press, 1993). Meron turns to Shakespeare's histories, notably *Henry V*, to illustrate the chivalric rules governing medieval armed conflicts. See also Lawrence Weschler, "Take No Prisoners," *New Yorker*, 17 June 1996, 50, 55 (reporting Meron's work).

119. Meron, *Henry's Wars and Shakespeare's Laws.* See also Allan A. Ryan, Jr., "Battle Cries: Why War Trials Matter," *Boston College Magazine*, summer 1996, 46, 47, for a discussion of medieval chivalry in contrast with contemporary human rights law that gives greater emphasis to the protection of noncombatants and civilians.

120. African scholar Ali A. Mazrui argues that "violations of human rights are preceded by the process of psychic subhumanization." Ali A. Mazrui, "Human Rights and the Moving Frontier of World Culture," in Diemer Alwin, *Philosophical Foundations of Human Rights* (Paris: UNESCO, 1986), 243. See also chapter 2, "Holocaust and Human Behavior (We and They)," in *Facing History and Ourselves Resource Book* (Brookline, Mass.: Facing History and Ourselves National Foundation, Inc., 1994), 58–109, hereinafter cited as *Facing History and Ourselves*.

121. Margot Strom, preface to *Facing History and Ourselves*, xvi.

122. Ron Gwiazda, assistant to the headmaster of the Boston Latin School, quoted in *Facing History and Ourselves*, xxv.

123. Planning meeting, Harvard Facing History Conference, January 1997.

124. Strom in *Facing History and Ourselves*, xix.

125. See Thanks to Scandinavia, Inc., "Human Rights Study in Denmark," June 1997.

126. Jamie Frederic Metzl, "Rwandan Genocide and the International Law of Radio Jamming," *American Journal of International Law* 91 (1997): 628.

127. Comments at Collective Violence and Memory: Judgment, Reconciliation, Education, Facing History and Ourselves, 12th Annual Human Rights and Justice Conference, 10 April 1997, Cambridge, Massachusetts.

128. Interestingly, the work is usually divided between those who address international politics and those who look at domestic violence internal to a nation. Perhaps there are important commonalities worthy of joint study. See Robert Harrison Wagner, "The Causes of Peace," in Roy Licklider, ed., *Stopping the Killing: How Civil Wars End* (New York: New York University Press, 1993), 235.

129. See Nygaard, "On the Role of Forgiveness," 1019: "forgiveness and revenge are attempts to deal with the same human need for balance, wholeness and healing." He continues with a defense of forgiveness: "Where revenge alienates, however, forgiveness heals."

130. "In nonhuman primates, peaceful post-conflict signals facilitate proximity, contact and affiliation among former adversaries." Joan B. Silk, "Making Amends: Adaptive Perspectives on Conflict Remediation in Monkeys, Apes, and Humans," *Human Nature* (draft, 5 December 1997): 25; Frans de Waal, *Peacemaking among Primates* (Cambridge, Mass.: Harvard University Press, 1989) (studies of bonobos, rhesus

monkeys and stump-tailed monkeys show ritualized methods for seeking contact with a former opponent to achieve reconciliation). See
also id., 270: "Forgiveness is not, as some people seem to believe, a
mysterious and sublime idea that we owe to a few millennia of Judeo-
Christianity. It did not originate in the minds of people and cannot therefore be appropriated by an ideology or a religion. The fact that monkeys, apes, and humans all engage in reconciliation behavior means that
it is probably over thirty million years old, preceding the evolutionary
divergence of these primates."

131. De Waal, *Peacemaking among Primates*, 233.

132. Ibid., 262.

133. Roskies, *Against the Apocalypse*, 303 (quoting Bak). In one
painting of Bak's, desecrated tablets of the law emerge both as gravestones and as fragments of new tablets. Id.

134. Rosenberg, *Haunted Land*, xxiv.

135. See Roskies, *Against the Apocalypse*, 135 (describing the literature of bearing witness and the need to cultivate it). See also page 133:
"If neither God nor His surrogates had any say in the course of Jewish
history, as the modernist pogram poem made amply clear, and if the
community no longer provided refuge in times of war and revolution, as demonstrated in a variety of shtetl novellas, then the last and
only holdout was the individual, emancipated from God and community."

136. Roger I. Simon and Claudi Eppert, "Remembering Obligation:
Pedagogy and the Witnessing of Testimony in History Trauma," *Canadian Journal of Education*, 23 (citing Toni Morrison, *Beloved: A Novel*
[New York: Knopf, 1987]). The process of "re-memory" takes a long
time, and shifts as new generations take part, in different political contexts. Robert Moeller offers these insights about struggles over memories of World War II in Germany more than fifty years later: "In the
1950s, most West Germans were able to interpret their experiences only
in absolute moral categories; a nation of victims confronted a handful
of perpetrators. The forceful reemergence of this postwar history in the
1980s and 1990s indicates how vivid this image of the past remains."
Robert G. Moeller, "War Stories: The Search for a Usable Past in the
Federal Republic of Germany," *American Historical Review* (October
1996): 1047. Moeller argues for an account of the past that "would
avoid any tendency to establish the moral equivalence of the victims of
Germans and German victims, just as it would reject an analysis that
explained the suffering of all Germans as the quid pro quo for the suffer-

ing inflicted on others by the National Socialist state. It would also move beyond a language in which the categories of victim and perpetrator were mutually exclusive; it would seek to capture the complexities of individual lives and 'mass fates' by exploring how during the Third Reich it was possible both to suffer and to cause suffering in others." Id., 1048.

Acknowledgments

I would like to thank Margot Stern Strom who asked me to join her in planning a national conference on contemporary responses to genocide and mass atrocity. I learned enormously in a year of study and planning with her and other members of her staff at Facing History and Ourselves, an organization that trains teachers to engage students in examinations of racism, prejudice, and anti-Semitism with the aim of promoting a more human and vibrant democracy. I would like here to express deep thanks to members of the conference planning group: Marc Skvirsky, Walter Robinson, Allan Ryan, Jr., Deanne Urmy, Kwame Anthony Appiah, Bernard Harcourt, Carol Gilligan, Jim Gilligan, Alan Stoskopf, John Stendahl, Phyllis Goldstein, Erica Stern, and Margot Strom. The planning and study work included a powerful series of lectures and films, organized by Bernard Harcourt at Harvard, and events with teachers and community members, organized by Facing History.

The conference, cosponsored by the Harvard Law School Graduate Program, assembled some 500 people in Cambridge in April, 1997. The event gave me extraordinary opportunities to talk with Dullah Omar, Margaret Burnham, Pumla Gobodo-Madikizela, Randall Kennedy, Michael Scharf, and Eric Yamamoto. Deanne Urmy of Beacon Press imagined a book emerging from the conference work. I thank her for vital encouragement and support at every stage of this book's development. I also thank many others at Beacon Press who also shared enthusiasm for the book and for public education on its themes.

I presented portions of chapter 1 and chapter 4 to audiences assembled by Facing History and Ourselves, and at the Commonwealth School, the Harvard law faculty, the Harvard Law School Graduate Program, the 1997 Law and Society Conference, Quinnipiac Law School, and also at Princeton University as the Inaugural Meredith Miller Memorial Lecture in memory of a young woman who was brutally murdered a few years after college graduation. Chapter 4 also benefited from comments by Abe Chayes, Cait Clarke-Shister, Patti Ewick, Phyllis Goldfarb, Jessica Mayer, Shani Pines, Austin Sarat, Anne-Marie Slaughter, and Ken Winston.

I presented Chapter 5 as the Frank Irvine Lecture at Cornell Law School; there I especially learned from comments by Kathryn Abrams, Cynthia Farina, John Siliciano, and David Wippman. Members of the Pentimento Reading Group—Kwame Anthony Appiah, Larry Blum, David Wilkins, and David Wong—afforded vigorous discussions of reparations. Avi Soifer gave me the distinct honor of teaching and learning with Boston College law students about the entire subject of this book.

Judge Richard J. Goldstone, whose own career exemplifies committed responses to mass atrocities, provided not only his wonderful foreword, but also crucial comments and corrections. Judge Antonio Cassesse kindly met with me, answered my questions, and gave me a tour of the War Crimes Tribunal in the Hague that I will not forget. Judge Albie Sachs wrote me a stunning letter about the South African Truth and Reconciliation Commission, and later discussed South Africa's recent history with me and with audiences at Harvard and Yale in ways that would renew even a skeptic's hopes for justice and human dignity. I learned a great deal with commissioners and staff members of the TRC during a World Peace Foundation meeting in Cape Town. I would like to thank the participants for their generosity and candor, and the organizers, Robert Rotberg and Dennis Thompson, for inviting me. Samantha Power guided my research into international trials in Bosnia and Rwanda, offered line-by-line commentary, and shared her own ongoing work on American failures to prevent genocides. Payam Akhavan also shared his writings and reflections on the war crimes tribunal for

Acknowledgments

202   the former Yugoslavia, and Henry Steiner invited me to join
Payam in a Harvard Law School Human Rights Program event
comparing prosecutions and truth commissions. I am also very
grateful to Henry for allowing me to join the unusual "interdisci-
plinary discussion" on truth commissions, held at Harvard Law
School in May, 1996.

   For his acute and timely reading of the manuscript, and for
involving me in the memorable Yale Conference on "Possibilities
of Memory and Justice: The Holocaust and Apartheid," Robert
Burt deserves special thanks. Avi Soifer and Shaun Ewen gave
valuable comments and corrections. Orli Avi-Yonah, Sally
Deutsch, Phyllis Goldfarb, Moshe Halbertal, and Ben Weiner
identified authors who became important companions in my
research and late-night thinking about memory, atrocity, and
lamentations. With speed and enthusiasm, Laurie Corzett,
Naomi Ronen, and Talya Weisbard tracked down hard-to-find
references. Vicky Spelman directed me to crucial texts and gave
repairing comments on the whole manuscript that combine ana-
lytic philosophic precision and humane compassion. Joe Singer
shared his work on reparations, editorial judgment, and sustaining belief in the project. Mira Judith Minow Singer restored
my hope each new day.

Index